Skills Development for Business and Management Students

Study and Employability

SECOND EDITION

Kevin Gallagher

OXFORD
UNIVERSITY PRESS

OXFORD
UNIVERSITY PRESS

Great Clarendon Street, Oxford, OX2 6DP,
United Kingdom

Oxford University Press is a department of the University of Oxford.
It furthers the University's objective of excellence in research, scholarship,
and education by publishing worldwide. Oxford is a registered trade mark of
Oxford University Press in the UK and in certain other countries

© Oxford University Press 2013

The moral rights of the author have been asserted

First edition copyright 2010

Impression: 1

British Library Cataloguing in Publication Data

Data available

ISBN 978-0-19-964426-1

Printed in Italy by L.E.G.O. S.p.A.—Lavis TN

 Skills Development for Business and
Management Students

Contents Summary

Detailed Contents

Setting the Scene: Study, Workplace and Personal Development Skills

This book has been written to help you to develop your skills in a variety of situations: study skills at university or college; skills for the workplace; and personal development skills. It is aimed at both full-time and part-time business and management undergraduate students, having a particular emphasis upon various business and management contexts. The text presents you with the foundational skills and knowledge required to ease you swiftly into your studies at university, while also introducing you to those skills and personal attributes that you need to develop for the workplace. The exercises encourage you to be proactive, questioning and reflective in your learning.

Workplace application of skills

Why do people study for business and management degrees? Well, to a great extent such degrees are a preparation for the world of work in business or management. The call for work-related skills for today's graduates has been growing stronger over recent years; in 2006 Carl Gilleard, Chief Executive Officer of the Association of Graduate Recruiters, stated:

> A degree on its own is not enough. ... Today employers look for a good degree plus a combination of skills, understanding, experience and personal attributes as well.
>
> (Carl Gilleard in the *Independent*, 13 October 2006)

Laura D'Andrea Tyson (2005), Dean of London Business School, echoed the need for workplace skills when she said:

> Business schools must move beyond their current focus of equipping future executives with knowledge, and instead furnish them with skills and attributes ... ways to nurture integrity, judgement intuition, and other essential leadership attributes ... the power to think, decide and act efficiently and innovatively in an unpredictable global business environment.
>
> (D'Andrea Tyson, 2005, p. 236)

In a sense, many management and business degrees now attempt to replicate those conditions under which you would be placed after graduating and going out into the 'real world' of business and management. Various methods are useful in addressing the theory-to-practice link outlined above: the use of the case study is a classic example; the placement year or internship is another; and the use of industrialists as visiting lecturers is a third. Another increasingly common approach is to incorporate 'employability' skills within the degree programme, either embedded or as separate modules. The emphasis here is on raising awareness of the business environment by working through activities (including business simulations) which attempt to recreate those that you are likely to face in the workplace. Soft skills, such as communication and teamwork, often feature strongly in these programmes.

Study skills

Your focus upon commencing your degree is likely to be upon study skills. You will need to know, for instance, where to find relevant information for your assignments, how to write in an academic way, how to interpret numerical data and how to present the findings of your research. However, if you later work in a business or management setting, you are likely to be using similar processes in your work situation (for instance, writing work reports, analysing sales data and conducting market research), so your study skills development serves a dual purpose. Even if you think you already have a reasonable level of ability in some (or all) of these areas, you should strive continually for improvements because these skills will be essential throughout your degree. At each successive year of your degree you will be expected to produce more advanced and skilful work, so you will probably need to upgrade accordingly. Perhaps one of the study skills that will assume greater importance (in terms of your knowledge and experience as you progress towards your final year) relates to your ability to approach a topic in a careful, questioning and reflective manner. You will begin to hear the word 'critical' to describe this approach to your assignments. Hopefully, your critical ability should increase from year to year. The exercises in this book are intended to assist you in this process.

Personal development skills

And finally—although some would argue principally—there is that character of your degree which relates to your personal development. The degree process should ideally be a means of self-development, a time for personal growth and new experiences, and a time for taking opportunities. The abilities to reflect and analyse are central to this process.

Reconciling workplace, study and personal development skills—a tripartite framework

The designer of your business/management degree needs to accommodate all three areas that are relevant to your skills development: the skills likely to be relevant to your future work situation; the skills for your university study; and your personal growth needs as an individual student. And, overarching all of this, is the aspect of transferability of skills between these contexts. This is not an easy task. Reynolds and Russ (2004) highlight the all-too-common attitudes of academics who belittle the importance of experience, and managers who regard theory as impractical.

This book provides a framework for skills development which recognizes the tripartite tension outlined above. It encourages you to monitor those times when you use specific skills and the context in which they are experienced—work, study or personal. It asks you to consider the transferability of the skills developed in one context to other situations; the inference is that there will often have to be adaptation on your part, or even that contextual barriers might enhance or preclude the use of such skills.

Thus, this book is not designed to be just a collection of tips and techniques but a means of active experimentation and reflection which you will carry out. Engagement equals confidence—an attitudinal factor which is given special mention in the Graduate Key Skills and

Employability (2002) Report of the Chartered Management Institute, which advises, 'The attributes most appreciated by managers [in the workplace] are graduates' receptiveness to training, their attendance record and *self-confidence*.'

The importance of feeling

In addition, there is a deliberate attempt to ask you how you *feel* about your abilities. The issue of feeling tends to be neglected by both tutors and students as something that comes second to thinking—and yet when it comes to self-development, how we 'feel' about some particular event or aspect of ourselves can reveal and clarify our true thoughts. Cunliffe and Easterby-Smith (2004) strongly support this view:

> Learning is ... intimately tied to how we feel, what we say and how we respond to others.
>
> (Cunliffe and Easterby-Smith, 2004)

The importance of context

From Chapter 2 you will be encouraged to keep a critical incidents journal—a log of those events in your personal, academic and work life which you feel are/were crucial in shaping your learning. The primary context level considered in this book relates to your personal, academic and work situations and the learning and transferability of skills between these contexts.

A secondary context level considers how you might sometimes have to use a different approach or skills mix, dependent upon the particular personal, academic or work situation. For instance, in a personal situation when communicating with someone who is angry, you would probably use a different approach to when communicating with someone who is happy; in the work context you could not speak to a new-starter with no knowledge of the business in the same way as a mature colleague. Of course, the book cannot show all of the possible contexts, but hopefully it will serve to illustrate contextual principles and some of the key contexts in which students/workers/people interact.

Skills and employability frameworks at degree level

Sometimes it helps to know a little about the background to what you are learning—in this case, skills and employability. If you were asking yourself 'Are skills really that important to my degree performance and do employers really rate them?', then this section will give you some relevant information. The book is based around these skills and approaches. However, you may wish to skip this section for now and return to it later.

There are now a range of skills frameworks following on from the influential Dearing Report (1997), which carried out an investigation into Higher Education within the UK with a particular emphasis upon what employers were looking for in graduates. The Report itself recommended 'Key Skills' of:

- communication;
- numeracy;
- the use of information technology;
- learning to learn.

The Report also recommended 'cognitive skills' such as the ability to *critically analyse*. Additionally, it recommended a structured period of work experience outside the university or college. Since this report was published there has been a great deal of further research on what is termed 'employability', which is generally considered to be a broader concept but still includes skills as a major building block. Two definitions are given by the Higher Education Academy, the first being the more basic. According to this definition, Employability is:

> A set of achievements—skills, understandings and personal attributes—that makes graduates more likely to gain employment and be successful in their chosen occupations, which benefits themselves, the workforce, the community and the economy.
>
> (HEA, 2012, p. 4, based on Yorke 2006)

The skills, attributes and knowledge given above, according to the joint report of the Confederation of British Industry and the National Union of Students (May, 2011) ('Working towards your future: making the most of your time in Higher Education') contribute towards a *positive attitude* [which] is the key foundation of employability' (CBI/NUS 2011, p. 13). The report (p. 13) lists the following 'key capabilities':

- self management;
- team working;
- business and customer awareness;
- problem-solving;
- communication;
- application of numeracy;
- application of information technology.

Another model of employability (Dacre Pool and Sewell 2007), again cited by the Higher Education Academy (HEA 2012, p. 23) has *self-esteem* at its core, this being a mix of your belief in your own ability to achieve a task (self-efficacy) and your self-confidence. Being able to *reflect* and make sense of your experiences and learning are essential. This model includes the following interlinking aspects, feeding into your employability:

- career development learning;
- experience (work and life);
- degree subject knowledge, skills and understanding;
- generic (e.g. transferable, such as report writing and research) skills;
- emotional intelligence (i.e. being aware of your own emotional triggers and those of others).

All of the above areas feature within this book.

Sequence of chapters

The sequence of chapters has been designed to help you in your learning. Even if you decide to skim it, you are advised to read Chapter 1 first, as this shows you why and how skills are important from the personal, academic and work viewpoints. Chapters 2 and 3 link aspects of personal development and are intended to be read together, and you may wish to read them before other chapters in the book if your intention is to develop your skills in line with a personal development plan. Chapter 4 on communication skills gives a general background to the other communication-related chapters of Chapter 7 (Reading), Chapter 8 (Writing) and Chapter 9 (Presentations). It is quite possible to access other chapters in any order, with the exception of Chapter 13 (Carrying your skills forward). This is meant to be read as the last chapter, looking ahead to continuing your professional development in the workplace.

Online Resource Centre

Answers to selected activities are given in the Online Resource Centre which accompanies the book. You will also find other information here: material which goes into further depth or raises interesting questions; updated and new information; and weblinks as they become available. These are updated regularly.

I wish you well in your learning endeavours—personal, study and work.

Kevin Gallagher

Acknowledgements

This book could not have been written without the assistance of many people. My heartfelt thanks to all of the people listed below:

The following persons for kindly agreeing to be interviewed for case studies included in the book:

Colin Briggs (Presenter, BBC Look North);

Keith Gill (Co-Founder, Tanfield Food Company).

The following staff from the Great North Air Ambulance Service:

Kevin Hodgson—Director of Operations, Northumbria Wing;

Dr Dave Bramley—Helicopter doctor.

Peter Harrington (Founding director of SimVenture) for allowing the use of the four business functions diagram in Chapter 1.

The following people shared their experience by contributing their own written accounts of 'Student tips on skills and employability' for particular chapters. Many thanks for your time and creativity:

Laura Berry—Chapters 1, 2, and 3;

Nadia Caney—Chapters 4 and 8;

Maggie Gallagher—Chapters 5 and 10;

Helen Charlton—Chapter 6;

Piotr and Wojciech Kublinski—Chapter 9;

Jen Gallagher—Chapters 7 and 12;

Stephen Wardropper—Chapters 11 and 13.

The following people contributed comments to the 'Student Viewpoint', given at the front of each chapter. Thank you for your time and thoughts

Chapter 1

Denise Graham
Trish Goss
Wes English

Chapter 2

Dawn Youssef
Lee Middleton
Paula West

Chapter 3

Denise Graham
Wes English

Chapter 4

Ummar Youssaf
Sarah Radford

Chapter 5

Maureen Crowder
Zena Henderson
Amanda Nichol
Kate Watson

Chapter 6

Maggie Gallagher

Chapters 7 and 9

Hannah Simpson
Sarah Cooper
Sarah E. Watson
Yasmin Mensli
Dan Baker
Sarah Fothergill
Jennifer Scullion
Nathan Sharp
Chris Hiscox
Adela Matei
Amanda Simpson
Jordan Huggins

Chapter 8

Ummar Youssaf
Sarah Radford

Chapter 10

Ronnie Barnett
Andrew Donkin
Denise Graham
Trish Goss

Chapter 11

Omar Hijab
Dirk Plaskuda
Katerina Spyou

Chapter 12

Ian Hayman
Elaine Kirby
Judith Lonsdale
Jeremy Manning

Chapter 13

William Alcock
Karin Bond
Maureen Crowder
Philip Humphrey
Linda Reiling

Alec Bickerton contributed Chapter 10 (Quantitative data presentation) in the first edition, and I have updated this for the second edition. Alec has extensive experience of Further and Higher Education and has taught with me at the university for a number of years. Many thanks for your contribution to a very relevant skills area.

I would like to thank the book reviewers, on behalf of Oxford University Press. Although protocol denies me your names I owe a debt of gratitude to all of you. Your comments throughout the review process have been as they should be—honest, detailed, critical, encouraging and filled with helpful advice.

To Francesca Griffin (Publishing Manager, Oxford University Press), many thanks for your guidance, enthusiasm and patience throughout the writing of this second edition.

And, last but not least, thanks to my wife Cath—thank you so much for your support and encouragement.

New to this Edition

- New employability skills focus that runs throughout the text to reinforce the importance and growing significance of transferable skills.
- New boxes entitled 'Student tips on skills and employability', in which students and graduates discuss their workplace experiences and how they have used the skills they learnt at university.
- Expanded coverage of referencing and plagiarism.
- New Chapter 6, which incorporates substantial material on critical thinking.
- Expanded coverage of intercultural communication.
- YouTube channel featuring relevant videos on skills, including interviews with students and graduates filmed to accompany the book.

How to use this Book

 By the end of this chapter you

- Apply a learning cycle approach to you Honey and Mumford)
- Outline the concept of learning styles (H
- Design your own learning journal

 Chapter Guide

Student Viewpoint

Denise and Wes were studying for a part-tir were asked for comments on how they h how useful the personal development pro

Introduction

You are constantly communicating in all so cesses are very familiar to you—however, th ment. Communication skills help you to e to others. The importance of communica

Chapter outline

This chapter gives you some basic but extr searching for information and referencing what sorts of journals, books and other in credibility of the information. You need tc

 Activity 5.1 Journal audit

For this activity you are asked to conduct an aud to Business and Management. List the journals a electronically. Quickly scan the contents pages t recommended. It is also worthwhile browsing th

Aims of the chapter

Each chapter opens with a bulleted outline of the main concepts and ideas. They include elements of understanding and application of skills with reference to the contextual environment of work, university and personal life.

Student viewpoint boxes

At the start of each chapter are Student viewpoint boxes where students speak about how they have used various skills in both work and university situations.

Introduction

Chapter introductions offer a brief synopsis of the subject topic that is about to be covered and serve as helpful signposts to what you can expect to learn from each chapter.

Chapter outline

Chapter outlines offer a succinct paragraph explaining how the chapter is structured and the key issues to be covered in that section of the book.

Activity boxes

These boxes include both 'thinking' activities and 'doing' activities to enable you to consolidate the theory and models you have just read.

Student tips on skills and em

Locating/searching for information

Maggie is working in her first full-time job after ;
company that publishes brochures for corporate

Student tips on skills and employability

This unique feature offers you first-hand comments and advice from students based on their own experiences of university and entering the professional environment.

 Skills Example 6.1   **The busi**

Gemma and Steve had a business plan to write.
mountaineering club and now that they had gra
allowed them to use their knowledge of climbir
was a qualified climbing instructor to join them

Skills example boxes

Skills example boxes have been integrated throughout the book and illustrate scenarios where a specific study, employability or professional skill is needed. This feature will exemplify how you can effectively translate the skills you have learnt into real-life situations and help you to avoid the common pitfalls.

 Case Study: The job intervi

Sarah worked as a team leader in the call centre
She was effective and well-liked. Recently, she h
that the prospects of advancement from her cu
answered an advert for a call centre manager v

Case studies

The book is packed with examples and case studies that link topics to real-life situations, and are followed by a number of questions to help you think about your own situation and how you might react.

 Chapter summary

You should now be familiar with some of th
information in a meaningful way as part of
career. There are many pitfalls in collecting
with is accurate and will enable you to focu

Chapter summary

Each chapter ends with a précis that summarizes the most important arguments developed within that chapter.

 End of chapter exercises

Exercise 1

Discussion question: 'In what sense can you

a. designing a logo or sign;

End of chapter exercises

Exercises have been included at the end of every chapter to check you have grasped the key concepts and also provide the opportunity to work in teams to discuss significant issues that have been covered.

 Further reading

Jobs and careers:

An excellent website to visit for details on s
be found at: http://www.thebigchoice.com

Further reading

An annotated list of recommended reading in each subject will guide you to further key literature in this area.

How to use the Online Resource Centre

www.oxfordtextbooks.co.uk/orc/gallagher2e/

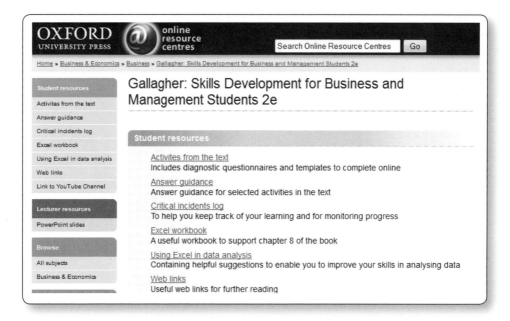

For students:

Activity 1.1: The good driver

As a car passenger or a driver, you have probably witness drivers' discourteous or poorly-controlled driving. These e *not* to be a good driver. However, being aware of what not focus upon what we should be doing. For this activity spe instances of poor driving. Now, construct a bullet point list should have to be a good car driver. Next, construct anoth

Activities from the text

Selected activities found inside the textbook are also available for you to access online.

Answer guidance

Activity 8.3: Using a narrative approach

1. Describe the database that is described in the paragraph.

Answer guidance on writing style and using a narrative approach

Suggested answers are provided for selected activities.

Critical Incident Sheet/Log

You may wish to use this as the format for your Critical Incid
build up your log you need to complete copies of this sheet.
to collate them in one place. You may decide that a simple d
most appropriate. Alternatively you may wish to keep log she
learning events together as these may represent how you ha
one learning cycle to the next.

Note: The other document associated with your Critical Incid

Critical incidents log

Here you can find a downloadable template of a critical incidents log which you are encouraged to use alongside the text to keep track of your learning as well as the positive and negative actions you take.

BA Year 1 rating of facilities (2009)				
	Very Good 5	Good 4	As expected 3	Poor 2
Refectory	0	0	23	34
Teaching	14	20	20	5
S. Union	6	10	19	11
Sports	6	10	18	10
Overall	9	17	30	4

Excel workbook

An Excel workbook is available to provide additional support in areas such as constructing pie charts, bar charts and line charts.

Using Excel in data analysis

This resource has been authored by David Whigham, Ser Glasgow Caledonian University.

The workbooks contain instructions and practical example using Excel in data analysis.

Information on using Excel in data analysis

Workbooks are also provided on the following areas: basic Excel techniques; descriptive statistics; contingency tables (cross-tabulation); charting and regression; and inference (statistical significance).

The following web links refer to *Example 1.1: The m* *example of multiple intelligences*. These are all credi

Sources
Love, M. (2008) Frankly we'd rather go to Dollywood. *The* [Online]. Available at: www.guardian.co.uk/travel/2008/jan [accessed: 6/12/2009]

Web links for selected chapters

Links to further information are provided where relevant.

Link to YouTube Channel

Access the link below to visit the YouTube channel featuri as interviews with students and graduates.

Skills Development for Business and Management Stude

Link to YouTube channel

The YouTube channel features relevant skills footage as well as interviews with students and graduates.

For registered adopters:

Introduction: chapter objectives

Chapter Objectives:

- Define skills, knowledge and competence
- Outline skills required for business and management education
- Give examples of learning that occurs when you

PowerPoint® slides

Chapter-by-chapter PowerPoint® slides have been provided for use in your lecture presentations. They are fully customizable, enabling you to tailor them to match your own presentation style.

1

Developing Skills for Business and Management Students

 Chapter guide

Student viewpoint

Denise, Wes, and Trish are studying for a part-time degree in Applied Management. They have been asked to give some examples of how they have recently used skills learned at university in the work situation. Their responses are given below:

'After reading about different team roles I carried out a study on my own QA team and was successfully able to analyse team members. I also became more aware of my own personal style [of leadership].'

Denise (Quality Assurance (QA) Manager)

'Studying management theory has helped me as a non-manager to better understand the styles of various managers I know. Also, through studying emotional intelligence I have a better understanding of how to manage upwards to obtain a satisfactory outcome. I have also learnt to adapt my approach to other people by recognizing what motivates them as individuals.'

Wes (works for a land and property company)

'Through studying the theories of learning I have a better idea of my own learning style, which I can use for both study and work situations. Other knowledge and theories in the course have enabled me to better understand the nature of the tasks which I am delegating to other people in my organization.'

Trish (works as a manager in the National Health Service)

By the end of this chapter you should be able to:

- Define skills, knowledge and competence
- Outline skills required for business and management education
- Give examples of learning that occurs when you memorize information, practise a skill, experience a particular event and when you reflect
- Define what is meant by 'transferable skills'
- Apply the concept of 'multiple intelligences' to a typical learning situation
- Discuss the relevance of emotional intelligence to work-based/managerial skills

Introduction

As a business or management student, you are faced with the immediate need to learn a variety of general skills, specific subject skills and masses of subject knowledge. You will write assignments, give presentations and perhaps take exams to demonstrate your grasp of your subject area. Hopefully, at the end of your studies, you will be awarded your qualification. Your following move may be to embark upon your new career. Your chosen field will depend upon circumstances and your personal preferences. However, it is likely that amongst the reasons your future employer will select you are your predicted abilities to plan, organize, lead others and control activities within your chosen area.

This book has been written to help you develop your general skills as a management student, which feed in to all areas of your studies, and provide a solid base of skills for your first managerial activities at work. This chapter will consider the nature of these skills.

Chapter outline

The chapter opens by exploring what we mean by knowledge, skills and behaviour. It shows, using the everyday example of someone driving a car, how these are all used by the driver to perform the task of driving. Acquiring knowledge and developing appropriate skills and behaviours through the process(es) of learning are outlined. At this point you will see that you can learn when you memorize information, when you practise a skill, when you experience a particular situation and when you think back over a situation.

The discussion then turns to the skills you require as business and management students. These cover, first, your academic and personal development skills during your course of study and, secondly, your future work-based and/or management career. You will see that there are four main areas of business activities in any organization and each area has skills you can develop. You will be encouraged to explore those aspects which are generic, transferable skills and behaviours—those which you can apply to different situations. You will see that many business and management skills are dependent not only upon your ability to think logically but also to use what are known as 'multiple intelligences'. Linked to this concept is that of emotional intelligence (EI)—how you become aware of, and work with, emotions in yourself and others—which has been proposed to be one of the key 'must-haves' for senior managers.

The chapter ends by way of a return to a discussion of what is one of the most useful skills in today's turbulent business world: the ability to learn new knowledge, skills and behaviours. Reflection is an essential element of this 'learning to learn'.

1.1 Introducing the concept of skills

1.1.1 Definition

The definition of 'skill' as *'the ability do something well'* (*Compact Oxford English Dictionary for Students*, 2006) establishes the essential nature of any skill. The possession of ability is fundamental to anyone who must do—rather than just talk about—something. In fact, even this is debatable—the best writers often base their novels upon their own experience. To put it simply, to be effective in our personal, academic and work lives we need to be able to actually do things—thus we need to be skilled.

Skills can take many different forms. Let's start by thinking of some types of skills with which you are already familiar: there are some skills which are quite task-orientated (reading a map, for instance), whilst others will be more behavioural in nature (calming someone down would be an example of this). Some skills are concerned with hand-to-eye co-ordination (typing, playing sports), whilst others are much more to do with thinking (playing chess would fall into this category).

Sometimes skills are divided into two categories: 'hard' and 'soft':

- *Hard skills* are technical in nature. Solving mathematical equations, using PowerPoint® and servicing a car engine would be classified in this way.
- *Soft skills* are people-orientated. Persuasion, discussion and leadership are examples of such skills.

In many situations you will have to use a combination of hard and soft skills.

1.1.2 The partnership between skills and knowledge

Although this book is dedicated to the development of skills, you should note from the beginning that without knowledge you may restrict your ability to use your skills to their full effect. You will generally learn and develop *both* knowledge and skills in modern universities. Course descriptions usually give 'learning objectives' in terms of not just 'skills' but also 'knowledge'. It is as well at this point to show the close relationships which exist between all of these aspects of learning. Let's consider an example with which you are probably quite familiar, either as a passenger or as a driver: driving a car.

 Activity 1.1 The good driver

As a car passenger or a driver, you have probably witnessed many instances of other drivers' discourteous or poorly controlled driving. These experiences clearly highlight how *not* to be a good driver. However, being aware of what not to do is one way of getting us to focus upon what we should be doing. For this activity, spend a few minutes thinking about instances of poor driving. Now, construct a bullet point list of the *skills* you think someone should have to be a good car driver. Next, construct another list, this time of the *knowledge* someone should possess to be a good car driver. Compare your (good) lists with the discussion below.

Author commentary on activity

Well, my list of skills included the following:

- Ability to move off and to stop
- Ability to manoeuvre the car (straight line, bends, emergency stops) at both slow and high speeds

(continued...)

- Ability to reverse between cars, around bends
- Ability to change gear and use other controls
- Ability to fill up with fuel and windscreen wiper fluid
- Being aware of other drivers
- Looking out for pedestrians
- Observing the speed limits
- Driving with care and attention
- Maintaining a calm approach to stressful situations
- Not driving when tired.

My list for 'knowledge' included:

- Knowing which controls to operate for various aspects of driving and how they work
- Memorizing layout of car controls
- Knowing the Highway Code (road sign meanings, speed limits, procedures for pulling out, overtaking, negotiating roundabouts, give-way junctions, etc.)
- Knowing the speed at which to change gear
- Knowing stress-busting methods
- Knowing the accident statistics showing a marked increase for tired drivers.

Of course, your list will not be identical to mine but it will probably have a lot in common with it. Note the various types of skills: we need to be able to physically move our limbs to manoeuvre the car, but we also need to think about what we are doing at the time; we also need to think ahead of our intended route and for possible hazards; an observer would be able to see (and hear!) our behaviour, which would probably reflect our competence. Of course, we need some basic knowledge, such as the Highway Code, in order simply not to crash into the next car that comes along. As previously noted, skills are not better than or inferior to knowledge: if you want to be a good driver, you need to have a certain level of both. This book focuses upon skills, but you will need to apply these skills to particular situations and have at least some basic level of knowledge to be effective in what you do (though we should note that gaining further knowledge is a skill in itself).

1.1.3 Competence and levels of skill

But there is more to this idea of 'skill'. Let us go back to the definition '.... the ability to do something *well*'. Our previous discussion of the car driver implied the possession of certain abilities as if the driver were at least competent in these—that is, 'can do', as opposed to 'can't do'. This idea of 'competence' is something which you will come across both at university and in the workplace. It carries with it the criterion of 'pass' versus 'fail' (or 'competent' versus 'not yet competent'). The inference is that 'competent' allows you to carry out the activity without direct supervision and gives you a particular status of skill attainment. In driving terms it is the equivalent of passing your driving test and being allowed out by yourself on the open roads for the first time. However, as most drivers will tell you, this does not mean that you are an expert driver. You may be able to perform the various skills well enough to be considered an acceptable risk on the road but you still have much to learn.

It is through further experience and a willingness to learn from your mistakes that you improve as a driver. So it is in other aspects of your life. However, you need the opportunity and the motivation to improve. Reflecting upon and then analysing your performance, and making appropriate changes for future events form the basis of this approach.

Of course, we all start from different base levels when it comes to skills. Some people are naturally more talented than others. However, to carry the driving analogy just one stage further, although few of us would aspire to, or be capable of, becoming a Formula 1 champion, most of us will be capable of driving successfully from A to B.

1.2 The learning process occurs when you...

The driving example assumes that, somehow, you acquire knowledge, skills and appropriate behaviours. You learn in a variety of different ways, as shown in Figure 1.1.

 Activity 1.2 Personal learning

Write down some of your own examples of learning through:

- memorizing
- experiencing
- practising
- reflecting.

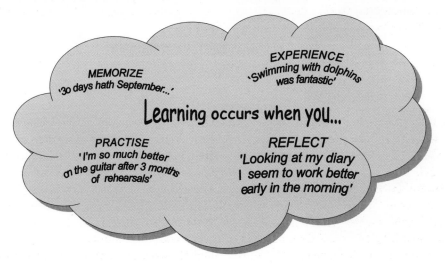

Fig 1.1 Learning occurs when you...

1.3 Skills for business and management students—four business functional areas

If you are studying, it makes sense to improve your study skills to make your studying more effective, and to achieve a better class of qualification at the end of it. Study skills, then, should be amongst the repertoire of skills you develop during your business or management degree. In the next chapter—concerned with personal development planning—you will be given the opportunity to diagnose your strengths and weaknesses in such skills. These study skills include:

- searching and evaluating information sources;
- reading and writing skills;
- skills in collecting and presenting data.

These skills are necessary no matter what type of degree you are studying for. What will differ will be the sites that you become acquainted with and the style of academic writing for your particular discipline.

The case for business and management skills has already been made in the introduction under 'Setting the Scene: Study, Workplace and Personal Development Skills'. At this stage you may be wondering what sorts of activities go on in a typical business organization. To give you an overview, you may wish to consider Figure 1.2, which illustrates four business functional

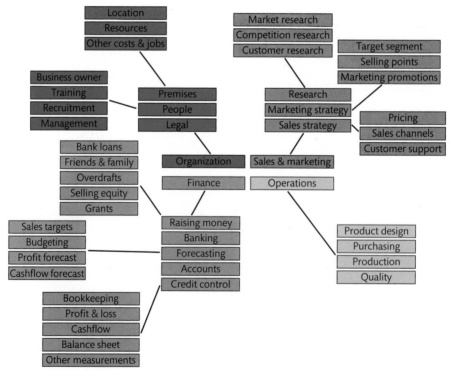

Fig 1.2 The four business functional areas

Source: Courtesy of Venture Simulations Ltd (http://www.simventure.co.uk)

areas involved in the successful running of an organization. These are also the areas you would need to consider if you were interested in writing a business plan.

Here, you can see the four main functional areas of Organization, Operations, Sales and Marketing and Finance. Each one of these areas is then broken down into typical business activities within the organization. Some of these names will vary from one organization to the next (some organizations, for instance, will favour 'Marketing' over 'Sales', others may talk about 'Service' rather than 'Product') but these areas are still quite typical of how many organizations arrange their business activities.

 Activity 1.3 Which of the four areas interest you? Which areas have you any experience in?

Having an overview of the four functional areas is very useful. It gives you an appreciation of what goes on in an organization. It shows how the organization is made up of different activities which make it viable when correctly co-ordinated. Even at this early stage of your degree, you may begin to develop a preference for what you would like to do in your career. One of the purposes of this book is to encourage you to think about your career and your employability skills. Figure 1.3 shows an example of a skills profile for a hypothetical company. You will note that there are many potential areas of skills development for this organization. Individuals within the organization may specialize in a particular skills area (e.g. Sales, Finance or Production) but will still need an appropriate level of skills in other areas (e.g. communication, IT skills, writing skills). In Chapter 3 you are directed to an online skills questionnaire which is designed to assess your current skills and help you to choose your future career direction.

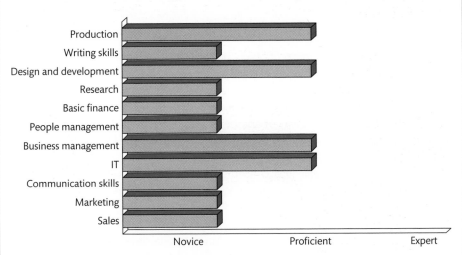

Fig 1.3 Different skills sets associated with different jobs and careers

Source: Courtesy of Venture Simulations Ltd (http://www.simventure.co.uk)

1.4 Transferability of skills

Clearly, the study skills of reading, writing, research and presentation will help you to get the most out of your studies at university. You will probably appreciate that these are very much 'generic'—that is, they can be applied to many different situations, and in various contexts; granted that a management presentation may be to a different audience and not require (for instance) details of theoretical models used, but it will still adhere to common principles of careful preparation, use of equipment and correct body language.

Other skills, such as teamworking, may not appear to be so obviously transferable from the university to the work context, especially if they require specific knowledge of company procedures, etc. However, there are often substantial aspects of such skills that can be transferred from one context to the other. Of course, it helps if students can see linkages between the academic and work contexts—this is why many programmes of study are now asking students to consider how skills may be used in the workplace. Case studies are another way to make these links. If you can immediately apply your newly learnt skills from university to your work situation, then you are in an even more fortunate position.

1.5 Skills development and multiple intelligence

Many of the skills included in typical business and management courses, cover both technical (hard skills) and people aspects (soft skills). A useful way of discussing skills further is to use the concept of multiple intelligences, as advocated by writers such as Howard Gardner, as it allows us to consider various aspects of our learning.

Howard Gardner (1993) talks of 'intelligences' rather than just a single 'intelligence'. He gives the definition:

> An intelligence is the ability to solve problems, or to create products, that are valued within one or more cultural settings.

> (Gardner, 1993, p. xiv)

In his ground-breaking book *Frames of Mind: The Theory of Multiple Intelligence* Gardner lists various aspects of intelligence. These intelligences are shown in Figure 1.4.

Linguistic intelligence relates to your ability to use language to speak, read and write. Studies have shown (e.g. Mintzberg, 1973) that up to 80 per cent of a manager's time can be spent in communicating in one way or another, so linguistic intelligence is of vital importance. We shall be devoting a considerable part of this book to exploring communication skills.

Logical–mathematical intelligence concerns your ability to reason and problem-solve using rational thought and using your ability to manipulate numbers and numeracy-based concepts. Again, these represent key abilities in terms of management and business operations. They are essential skills for many business functions but in particular for Strategic Management, Operations Management and Finance. Your personal development plans are highly likely to feature these 'hard' skills. We will cover some of these skills later in the book, but you should note that they will feature heavily in many business activities that you will encounter elsewhere.

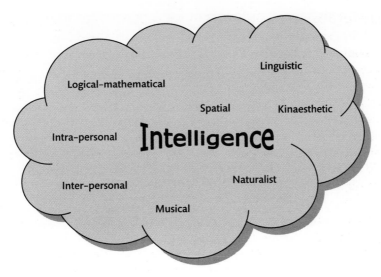

Fig 1.4 Gardner's multiple intelligences

Source: Based on Gardner (1993)

Spatial intelligence relates to the ability to visualize objects in two or three physical dimensions. Professionals such as architects typically have (and develop) this. If you use a map to navigate and are able to 'see' the rise of a hill or the trough of a valley, then you too are using this intelligence.

Musical intelligence covers the ability to recognize musical notes and form, to create songs and music, to read and write in music notation, to sing and play musical instruments, to recognize and use different timings and rhythms, including the use of poetry and rhyme. Music can be a powerful means of evoking your emotions or simply of reflecting them; it can add to your ability to communicate to others. Rhymes can help you to memorize facts.

Kinaesthetic intelligence is concerned with the movement of your body. Top gymnasts have honed this intelligence to a very high level, although of course the majority of us have learned the balancing act of walking. The term 'motor skills' describes the fine movements involved in typing on a keyboard, driving a car, playing a musical instrument or surgery skills. Hand-to-eye coordination is another example of kinaesthetic intelligence. Sometimes you depend upon this until you reach a point when you no longer need to look at what you are doing to perform the task—for instance, being able to type without looking at the keyboard.

Intra-personal intelligence is inward looking. It relates to our ability to recognize our strengths and weaknesses, what motivates us, why we behave as we do and our ability to reflect upon our performance. This is the intelligence we use when engaged with personal development plans.

Inter-personal intelligence looks outwards at how you interact with other people—your ability to 'connect' with them—to communicate and influence both individuals and groups. Clearly this is an essential requirement for anyone who has to work in or manage a team or develop strong relationships with customers.

Skills Example 1.1   The multi-talented Dolly Parton—an example of multiple intelligences

You don't have to be a country music lover to have heard of one of the world's greatest country singers—Dolly Parton. Larger than life, and instantly recognizable by her trademark white blonde wigs and enhanced figure, her songs of life in the country and her beloved Smoky Mountains have sold in their hundreds of thousands. But dig a little deeper, and you will notice that she is much more than a singer who has become rich purely on the basis of her attractive looks and a few one-hit wonders: she has also written many of these hit songs. Indeed, her autobiographical 'rags to riches' story is reflected in songs such as 'The Coat of Many Colours' (which tells of a girl who proudly wears a coat sewn together by her mother from various cast-off garments). Dolly is thus a singer/songwriter with a proven ability to excel in both her music and her story-telling—and she does it in such a way as to empathize with her many listeners, showing that she can explore her own feelings while also knowing how to connect with her audience. Additionally, she has also starred in a string of movie hits.

However, Dolly's talents are not restricted to singing and acting; she is a high-flying business woman too with her very own theme park—Dollywood. In his article 'Frankly we'd rather go to Dollywood' Martin Love of the *Sunday Observer* (Sunday 27 January 2008) reports that, far from her theme park being 'a hymn to kitsch and rhinestones', it is a place which 'thrilled with its vivid re-creation of life in the Smoky Mountains'. Some 3 million people visit Dollywood each year.

Then, just when you thought that singing, acting and theme parks would be enough for anyone to fit into a busy life, up pops Dolly again; Len Tingle, the BBC's editor of The Politics Show, leads his article (Friday 30 November 2007) with 'If you have a problem teaching young children to read, who do you call?' The answer is ... Dolly Parton! Tingle explains how Dolly, recalling her own childhood (in a replica at Dollywood of the log cabin where she grew up, there is not a single book), established a scheme providing free books for children under 5 in the area around the Smokies. Called 'The Imagination Library', the idea has taken off and rooted in England too; in Rotherham the Imagination Library is now established—its credibility enhanced by the presence of prominent council members and a director of the national education body QCA (Qualifications and Curriculum Authority).

Sources: Love, M. (2008) 'Frankly we'd rather go to Dollywood', 27 January. *Observer* [online]. Available at: http://www.guardian.co.uk/travel/2008/jan/27/usa.familyholidays?page=all (accessed: 25 May 2012). Dollywood.com (2012) *Imagination Library* [online]. Available at: http://www.dollywood.com/learn-about-dollywood/Imagination-Library.aspx (accessed: 25 May 2012). Rotherham Metropolitan Borough Council (2011) *Rotherham's Imagination Library* [online]. Available at: http://www.rotherham.gov.uk/info/200071/parental_support/557/rotherhams_imagination_library1 (accessed: 25 May 2012). Book2Book (2012) *Press release: Miscellaneous announcements: Dolly Parton announces UKi Imagination Library Selection Committee* [online]. Available at: http://www.booktrade.info/index.php/showcomments/15572 (accessed 25 May 2012).

The final term—**Naturalist** intelligence—is your ability to work in harmony with nature. The obvious people to exhibit this are those who work in farming or who live in close proximity to their natural surroundings, living off the land. However, this may be seen today in terms of public ecological awareness—a factor which a large number of organizations are now attempting to capitalize upon. Many people have a strong need to connect with their natural surroundings—for instance, it has been shown that hospital patients who have a view of trees and sky tend to recover more quickly than those whose only view is that of concrete buildings (Roe, 2003; Gizowska, 2005).

1.6 Skills development and emotional intelligence

1.6.1 The concept of 'emotional intelligence'

Another popular concept of intelligence in recent years, owing some debt to Gardner, has been that of 'emotional intelligence', which has been popularized through Daniel Goleman's international bestseller of the same name. Goleman describes emotional intelligences as a 'key set of ... characteristics' which include:

- *abilities such as being able to motivate oneself and persist in the face of frustration*
- *abilities to control impulse and delay gratification*
- *[ability] to regulate one's moods and keep distress from swamping the ability to think*
- *[ability] to empathize and to hope.*

(Goleman, 1996, p. 34)

Essentially what Goleman says is that, whilst technical skills and thinking (cognitive) abilities rely on more traditional intelligence (as in IQ tests), there is a whole range of what he calls 'emotional competencies' linked to emotional intelligences such as being emotionally self-aware and being able to empathize with others. Moreover, in his more recent book, *The New Leaders*, written with Richard Boyatzis and Annie McKee (2002), he goes on to make a strong case for a predominance of emotional intelligence (EI) factors as being the final determinant in separating the excellent from the average business leader. As if to emphasize this, he goes on to say that the further up the organizational ladder the manager is, the greater is the dependence upon EI factors. As one of the aims of most business and management degrees is to promote the development of future business leaders, it would seem appropriate to consider such EI competences.

As if to emphasize that there is more to being successful in life than being technically competent or a good problem-solver, the concept of emotional intelligence, like that of multiple intelligence, considers other factors—in this case, our awareness of and ability to control our emotional response to situations. Comparing it to Gardner's theory, there are perhaps some basic parallels in that Gardner considers intra-personal and inter-personal intelligence. However, EI as a subject has a very specific focus—emotions. The point of studying EI according to Goleman is that those people who score highly in terms of the various EI factors have been shown to be significantly more effective in their managerial and leadership roles than those who (equally competent in other technical and cognitive skills) score poorly. To make use of this yourself, you need to become aware of your emotions and how they impact upon your everyday and working life. This includes not only your own direct performance, but also how you interact with others. It also includes getting a better understanding of how emotions affect other people and how you might best handle emotionally charged situations.

Goleman, Boyatzis and McKee (2002) state that there are four major categories of EI for the business leader:

1. self-awareness;
2. self-management;
3. social awareness;
4. relationship management.

Self-awareness

If you are 'emotionally aware', you know your emotional strengths and weaknesses and can discuss them with others. 'Emotional self-awareness' is present when leaders are:

> attuned to their inner signals, recognizing how their feelings affect them and their job performance. They are attuned to their guiding values and can often intuit the best course of action, seeing the big picture in a complex situation. Emotionally self aware leaders can be candid and authentic, able to speak openly about their emotions or with conviction about their guiding vision.
>
> (Goleman, Boyatzis and McKee, 2002, p. 327)

Typical emotional strengths and weaknesses include:

- keeping calm versus getting in a panic;
- keeping going versus giving up;
- seeing the bright side of things versus becoming sad or despondent;
- controlling your anger versus losing your temper;
- feeling confident versus feeling afraid.

 Activity 1.4 Emotional SWOT

1. Draw an emotional SWOT framework, as shown in Figure 1.5. As you might behave differently in study, work and personal situations, you might decide to limit your analysis to a particular context.
2. Now, think of how you react emotionally and enter at least three strengths and three weaknesses for yourself.
3. Next, think of times when you could make use of your emotional strengths, and label each of these as an opportunity.
4. Next, think of times when your emotional weaknesses might put you at a disadvantage, and label each of these as a threat.
5. Analyse your SWOT diagram: do you wish to improve your emotional strengths further? Do you wish to tackle your emotional weaknesses? You might want to refer back to this exercise when you read Chapters 2 and 3, which deal with personal development. The process in this step corresponds to the second of Goleman's EI categories—self-management.

Fig 1.5 Emotional SWOT

Skills Example 1.2 Empathy

In some organizations it is usual for trainee managers to spend some time working on the shopfloor. This allows them to learn how operations are carried out. However, there is also another benefit to this: it gives trainees an insight into what it feels like to work that overtime shift after a hard day, what it feels like to do a repetitive task, what it feels like when no one thanks you. Good managers will remember those trainee days and be able to empathize with their staff—and be better managers as a result.

Understanding and sharing another's feelings—empathizing

An area which you might find it useful to develop is what Goleman *et al.* (2002) call 'social awareness'. One aspect of this is your ability to empathize with someone else.

The ability to inspire others

Another area that you might wish to develop (part of Goleman *et al.*'s (2002) 'relationship management') is the ability to inspire others.

1.6.2 **Managing your emotions**

When your emotions take control

If you can't control your emotions, they may increase out of all perspective; you will then be in danger of focusing upon them and the feelings they bring, rather than the task at hand. Have you ever noticed how someone who is prone to angry outbursts can be 'ignited' by something which then grows rapidly and is disproportionate to the 'problem'? (In everyday life we talk of 'road rage', when otherwise sensible people become violent and abusive over seemingly innocuous acts by other drivers—they have literally lost their ability to control their emotions.) Goleman explains this by showing that activity in the parts of our brain which control our feelings, emotions and intuition swamps that part of our brain which we use for reasoning.

Can you improve your emotional response?

So, what are we to do if we recognize that our emotions are at best not working in our favour and are at worst hijacking our attempts to excel in a desired performance area? Are we doomed to forever repeat the same emotional response and subsequent behaviours? The answer is, not necessarily. But change will take time and require the repetition of actions. Goleman states that EI learning can take place but that the emotional part of your brain (unlike the thinking part of your brain, which can learn a new method of thinking in a single session) may take weeks or months to establish new neural linkages and that learning is implicit—it is absorbed without us being directly aware of it over a period of time.

Skills Example 1.3   Inspiring others

Many organizations seek to improve the leadership abilities of their staff. At one level leadership is about giving your staff direction. At a higher level it is concerned with inspiring people to give their best. This is an elusive quality. It requires being skilled at the task requirements of your job, being confident in your own abilities, having personal integrity and being willing to trust in others. Others need to observe your own personal commitment and energy and take their lead from this. All of these may be highlighted in management annual appraisals as areas for personal development.

Setting yourself emotional goals

Thus, emotional intelligence cannot be 'learnt' in the conventional classroom sense of listening to someone or reading a book. These are only starting points to guide your actions. It is the actions themselves and their repetition which forms your new emotional response. So, for instance, to gain in confidence, you need to practise. What you can do is to set yourself a series of increasingly more challenging targets, which with luck will lay the foundations for more appropriate emotional responses. For young people whose brains are still developing this is an ideal time for careful training and development. However, Goleman insists that whatever your age, you can develop new neural pathways—but that it will take time and a good deal of motivation. The message is clear—set yourself manageable but challenging targets, endeavour to put yourself in situations where you can experience these challenges, and be determined to stick at it!

 Student tips on skills and employability

Using emotional intelligence—retaining self-composure

Laura is a part-time business student. She is in a trainee managerial role with a NHS Foundation Trust hospital. Here, she gives an example of how she has used her new knowledge of emotional intelligence in her job:

> Within the organisation I worked for there had been a recent change of operational process. I attended a meeting, held by the service manager, to discuss the changes—changes which I felt very passionate about. Previous discussions had triggered emotional responses in me, such as anger and frustration. However, at recent university sessions I had been introduced to emotional intelligence, so I decided to take a different stance at this meeting.

> I successfully attended the meeting and calmly discussed with the service manager the progress by her team. Being able to maintain my composure and keep the situation under control made me feel elated. It also meant that I did not feel disappointed with myself; many times the 'come-down' after an emotional response can be the worst, filled with regret and embarrassment! This occasion marked the start of a new me.

1.7 Learning to learn

Of all the skills, that of 'learning to learn' is perhaps the one which, over time, will become the most important to you. You will continue to learn long after you have completed your present 'academic' studies. This learning will often be informal. It will happen in your work-place; it will happen in your personal time. It is unlikely that you will remain in a 'job for life'. It is much more likely that you will have several jobs, if not career moves, during the years ahead. It is also unlikely that you will have sufficient knowledge to perform tasks on a solitary basis; increasingly you will have to link to others in social/learning networks. George Siemens (2005, p. 3) reflects that learning in the 'digital age' means that 'Know-how and know-what is being supplemented with know-where (the understanding of where to find knowledge needed)'.

 Case Study 1: New starter at Supreme Life Insurance

Jamie Andrews had recently completed a business studies degree and was now employed as a management trainee in Supreme Life Insurance, a major insurance company which specialized in over-the-phone and online selling of insurance policies for contents, home, holiday and motor insurance. Jamie was sure that he would soon be on his career path to senior management. He had graduated with a first class honours degree at a prestigious university and had prided himself in always being able to devise novel solutions to problems which others found perplexing. The personality test which he had taken as part of the selection process for the trainee manager's position had noted that he was 'conscientious, does not suffer fools gladly, results-driven but could be impatient, highly intelligent in abstract concepts, could be outspoken'.

He had a high-ranking company mentor—Peter White (a senior manager in the Human Resource Development department)—who was in overall charge of his development. Peter had devised a schedule of developmental activities which involved Jamie spending three months working with various departments, a system which he had devised as a 'graduate fast-track' approach for 'high fliers'. At the end of this time Jamie would begin his managerial career as a team leader in one of the customer adviser departments, where he would be in charge of eight staff dealing with incoming telephone calls from the general public.

For his first month's experience, Jamie had been working as a customer adviser in the largest team of the company's central call centre environment, taking phone calls from the general public. This entailed dealing with incoming calls for insurance from private individuals. He followed a scripted response from the company's comprehensive training manual when dealing with incoming calls. In addition to giving quotations for insurance and inputting the clients' details to the computer, he was also to ask if the client had any other insurance needs which he could then pass on to other departments. A further requirement was that he had a maximum 'wrap-around' time—i.e. the time for a complete 'customer transaction'. He was timed against company standard wrap-around times and the number of clients he successfully dealt with: his team leader would occasionally listen in to calls and assess his performance. His performance as a customer adviser was measured against these standards, and each week he had a meeting with his team leader (Jill Bradley, an enthusiastic individual who took her role in developing staff seriously) to discuss his progress. A typical shift was 6–8 hours with a short break for lunch. *(continued...)*

His next month had been spent working in the corporate accounts section. This involved some data inputting. However, to expand his knowledge of the company's activities, a significant amount of his time was spent contacting existing account holders of large organizations, and he was gradually allowed some amount of discretion (within given boundaries set by the section's line manager, Roger Knowles) for negotiation with clients. As part of the corporate accounts team he was asked to prioritize a number of corporate accounts in terms of present sales value and projected growth for the next 2 years. He was then asked to present his findings back to the team at one of their weekly meetings. Some of the data input officers in the team who were permanent members thought that this was something which only they should do as they had far more experience of the clients and their needs. Also, they had been used to a fairly basic form of presentation and statistics, but they noted with concern that Jamie was using much more advanced techniques than they normally used in their presentations. Jamie soon sensed that he might have to 'dumb down' his presentations.

During his third month he was invited to accompany Roger Knowles to several meetings with clients. Some of these were fairly casual discussions which gave both parties a chance to catch up with any gossip and developments whilst reviewing ongoing contracts. Some of this work was conducted in the office, but quite a lot of time was spent in business lunches. Upon completion of these 3 months, Jamie was to take up his new role as team leader.

 Case Study 2: Eco Day display

Stephen considered himself an active member of the work group he had been allocated to at university. He always showed up on time to meetings, he always did what was asked of him at the time—usually some research on a specific topic (he was good at retrieving information from the various electronic sources available at the university.) Recently his group had been asked to design a display which would be part of a university 'Eco Day' to promote ideas to educate people in environmentally friendly ways of carrying out their business and in particular the need for people to think more about their 'carbon footprint'. He realized that if his display was to be really effective it should appeal not just to one sense and intelligence (as given by Howard Gardner) but a variety. He wondered how he might incorporate elements of these in his display. His initial idea was a simple one—to try to show in a novel way how, on an everyday basis, people could save fuel and cut gas emissions by either sharing a car, by taking a bus or train or by walking or cycling into work.

 Chapter summary

The aim of this chapter has been to introduce you to some definitions and underlying principles of skills and learning. In addition, you have explored the links between knowledge, skills and behaviour. You have seen that to be an effective student you need study skills as well as subject-specific knowledge. You have seen that effective managers need a range of skills, some analytical/task-based, others related to how they interact with individuals and groups. To reinforce the social nature of managerial skills you have been given examples of multiple intelligences and emotional intelligence. The concept of transferability of skills between contexts has also been covered.

End of chapter exercises

Exercise 1: New starter at Supreme Life Insurance

Read Case Study 1—New starter at Supreme Life Insurance, then answer these questions:

1. What sorts of skills do you think Jamie needs for his new role as team leader?
2. Do you think he could have developed any of these skills during his degree studies?
3. How important do you think the following are to his successful development of these skills:
   - his own motivation and self-belief;
   - feedback during his training;
   - the content of the training?

Exercise 2: Eco Day display

Read Case Study 2—Eco Day display. Then, using Gardner's ideas on multiple intelligence, suggest how Stephen could design the proposed 'Eco Day' display to appeal to his audience. You might wish to consider what special features and what types of media he might employ.

Exercise 3: Emotions

Think of a time when you lost control of your emotions in a work or study situation. Do you think this was an appropriate response? What have you learnt from this episode? What might you try to do differently next time?

 ## Further reading

To read Gardner's original work on multiple intelligences, look for the following book in your library: Gardner, H. (1993) *Frames of mind: The theory of multiple intelligence.* New York: Basic Books.

 For further information on the concept of skills transferability, please visit the Online Resource Centre at **http://www.oxfordtextbooks.co.uk/orc/gallagher2e/**

2 Foundations for Personal Development

 Chapter guide

Student viewpoint

Dawn, Lee and Paula were studying for a part-time degree in Applied Management. At the time of writing they had been working together for almost 2 years in the 'learning set'. They were asked how useful they had found personal development within their course. Their responses are given below:

'good to have protected time to review and reflect own personal development, to analyse strengths and weaknesses and to identify a plan'

'wouldn't normally look at personal development on a day-to-day basis but having to engage with the exercises [as part of the course] has in fact proved very beneficial'

'has helped me to look at career planning'

 By the end of this chapter you should be able to:

- Apply a learning cycle approach to your own learning (we will look at Kolb, Honey and Mumford)
- Outline the concept of learning styles (Honey and Mumford)
- Design your own learning journal
- Explain the concept of 'self-efficacy' and how this is linked to experience
- Apply the principles of 'cognitive apprenticeship' to your own learning
- Describe conscious and unconscious competence

Introduction

The main thrust of this chapter is about preparing you for the personal development exercises throughout the rest of the book. Essentially you need to be aware of the underlying learning philosophy. This is centred here around a reflective, experience-based ('experiential') approach to personal development. The idea that you develop confidence (self-efficacy) through having experiences is introduced.

Some of your learning experiences will be planned, others will happen anyway. However, you should not think that you always have to go through this process alone. The personal development process is ideally one that you share with others, where you seek advice and appropriate help as necessary.

Chapter outline

The chapter begins with a reminder from Chapter 1 that personal development is important from both academic and employment perspectives. The role that reflection plays in personal development planning (PDP) is introduced. This leads into a discussion of how you learn through experience—experiential learning. Various models of this are given, and you are shown an example of a typical learning sequence using one of them. You will then consider your different 'styles' of learning. To help you in your reflection, the discussion then turns to how you might use a learning journal to record your progress and to think about how you have learnt, and perhaps what you might do in similar situations in the future. The final part of the chapter is about the help, support and advice you might receive from a mentor or other person. This person may be able to tell you things about yourself that are not obvious to you.

2.1 Introducing personal development plans

At university the focus of personal development plans is upon personal, academic and career-related goals during each of your years' studying, with an eye to the future. It is important to fully engage with them, for as Garavalia and Gredler (2002, p. 221) point out, 'students who set effective goals, utilize appropriate learning strategies, and evaluate the requirements of learning tasks adequately tend to achieve at higher levels than other students'.

In the world of work you will probably be given annual appraisals which look back over the previous year and forward to the next in terms of your performance, training needs and career aspirations. Some professional institutions, such as the Chartered Institute of Personnel and Development and the Chartered Management Institute, require that you keep your 'Continuing Professional Development' (CPD) up to date and keep an ongoing portfolio of your professional development. Many organizations ask you to keep a diary or a log of your personal and professional development. In other words, personal development planning is going on not just in schools and universities but 'out there' in the world of work.

2.2 The importance of reflection

Personal development planning requires careful thought. You need to think about what you want to improve. This means you need to decide what is important to you at the moment and what is likely to be relevant to you in the future. You need to investigate and somehow measure your current levels of skills and knowledge. To do this you may have to look back in time (to reflect) to consider your recent performance. Armed with these 'baselines' you have the starting point of your plan and a means of monitoring future improvements. Thus, reflection is part of the initial planning process.

Boud, Keogh and Walker (1985) talk of reflection as 'turning experience into practice'. They state that:

> Reflection is an important human activity in which people recapture their experience, think about it, mull it over and evaluate it. It is this working with experience that is important to learning.
>
> (Boud, Keogh and Walker, 1985, p. 19)

The whole purpose of a personal development plan is to give direction to what you are going to do—those experiences which will allow you to develop your abilities and knowledge. Reflection enables you to derive the fullest benefit from those experiences. To do this you need to be constantly reflecting upon your learning experiences. You should note that the term 'experience' can constitute all aspects of our actions, behaviour, thoughts and emotions.

2.3 Experiential learning

You will recall from Chapter 1 that one of the ways through which you learn is by memorizing information—but there are other methods by which you learn, learning from experience being at the forefront. Kolb, Rubin and Osland (1991) remind us:

> For most of us, the first associations we have with the word 'learning' are teacher, classroom and textbook...
>
> As students, our job is to observe, read and memorize what the teacher assigns and then to repeat 'what we have learned' in examinations. ... The textbook symbolizes the assumption that learning is primarily concerned with abstract ideas and concepts. The more remembered, the more you have learned. The relevance and application of these concepts to your own job will come later. Concepts come before experience.
>
> (Kolb, Rubin and Osland, 1991, p. 59)

These researchers talk of learning from our experiences and regard learning as a continuous process in which you take charge of your learning. What you learn is what you choose for your own particular situation. The following quote emphasizes that what you really need to acquire is the ability to keep learning from your experiences:

> And yet ... in a world where the rate of change is increasing rapidly every year, in a time when few will end their careers in the same jobs or even the same occupations they started in, the ability to learn seems an important, if not the most important, skill.
>
> (Kolb, Rubin and Osland 1991, p. 59)

In experiential learning it is not just the immediate content of what you have learned that is important but your ability to think back to previous experiences and to make some sort of sense of what has happened in a particular situation(s), and then to construct plans for what you might do if a similar situation were to confront you in the future. You also carefully consider the worth of any new learning in terms of cost/benefit. Both of these processes are 'cognitive'—they engage you in deliberate conscious thought.

Perhaps the most defining of the work of Kolb (1984) was his 'experiential learning cycle', which depicted learning as a cycle of four consecutive stages. The four stages are: concrete experience, reflection, theorizing and testing.

Concrete experience

Typical examples of learning experiences are:

- field trips;
- training sessions;

- mistakes;
- giving/listening to presentations;
- reading;
- arguments;
- team discussions;
- creating something;
- watching someone else do a job.

The list goes on. Experiences may be physical—that is, feeling, doing or thinking/emotional—or a combination. They might happen to us or we might observe them happening as events and be affected by them in some way.

Reflection

The reflection stage is where we give our own initial thoughts on what happened. This may also take into account initial observations from others. For instance, let's say that your learning experience was giving a presentation in class. Then, your initial thoughts may be 'Yes, that went well, particularly the concluding remark.' At this point all you are doing is observing.

Theorizing

In the next stage—theorizing—you try to make sense of what happened. In this case, why did people like that concluding remark? Was it because it was interesting? Was it humorous? You will think of other similar situations that you have been in. Is there some sort of general rule that you think applies? What have the textbooks told you about concluding remarks?

Testing

At this stage you may decide to test out your ideas for improvement before applying them to the next time that you have a similar experience. In the above case, you might want to try writing different types of concluding remark and experiment to see how effective they are. You are, in effect, planning for your next experience. (Sometimes you will see the 'testing' stage replaced by 'planning' for this reason.)

The cycle was normally shown to start with the experience (or 'concrete experience' as Kolb described it) in the 12 o'clock position, the cyclical arrow from this leading to the next stage at 3 o'clock, which was the 'reflection' stage. The stages of 'theorizing' at 6 o'clock and then 'testing' at 9 o'clock followed in the cycle. (You may wish to note, however, that Cowan (2006, p. 46) says that it is quite possible to begin the cycle at the theorizing stage.) Being cyclical, Kolb said that we go around a new cycle the next time we have a similar experience.

Following on from the popularity of Kolb's work on the learning cycle, many other theorists adopted the learning style approach, perhaps none more successfully than Alan Mumford and Peter Honey. Indeed, over recent years their work on learning styles has become the preferred choice for many trainers and tutors involved in management development (and, by implication, for students studying business and management). Honey and Mumford's model of the learning cycle is shown in Figure 2.1.

Skills Example 2.1   The adult swimmer

To illustrate how the Honey and Mumford model in Figure 2.1 works, let us take as an example James, a poor adult swimmer who wants to improve his swimming technique. Tired of fit twenty-something swimmers who seem to delight in speeding past and cutting in front of him, and embarrassed that he struggles to keep up with the old-age pensioners in the pool, James has decided that he must do something to improve his swimming finesse and pool image (note how feelings are very important to spur us on to learning!).

First cycle

Having an experience Relating James' learning to the learning cycle, you can see that he has had an experience (swimming poorly).

Reviewing He has then immediately reviewed this experience; he is far from happy with his performance. Had an instructor been present at the poolside, James' performance might have been observed and he might have received feedback at this stage, but in this particular case the feedback is the result of self-assessment only.

Concluding James then enters the 'concluding' position: he wonders what he is doing wrong—he seems to be putting a lot of energy into not getting very far or going very quickly. He starts to observe fast swimmers to see what it is that they do which he doesn't. He finds this of limited use as it is difficult to see precisely what they are doing, but he notes that they don't seem to expend energy frantically like he does. Then, browsing through his local bookshop one day he has a breakthrough; there on the shelf is a book entitled *Total Immersion*, which almost unbelievably says that by following a few essential changes in technique, the poor swimmer should quickly be able to progress to competence. James buys the book. He notes the main points: try to maintain a horizontal position so as to minimize drag from the water; try to make yourself long and pointy in the water—like a sleek yacht hull, rather than a squat tugboat—for as long as possible throughout the swimming stroke; finally try to think as if you are a fish slipping through a small hole in the water in front!

Planning Armed with these 'theories' he progresses to the 'planning' phase—the next time he is in the pool. Achieving a horizontal position in the water is difficult at first, but by following the book's advice on imagining oneself as swimming 'downhill' he manages this. He practises being long and thin in the water by trying to glide in the water fully outstretched. He spends the rest of the session trying these techniques, planning to incorporate them into his swimming in future. James has now completed one learning cycle.

Second cycle

The next time he goes to the pool he incorporates everything he has learnt into his swimming: this is his next experience. He might then go through a second learning cycle. For instance, almost straightaway he notices a significant improvement in his swimming (reviewing). Amazing! The book was right. Later that night he re-reads the chapter (further concluding). In future he can feed experiences into his own theory. (Cowan (2006) talks about 'generalizing'—from our experiences we are able to say 'aha, ... so it would seem to me that in general the following seems to be true ...'). And so the learning cycle continues. James is now swimming faster and with more efficiency. But note—it's not because he is fitter, it's because he took time to review, conclude and plan.

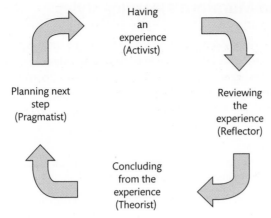

Fig 2.1 Honey and Mumford's learning cycle

Source: Mumford (1997, p. 32) with the permission of the publisher, the Chartered Institute of Personnel and Development, London (http://www.cipd.co.uk)

 Activity 2.1   Learning from Intute

For this activity you will need to have access to the Internet. The aim of the exercise is to learn something of value to you as a student and to analyse how you learnt it in terms of the learning cycle.

You are about to use a website called 'Intute'. The easiest way to explain the website's function is to quote from the site itself: 'Intute is a free online service providing access to the very best web resources for education and research.'

- On your computer, access the Internet and then go to the address http://www.vtstutorials.co.uk/ (accessed: 9 March 2012), which will take you to the 'Virtual Training Suite'.

- Next, scroll down to 'Business and Management' (materials author for this section of the site is Angela Joyce, ILRT, University of Bristol, 2009).

- Clicking here brings you to 'The Internet for Business and Management' and an interactive tutorial.

In this exercise you may choose what you spend your time on. However, it is suggested that you spend half an hour on whatever section(s) this is. (Do not expect to finish the whole tutorial in this time; you may decide to overview the whole tutorial, or focus on particular sections.)

Q1. Which sections of the tutorial did you access? (This is your learning experience in the learning cycle.)

Q2. What, in particular, did you learn? Was it interesting? How easy did you find accessing new information? (This is your initial review, the next stage of the learning cycle.)

Q3. In general, what can you say about what you have learnt in your chosen section? For instance, how might you summarize this as an approach to researching companies, government websites, famous business writers, etc.? Does what you have learnt agree with any previous knowledge you have? (This is the concluding stage of your learning cycle.)

Q4. Finally, how might you use what you have learnt (in future research, for example)? What will you do differently in future as a result of this learning? This can also include learning more about some of the websites, as well as using them. (This is the planning stage of your learning cycle.)

Please note: as this web-based exercise is subject to change, should you encounter difficulties, you should consult the Online Resource Centre, where alternative exercises may be available, for further information.

2.4 Honey and Mumford's learning styles

In the late 1970s Peter Honey and Alan Mumford introduced their learning styles theory. This linked the four stages of Kolb's learning cycle to particular styles of learning: an 'activist' style corresponding to the experience part of the cycle, a 'reflector' corresponding to reflection, a 'theorist' corresponding to the theorizing stage, and a 'pragmatist' corresponding to the testing/planning phase. The four learning styles in the Honey and Mumford Learning Styles Inventory are defined in summary below:

- Activists like: to think on their feet; to have short sessions; plenty of variety; the opportunity to initiate; to participate and have fun.
- Reflectors like: to think before acting; thorough preparation; to research and evaluate; to make decisions in their own time; to listen and observe.
- Theorists like: concepts and models; to see the overall picture; to feel intellectually stretched; structure and clear objectives; a logical presentation of ideas.
- Pragmatists like: to see the relevance of their work; to gain practical advantage from learning; credible role models; proven techniques; activities to be real.

(Honey and Mumford, 2006, pp. 19–20)

You can see how this maps on to Honey and Mumford's learning cycle if you refer back to Figure 2.1. By completing a questionnaire, students can be 'scored' against each of the four styles. Honey and Mumford say that ideally someone has a balanced learning style, which means that he or she will go through all stages of the learning cycle. However, some people have a strong preference for a particular style. Whilst this can have benefits in terms of that particular style's strengths, it may miss out on the desirable qualities of the other styles. Thus one of the uses of the Learning Styles Inventory is to allow the learner to build developmental objectives for expanding their competence in the under-represented styles: for instance, someone who is a poor activist might deliberately plan to carry out more activities to learn from; a poor theorist might plan to find out more about how and why a particular experience turned out as it did. Alternatively, the learner might choose a method of learning which best suits their particular learning style strength. Another use of the Learning Styles Inventory is to form teams of people who as a group exhibit all of the four styles in a balanced fashion.

2.5 Reflecting—using learning journals

2.5.1 Why keep a learning journal?

You may be asked to keep a learning journal for your personal development. This helps you in your reflection. It helps you to move around the learning cycle. But how many of us keep a diary? Perhaps not many. Anna Bolling (1994, p. 47) quotes the American novelist Mark Twain writing in 1867—probably with tongue in cheek—'If you wish to inflict a heartless and malignant punishment upon a young person, pledge him [her] to keep a journal for a year', before she then goes on to state that Twain did in fact keep many journals himself.

If you have ever kept a diary or journal, it has likely been at a time when you were reflecting upon your life—for instance, when moving away from home for the first time. However, the action of writing down your thoughts can be very powerful when it comes to your personal development. You may see the terms 'learning journal', 'learning log', 'personal review' or simply 'workplace diary' used when referring to this activity.

Learning journals can come in many different formats: at the simplest they are merely notes recording what we did that day; they might be completed on a daily or regular basis; they might be completed only when we feel that we have something significant to say; they might be more akin to a series of question prompts that we complete; they might be linked to our personal development objectives.

If you want to read up on the use of journals, the work of Jenny Moon is highly recommended. She quotes Richardson (1994, p. 517) as saying, 'I write because I want to find something out, I write in order to learn something I didn't know before I wrote it' (Moon 2006, p. 33). She goes on to add that journals offer the development of 'voice' (p .72). Also, quoting Richardson again, she points out that 'Journals acknowledge the role of emotion in learning' (p. 27). Once again—feelings matter!

You may say things in your journal that you feel you cannot say to others; for this reason, you may wish to keep your journal private. However, if you are required to keep a journal for professional development purposes (for example, by a professional institution), you may have to give access to certain individuals. Certainly, journals can record your fears, doubts, joys, highs and lows in a very personal manner. You are encouraged to keep a learning journal for these reasons.

2.5.2 Thoughts on the learning journal format

Critical incident versus diary

Your learning journal may simply be a collection of such critical incident sheets in a folder (hard copy or electronic). See Figure 2.2 for an example of a critical incident sheet. Alternatively, you may prefer to write in diary fashion what you have learnt that particular day or week. The important thing is that you establish a routine of entering comments.

Hand-written versus electronic

If you decide upon a hand-written journal, buy a good quality hardback notebook that can take a little rough treatment over the next 6 months or so. A good ringbinder file is another option—this will allow you to add supplementary sheets. The beauty of hard copy is that you have the ability to easily add freehand notes or diagrams, and you are not dependent upon technology. However, you may decide to keep your learning journal electronically— you can devise your own, or you may already be using computer software for this purpose (for instance, capturing additional information such as photos and relevant links to websites). Or you might have some combination of the two media—for instance, downloading key information to hard copy.

LEARNING JOURNAL: *Name*	
Date:	
What was critical incident concerned with?	
Details of what happened	
My initial thoughts	
My initial feelings	
What skills/behaviours did I use?	
Performance rating of my skills (1 poor–5 good)	
Confidence rating of my skills (1–5)	
What have I learnt?	
What will I do differently next time?	

Fig 2.2 Critical incident sheet

 Activity **2.2** A personalized learning journal

Read the above section on learning journals again. You are asked to:

1. Choose or design your own learning journal format.
2. Write in your learning journal for 2 weeks.
3. Review its usefulness to you at the end of this period.

Requirements of your journal

As a minimum your learning journal should serve the following purposes:

- provide a record of your daily/weekly learning;
- give a brief description of what you did/what happened;
- include a reflection on what you did/what happened;
- include your thoughts on what you have learnt.

Additionally, you may wish to add sections which cover:

- follow-on actions;
- useful information sources/websites;
- ideas for future projects.

2.6 Albert Bandura: confidence and self-efficacy

Were you to ask fellow students who had been working on a 6-month work placement what they think they had learnt, one of the phrases you would probably hear them say is 'increased confidence'. Ask a group of managers at the end of a part-time degree in business studies what they had learnt and you are likely to hear the same phrase. 'Confidence' is not an easy concept to discuss; however, we should differentiate our feeling of confidence in performing specific tasks from our general sense of self-belief. In terms of learning theories, what is often referred to is 'self-efficacy', which is our perceived ability to achieve given results. This definition would seem to cover the notion of feeling confident in performing given tasks but would not seem to be sufficient to describe 'self-belief', which is much more complex, involving for instance, aspects of our personality. This explains why a person may feel perfectly confident in one situation but not in another.

Bandura (1997), who views learning as the interaction between environment, behaviour and the learner's internal processes, has written extensively on 'self-efficacy'. He states that there are four sources of this:

- Mastery experiences—we become more confident after successfully doing something that is difficult.
- Vicarious experiences—we observe others doing something and think that we should be able to do the same (albeit at a lesser, similar or greater level).
- Social persuasion—others tell us that we can do it!
- Physiological/emotional states—feeling 'good' emotionally and physically tends to help us feel that we can achieve something.

There are links between our self-belief and the goals that we set ourselves in our personal development. Therefore, we will expand upon self-efficacy in Chapter 3.

 Skills Example 2.2 Otto Rohwedder: sliced bread—his greatest invention

Sliced bread—that packaged loaf you turn into sandwiches and put into your toaster—is something you probably take for granted. Yet, it was not always so. Before 1928 people had to be content with cutting their own slices of bread, a process essentially simple in nature, yet infuriatingly difficult for some: slices of uneven thickness, misshapen chunks, and squashed wedges of bread were to be found in the lunch boxes of workers across those great sandwich-eating nations of the United States and Great Britain. Then, along came Otto Frederick Rohwedder with his US-patented breadslicing machine, and the world welcomed with open arms (and mouths) the arrival of the uniformly pre-sliced loaf.

However, Otto's story is one of persistence in the face of technical and financial problems, and ridicule from bakers who thought the concept of sliced bread was fundamentally flawed (it would, they said, go stale). He formulated his original idea in 1912 but it was not until 1916 that he began to build a prototype machine—thus spending quite some time on the first phase of his 'learning cycle'. Then disaster struck in 1917, when a fire burnt down his new factory and his precious machine.

(continued...)

Undeterred, he worked as an investment agent and saved until he had sufficient funds to once again build a mechanical bread-slicing machine. This he patented in 1928, the first sliced bread going on sale in the same year. The technical problems Otto faced in successive learning cycles included: holding the cut slices together—his first method, which involved temporarily securing it with metal pins, failed (eventually a collapsible cardboard box was used); keeping the cut slices fresh—to combat this he mechanized the wrapping process; and cutting multiple slices of bread without crushing the loaf—a problem he solved by devising a system in which the bread was sliced from different directions at the same time. Fortune too, played a part—the invention of the first pop-up toasters in 1926, with their own appetite for evenly sliced bread, fuelled demand.

We might conclude the following from Otto's example:

- learning takes persistence and self-belief: perhaps the most striking aspect of this case is how Otto showed great determination throughout his new project;

- the discovery of new knowledge can challenge the status quo—we need to keep an open mind: Otto was up to the challenge, while other bakers were not prepared to change their mindset;

- learning sometimes takes the form of an intuitive leap: Otto's initial idea of producing sliced bread for a hungry workforce, for instance;

- learning often occurs as improvements through repeated cycles of experience: Otto's innovations to overcome various technical problems with his machine is a good example of this;

- the internal and external environment (in this case, financial backing and the invention of pop-up toasters) can promote or restrict learning.

Sources: DesmoinesRegister (2004) *Rohwedder, Otto* [online]. Available at: http://www.desmoinesregister.com/article/99999999/FAMOUSIOWANS/41217023/Rohwedder-Ottto (accessed: 27 May 2012).
The Great Idea Finder (2005) *Bread Slicer* [online]. Available at: http://www.ideafinder.com/history/inventions/breadslicer.htm (accessed: 27 May 2012).
Falzini, M.W. (2008) 'The greatest thing since Otto Rohwedder', *Archival Ramblings*, 7 July [online]. Available at: http://njspmuseum.blogspot.com/2008/07/greatest-thing-since-otto-rohwedder.html (accessed 27 May 2012).

2.7 Cognitive apprenticeships

2.7.1 Learning from others

'Do we always need to learn alone? Can we benefit from others helping us?' The clear answer to these questions is: there are often times when the help of others is useful, if not essential, if we are new to some aspect of learning. However, sometimes we need lots of help; at other times we only need a reassuring word of advice. If we are going to make swift progress in our learning and personal development then we should be aware of how others might help us. In this section, we explore these ideas further under the heading of 'cognitive apprenticeships'.

2.7.2 Levels of learning

Collins, Brown and Newman (1989) show that just as a skilled craftworker can serve an apprenticeship under the guidance of an expert and go through various stages of development, so too can a person be helped to develop in terms of their analytical and reasoning ability in higher-order (non-craft) skills. The example they cite relates to students becoming better writers. The cognitive apprenticeship has five stages in its hierarchy: modelling, coaching,

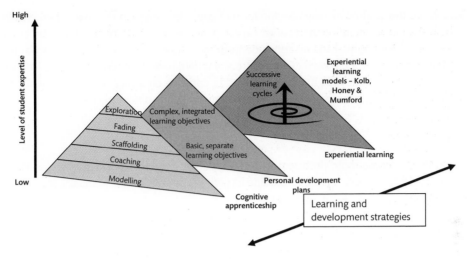

Fig 2.3 Levels of student expertise versus learning and development strategies

scaffolding, fading and exploration. Figure 2.3 shows the level of student expertise increasing with each level attained. By way of comparison (and not to forget that students might also simultaneously be engaged with them), the diagram also shows other strategies and theories such as personal development plans of increasing complexity, and the increase in expertise which comes from students completing successive learning cycles using the experiential learning models of Kolb and Honey and Mumford, as recently outlined. The section that follows expands upon Figure 2.3.

Modelling

The idea of modelling is that of the expert demonstrating to the student the task which is to be learnt, explaining at the same time what needs to be considered and the reasons for their consideration. We have seen an example of this earlier in the chapter in the case of James, the poor adult swimmer, which illustrated the use of Kolb's learning cycle in action.

Coaching

In the case of James, the reader was encouraged to think of an example of their own and to follow Kolb's learning cycle through each of its stages. Under coaching conditions the reader would be observed by the teacher or expert and, where necessary, be given advice (either during the activity or upon completion of it).

Scaffolding

Scaffolding provides a framework for students as they engage with the task. This framework is just sufficient for them to keep heading in the right direction, to keep asking themselves relevant questions along the way so that they do not become 'stuck' and unable to continue.

Sometimes this scaffolding may take the form of cue questions such as 'what, where, when, who, why, how' analysis. In the case of experiential learning, students may also be asked questions such as: 'What can you conclude from this experience? Are there any similarities to other experiences you have had? Are there any differences? Are there any trends you see emerging?' Later on they might be encouraged to consider cues such as: 'How do you now feel about performing this particular task? What might you do differently next time?'

Fading

As students become more proficient with the task, the need for coaching and scaffolding reduces, and so it is appropriate to provide less—the support is 'faded' gradually, leaving the student to become more self-sufficient.

Exploration

Whereas initial tasks are quite explicit, demanding a fairly direct approach and probably expecting that a particular technique be employed, more complex or ambiguous tasks might require the student to frame the problem itself and then to decide which approach would be the best one to use. This process is called 'exploration' and is much more relevant to the 'real world of business': in a business context, there are often unclear and sometimes conflicting symptoms of an undesirable situation: is it a financial problem, a human resources one, a marketing one or a mix of these? What can be done about it?

2.8 Mentors

2.8.1 **Need for guidance**

One thing you will notice about personal development planning—whether or not you encounter it at university or in the work situation—is that it is an activity that will probably involve someone who takes it upon himself (or more usually is required as part of their job role) to guide you through the process. In the case of the mentor at work, this person may well be

---

 Student tips on skills and employability

Use of mentors

Laura is a part-time business student. She is in a trainee managerial role with a NHS Foundation Trust hospital. Here, she gives an example of her personal experience with her workplace mentor.

> I was working within a busy department as a line manager to 26 members of staff when I first began my degree. My line manager had completed the same course a few years earlier and so she was a great inspiration and kept me grounded by listening when I was struggling and providing advice on work–life balance. Although I never referred to her as my 'mentor' I now realize that she provided regular support and guidance to me, which was invaluable. Sometimes you may not need any guidance—but just having someone to talk to can provide the reassurance that you are heading in the correct direction.

Activity **2.3** The perfect mentor

Many successful business people have benefited from having mentors who they could relate to directly. Others have modelled themselves upon the writings of well-known figures from past or present. Imagine you could choose your ideal mentor, someone who could help you to achieve your goals, someone who you could aspire to be like. What qualities would that person possess? (You may wish to consider not only their knowledge and technical skills, but also their behaviours, attitudes and values.)

involved in your annual appraisal; at university this person might well be your personal mentor or tutor. The reason for this involvement is twofold: to help you to complete the process stipulated for the organization and to help you to explore your development objectives. Let's just take a little time to consider the second of these reasons: it assumes that you are likely to require help in addition to your own self-analysis. Why should this be? The answer, quite simply, is that often we are not capable of seeing ourselves in all aspects and can benefit from the observations of someone who has worked with us.

 ## Chapter summary

This chapter has covered a range of concepts that underlie the personal development planning process. At the heart of this process are the themes of personal reflection and experiential learning. The mainstream theories of experiential learning have been introduced; these have included the 'learning cycle' and 'learning styles'. Finally, the concept of 'cognitive apprenticeship' has been covered, reinforcing the view that much of our learning is a socially based experience in which we learn with and through others. The fact that we can't always (accurately) see our own strengths and weaknesses lends weight to the argument that others (e.g. mentors) can help us in our learning.

 ## End of chapter exercises

Exercise 1: Looking ahead

It is sometimes useful to look at the broad picture. In terms of personal development this suggests that you might want to think about not just your immediate situation but also your past development in more general terms, and think ahead to where you eventually would like to be. Your present programme of study is a step in this process. Ideally, it should help you to achieve your broader, longer-term goals. In Chapter 3 you will consider the more specific personal development goals during your programme of study.

For this exercise, look back over your life to the present, in terms of key events or times or achievements in three areas: personal life, academic life and work/career life. (If you have not yet had any work experience you will need to consider this only for the future part of the Activity.) Use the template in Figure 2.4 as a guide.

Can you think of a picture that would show what you would like your future life to be like—what you might be doing, how you would be feeling?

Exercise 2: Your strengths

Peter Honey (2008) and Malcolm Gladwell (2001) ask us to consider improving our strengths, rather than focusing on our weaknesses. Sometimes, however, we do not always appreciate fully what our

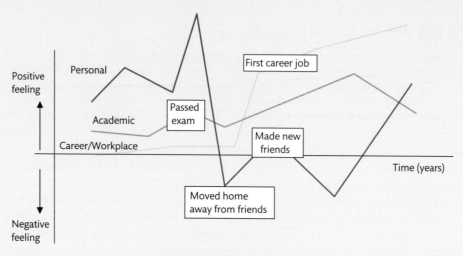

Fig 2.4 Personal, academic and career/workplace highs and lows

strengths are. For this exercise, you are asked to gather the opinions of others, specifically on what they regard as your strengths. This may be dependent upon the context (work/home/academic), so you should take this into account. You may wish to revise your own opinion of your strengths in the light of what your friends/colleagues have said. How might you develop these strengths in the short term/long term?

Exercise 3: Cognitive apprenticeship

As a student, apply the model of cognitive apprenticeship, as given in Section 2.7, to several specific aspects of your own personal development. Ideally, your examples should show how the strategies of modelling, coaching, scaffolding, fading and exploration have been used by your tutor or mentor. However, you might have learnt without such support—in this case, say how further support might have been useful to you.

 ## Further reading

Well worth a look for her work on reflection are the books of Jenny Moon. The one below considers learning journals in particular:

Moon, J. (2006) *Learning journals: A handbook for reflective practice and professional development.* 2nd edn. London & New York: Routledge.

To read Bandura's original work on self-efficacy you may wish to consult:

Bandura, A. (1997) *Self-efficacy: The exercise of control.* New York: W.H. Freeman and Company.

 For further information, please visit the Online Resource Centre at http://www.oxfordtextbooks.co.uk/orc/gallagher2e/

3 Personal Development and Career Planning

 Chapter guide

Student viewpoint

Denise and Wes were studying for a part-time degree in Applied Management. They were asked for comments on how they had identified skills for development and how useful the personal development process had been for them. Their responses are given below:

'identifying study skills in year 1 was very beneficial, especially for those of us who had not studied for a long time'

Wes

'I found the management skills and competencies identified in year 2 of my personal development really useful'

Denise

 By the end of this chapter you should be able to:

- Recognize the need for balance between social life and academic study
- List five ways to well-being
- Conduct a personal time audit
- Construct an activity (Gantt) chart
- Conduct a personal skills audit
- Identify aspects of jobs/careers that interest you
- Construct a personal development plan using SMART goals
- Explain the role of self-belief (self-efficacy) in goal-setting

Introduction

The aims of this chapter are to encourage you to consider your own personal development and then to give you some tools and techniques to assist you in this process. The actual process of looking at your personal development is something that you may already do in an informal way. However, in this chapter you will approach it in a more purposeful way, using supporting documents.

Chapter outline

The chapter begins by asking you to reflect upon how you currently organize your work and leisure activities. Getting the right work–life balance is important for your long-term mental and physical health. You will need to keep this very much in mind when you are establishing your personal development goals. In the opening sections you will also cover various time management and well-being approaches. You may wish to carry some of these forward into your personal development plan for this year.

Personal development planning requires a careful, thoughtful approach. Typically, at university you will need to consider three sets of goals:

1. academic—relating to your university studies;
2. career—relating to your future job role;
3. personal—relating to areas of personal interest.

You will need to establish a baseline of your levels of ability and knowledge in the areas you think are appropriate. From this baseline exercise, you will set yourself goals that you will monitor over time. The level of difficulty and challenge that you set yourself in these goals is important: too easy, and you will achieve little from the exercise; too difficult, and you may become dispirited at a lack of progress and give up. Therefore, we will spend some time in this chapter looking precisely at the issue of setting goals, which, as we shall see, is linked to our level of self-belief in our ability to achieve them.

3.1 Personal well-being and organization skills

3.1.1 Achieving balance

Work–life balance is a hot topic. The UK government continues to invest significant sums of money investigating the productivity of people in the workplace (Government Office for Science, 2008). It wants to avoid the huge drain on the national purse caused by workplace stress. It wants 'switched-on' workers who actually want to go to work. 'Well-being' is the word on the ministerial street.

Does this apply to you as a student? You bet it does! Work–life balance is relevant to you right now; it is an approach, a philosophy which becomes a habit that you will take with you from the world of academic study to the world of work. For those of you who already juggle a part-time job to fund your study, work–life balance is even more crucial for success.

So, before you sit down to plan your personal development goals in detail, consider three possible scenarios. The first (Figure 3.1) is tempting, but carries with it the sorts of problems your tutor warns you against, particularly in your first year at university—too much socializing!

The second scenario may be less familiar to you, but it is equally problematic—too much academic study at the expense of other activities (see Figure 3.2). You need time for friends and social activities. University is a great time for trying out new sports and social activities and joining clubs with fellow enthusiasts. Your personal goals should be included with your academic and career goals. Remember that social skills and organizing others are really important management skills too—good for your CV!

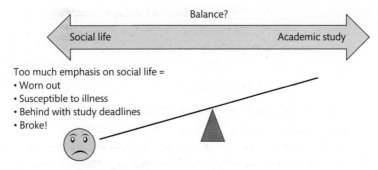

Fig 3.1 Too much emphasis on social life

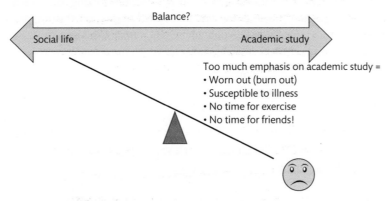

Fig 3.2 Too much emphasis on academic study

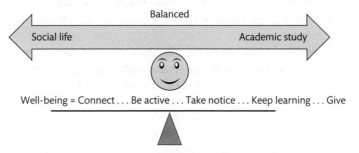

Fig 3.3 Balanced social life and academic study

Ideally (yes, it is easy to say this, but true nevertheless) you should be aiming for a balance of social life and academic study. Figure 3.3 indicates this in a simplistic way; however, it introduces five important areas for your well-being, which we will discuss next.

Five ways to well-being

In its 'Foresight' projects (BIS: Department for Business Innovation and Skills, 2012) the UK government asks groups of experts to undertake projects of national interest. These projects

Activity 3.1 The five ways to well-being

Consider the five ways to well-being.

Make notes against each area of things that apply to you now.

Do you think you need to improve in any area?

If so, how might you achieve this in your social life or academic study?

are designed to look 20–80 years into the future. The aim is to provide guidance for the future social and economic growth of the country. 'What has all of this got to do with me as a student?' you may ask. Well, apart from the fact that you may be working to the recommendations of these reports when you enter the workplace after graduation, the reports offer some very useful advice for you, right now. In particular, the report 'Five Ways to Wellbeing' (nef, 2011) concludes that the evidence heavily suggests we all need to take account of five key areas to be physically and mentally well, as follows:

1. Connect—we need other people, we need to connect with them.
2. Be active—this helps to keeps us physically healthy and also is great for beating stress.
3. Take notice—we need to slow down at times, and appreciate what is around us.
4. Keep learning—this is a natural activity, which is stimulating.
5. Give—helping others makes us feel better about ourselves.

(NEF, 2011, p. 8)

When you are setting your personal development goals for the year, try to ensure that you include all of these in some way—you will be doing yourself a favour!

3.1.2 Do you need to improve your time management?

Any plan requires that you manage the resources available to you. Most textbooks will tell you that, in management terms, these include people, materials, equipment and money. Some then add another 'resource'—time. We all have the same amount of time allotted to us, but managing it is a skill. Before you devise your personal development plan it is therefore appropriate for you to review your time management skills; you may wish to improve these before you commence your plan. Alternatively, you may include 'improving time management' as one of your personal/academic goals for the year.

Notes on 'time waster breaks'

Is a coffee break or a chat with your colleagues or friends a 'waste of time'? Be wary of cutting out altogether breaks that will refresh you physically and mentally and help connect you with your social world. Again, it is a question of balance. If you find yourself having coffee/lunch breaks for as much time as you spend working (this is not as preposterous as it sounds!), then you may wish to focus more on work. Really, the decision is yours. But know how you are spending your time.

Activity 3.2 Managing your time

Case Study 1

Ian was in the second year of his BA Management Studies degree. He was living away from home, sharing a flat with some friends—all in their early twenties. As a group they thought themselves to be fairly conscientious students, but they did still tended to spend most nights socializing. The first year had been relatively easy, as Ian already had a background in A-level business studies. The second year, however, was starting to get difficult, especially as he had recently taken on a part-time job in a fast-food restaurant to cover his living expenses and to fund his socializing. He also tended to eat there as well, as the culinary expertise of both himself and his friends at the flat was somewhat limited to breakfast cereal and spaghetti bolognaise. He had also recently taken up with the delightful Sophie, another student, and was spending quite a lot of time with her. Consequently, his grades had started to suffer—not drastically, but there was a definite trend. This had not been helped by the number of minor colds and ailments that he seemed always to be suffering from.

Case Study 2

Jane was a mature student studying for a part-time business degree. She worked as a team leader in a call centre and had a 2-year-old child with her long-term partner. She was always trying to 'do her best', even if this meant working late into the night on assignments. She prided herself on being good at whatever she did. Her work at the call centre had always been of a very high standard and her assignments in the first two years of her degree had always been very thorough—hers were also usually the longest (she frequently exceeded word limits). However, she was now finding that she was becoming increasingly tired in the mornings and was becoming dependent upon regular coffee 'fixes' to keep her going. Her last assignment had been disappointing—her tutor had described her work as 'too descriptive' and 'wandering away from the point'—this despite it being on a topic about which she knew a lot because of her work background.

Consider Case Studies 1 and 2 above. Comment upon how Ian and Jane are spending their time. Can you see any similarities with how you manage your own time?

 Activity 3.3 Improving your time management—time audits

Have you ever tried to carry out an audit of how you spend your time during a typical working week? If you have not done so recently, then you are recommended to try such an exercise—but be warned that some people discover that it can be a rather tedious and (yes!) time-consuming business. No matter—arm yourself with a notepad and pencil and doggedly determine to carry out such an audit if you wish to improve your time management. Then, at regular intervals during the day (Adair (1987) recommends every 15 minutes, which is probably excessive; you may wish to consider hourly intervals) note down what you are doing (you can categorize into types of activity such as reading, sending emails, having coffee, chatting, work discussions, writing, etc. if you wish). Do not be too surprised if much of your 'work day' is not 'work'. The important thing is for you to be able to identify where you spend the majority of your time. You can then use this information as a baseline of your current activity levels and identify priority areas to be tackled.

3.1.3 Plan the semester/term—diaries and schedules

It's probably an inevitability that those coursework assessments you receive at the beginning of the term/semester will be due in at approximately the same time. This may also include your personal development plan. Why does this bunching occur? Quite simply, your tutor will wish to assess as much as possible of the available teaching time. This, plus the requirement to mark your work and present it to an examinations board, tend to be the deciding factors.

Of course, tutors will try to introduce some early or mid-assessment and some may consult with others so that there is not such a bulge of assignments due in at the same time. However, tutors will tell you that it is up to you to 'manage your time'; whereas it is possible to burn the midnight oil for one assignment, if you try to do this for an assessment 'glut' then you are likely to perform badly. The sensible way is to plan. This means looking ahead to the various submission dates and putting them in your diary. You then need to schedule your work over the coming weeks so that you do not leave everything to the last minute.

One simple but effective way to schedule activities is to use an activity chart (sometimes called a Gantt chart after the early twentieth-century time-and-motion study engineer, Henry Gantt). You can, of course, use computerized versions, but they are easy to draw and show an obvious logic. An example is shown in Figure 3.4.

ACTIVITY / DATE	Week 1	Week 2	Week 3	Week 4	Week 5	Week 6	Week 7	Week 8	Week 9	Week 10
PDP coursework										
Self-audit	░	░								
Research/read	░	░								
Draw up plan			░							
Carry out PD plan (see detail)				░	░	░				░
Write report on PDP (Term 2 Week 16)										
Submit report (Term 2 Week 18)										
Finance coursework										
Research/read	░		░			░				
Mid-term test					░					
Write part A						░				
Write part B								░		
Submit A and B									░	
People in Organizations coursework										
Research/read					▓	▓	▓			
Work on group presentation			▓							
Present in this week				▓						
Work on case study						▓	▓			▓
Submit case study										▓

Fig 3.4 A typical activity (Gantt) chart for term 1

Note: This only shows term 1, 10 weeks—you would add further weeks for term 2, weeks 11–20, as necessary

3.1.4 **Plan the day**

In addition to your long-term planner, you need to spend 5–10 minutes each day planning out what you are going to tackle for that particular day. Adair (1987) urges that we prioritize. This might be by labelling activities as 'urgent'—which means that they should be done soon, and 'important'—which means that they have significance. Important activities are not always urgent; however, if we continue to ignore them they will at some stage become urgent. You need to judge which urgent tasks to carry out that day. Some of these might be easy 'hits'. Be wary if your to-do list never seems to get around to carrying out a particular task and ask yourself if you are guilty of simply putting off doing it because you do not want to do it. Another way of itemizing tasks might be to use a priority such as A—Must do; B—Should do; C—Might do.

3.1.5 **Don't wait for the mood!**

I like this advice, as it applies to writing. Rowena Murray (2005) encourages fellow academic writers (you see, it is not only students who find it difficult at times to engage with the writing process) to force themselves to write something every day. She exhorts writers not to 'wait for the mood'; rather, she advocates 'snack' rather than 'binge' writing. And, it is surprising how effective this strategy can be in keeping you moving forward. I find it reassuring to know that getting started each day is sometimes difficult for the professionals too and that they often have to adopt this gritty approach.

 Student tips on skills and employability

Stress/time management

Laura is a part-time business student. She is in a trainee managerial role with a NHS Foundation Trust hospital. Here, she recalls how she has learnt ways to manage her time and thus alleviate stress. However, she still admits to putting pressure on herself with her perfectionist tendencies—deeply engrained attitudes such as this are hard to change, especially if deep down we feel that we do not really wish to change them.

> I did not have family pressures like other students on the course—but that did not mean that I didn't suffer from pressure and stressful situations. Having strong perfectionist tendencies means that everything I do has to be completed to a certain standard. Evaluating my time, I found that there was a lot of 'down time' in between meetings at work. I therefore rearranged my diary and blocked out at least one admin day per week to allow me to undertake desk-based work, moving meetings to the other days. At home, when I was studying, I made little changes such as not turning on the tv—I started listening to the radio instead—which meant that I was less distracted.
>
> The changes I made resulted in reduced stress at work and my university assignments were also completed on time, meaning that I wasn't panicking at the last minute trying to squeeze everything in. I also found the use of planning aids effective: using a GANTT chart helped me keep track of various assignments, goals and deadlines. A 'to-do list' helped me to focus and to continue work from a previous study session.

3.2 Personal development planning

3.2.1 Career, academic and personal goals

Why did you come to university? The answer to this question will vary from one person to the next, and it is likely that you will have a number of reasons. Here are some possible responses for wishing to attend university:

- I want to get a specific degree to secure the first step on my career ladder.
- I am interested in learning more about my subject area.
- I want to get a 'good' job with a major company and I need some sort of degree— preferably a 2:1.
- I believe spending time at university will be enjoyable and give me a range of life-enriching experiences as a student.
- I think of it as a time to do more of the pastimes I love (e.g. sports) before I settle down to a full-time job.
- I'm not sure yet what I want to do with my life, but my time at university may help me to decide.

In the present job market the competition for many jobs is fierce. This, coupled with the growing cost to students of financing their studies, has tended to put more emphasis upon linking degree attainment to obtaining jobs. Employers are able to be much more selective in their recruitment strategy (HECSU and AGCAS, 2011). With this in mind, this chapter is somewhat biased towards employability as the primary reason for students doing Business and Management degrees. So, for instance, you will be asked to consider what you might wish to do as a future career—even though at this stage you may not have given this much serious thought. Clearly, academic success is necessary to achieve a good degree (and hence a good job), so you will also be asked to consider your academic strengths, weaknesses and goals. But to ignore personal goals would be foolish, as we have just seen in the discussion on work–life balance, and many would rightly argue that life at university is much more than just gaining an academic qualification. So, these too will be covered.

3.2.2 Initial assessment of self

Armed with the knowledge that we might not be aware of every aspect of our personal strengths and weaknesses, we must nevertheless begin our journey of self-development. It is common for students to say, 'If only I had known X at the beginning of the year or could perform skill Y better, then I could have done so much better!' This is a perfectly natural reaction—but don't beat yourself up about this. Focus rather upon what you will be able to do in the future.

No matter, the first step in your personal development planning needs to include an initial assessment of yourself in as valid a fashion as you can muster. This will include your own self-assessment (it is surprising what you can uncover, given a little time to quietly think about yourself) and may well include discussions with others to find out how they see you. These other people can be your family, friends or colleagues. They may be your university tutors (in which case, you may also have written feedback—for example, from assignments). Perhaps you have also recently been through a work appraisal and discussed your work development with your boss. Perhaps you applied for a job and were asked to complete a personality or skills questionnaire—in which case, you might have a print-out showing various aspects of yourself. The idea is to get other sources of information in addition to your own self-knowledge.

'What if I don't agree with what I hear?' Well, of course you would think that you would know yourself better than anyone. You may well decide that the other person is off the mark. However, you may still wish to question yourself to see if there is anything in what the other person is saying—perhaps more so if other people are saying similar things about you.

'What if people only tell me the "good things"?' This too, can be a problem—especially if it's your friends who don't want to sound ungracious. However, if you concentrate on your specific behaviours, knowledge and skills (for instance, 'You can be rather impatient in situation A') that are capable of being improved, rather than focusing upon some aspect of yourself which cannot be changed (for instance, 'You would have made a great guitarist if only your fingers were longer', or another lament, 'You would have made a great dancer if only you had been trained as a child!'), then you are more likely to approach the activity in a problem-solving way.

Personal audits, skills audits, benchmarking, skills assessments

You may well come across some or all of these different types of assessment in your reading. These are just names given to the particular method being used to help you gather your initial self-assessment information together. They also provide a record of your self-profile at the beginning of your personal development plan. The forms which you use will vary according to your university/college/organization. They will have been designed to help you focus your thoughts on something that your tutor can relate to with some form of consistency between you and the next student. A 'house style' is common, with universities adopting their own layouts. Alternatively, you might go with an 'off-the-shelf' product, such as those produced in self-development/skills books.

Using the 'Prospects' website

An excellent website to go to for an in-depth exploration of your future career is 'Prospects', advertised as 'the UK's official graduate careers website' and available at http://www.prospects.ac.uk (accessed: 17 March 2012). Figure 3.5 is a screen shot of the opening page showing the drop-down menu for 'Jobs and work experience'.

 Activity 3.4 Employability questionnaire

Here's a quick online employability questionnaire for you to try in addition to the previous self-assessment. It assesses the sorts of skills that employers seek when recruiting graduates, and you can print out your own profile from it. This site also shows you some examples of how to improve these employability skills at university, socially and in vacation work.

   Please go to http://www.rlo-cetl.ac.uk/whatwedo/rlos/completedrlos.php (accessed: 17 March 2012), then click on 'Business Studies', then 'Employability' and complete the questionnaire.

Used with kind permission of rlo-cetl: developed by Debbie Holley and Carl Smith at the Centre for Excellence in Teaching and Learning in Reusable Learning Objects, London Metropolitan University.

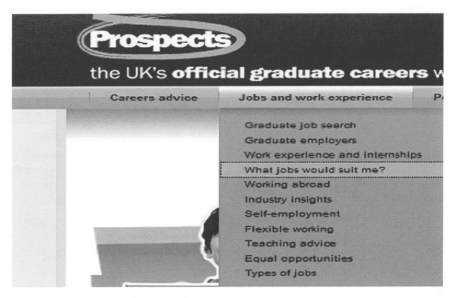

Fig 3.5 Prospects website

Source: © Graduate Prospects Ltd. Used with kind permission of the Association of Graduate Careers Advisory Services (AGCAS) (http://www.prospects.ac.uk)

You will need to register to use the site, but everything is free. You may find that your University Careers Services already use and recommend the site. Of particular interest at this point is the section 'What jobs would suit me?' and 'Types of jobs'. The section 'Industry insights' gives you a lot of useful, concise information, including case studies of people working within the sector. These sections may give you ideas if you really haven't thought much about your career at this point; they may also give you further information on any tentative thoughts you might have. However, to get a fuller picture, you should consider speaking to persons who have worked in, or have contacts with the profession, including relevant university tutors and your Careers Advisory Service.

Clicking under 'Job sectors' brings the screen shown in Figure 3.6, which has a section entitled 'Business and management' (although you may wish to look at other sectors, as many of them recruit students with business and management degrees).

Job adverts

When you read adverts for specific job vacancies you will note that they often provide information in the form of job descriptions and person specifications. A job description outlines the key tasks and responsibilities of the job holder and usually gives details of terms of service, such as your pay, holidays and benefits. A person specification links the job to the characteristics expected of a suitable candidate; these are often listed as either 'essential' or 'desirable' and may include prior knowledge/experience/qualifications, and particular skills—both technical and inter-personal.

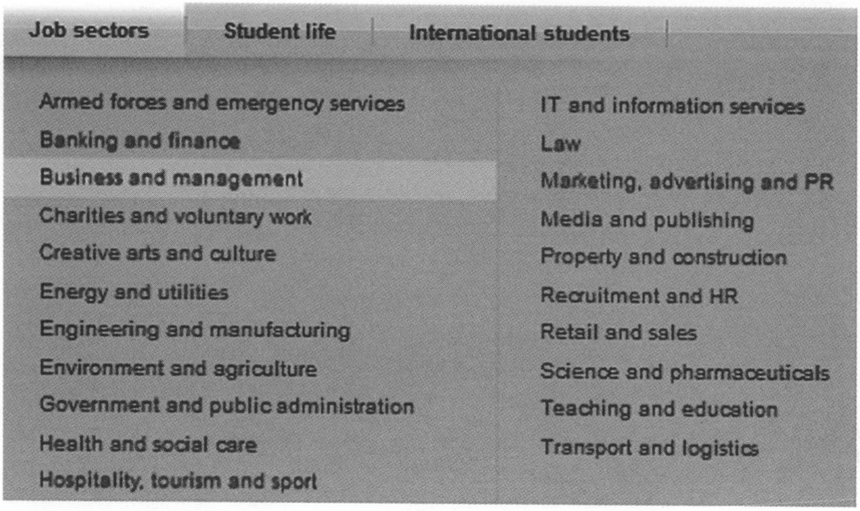

Job sectors	Student life	International students	

Armed forces and emergency services	IT and information services
Banking and finance	Law
Business and management	Marketing, advertising and PR
Charities and voluntary work	Media and publishing
Creative arts and culture	Property and construction
Energy and utilities	Recruitment and HR
Engineering and manufacturing	Retail and sales
Environment and agriculture	Science and pharmaceuticals
Government and public administration	Teaching and education
Health and social care	Transport and logistics
Hospitality, tourism and sport	

Fig 3.6 Job sectors (Prospects website)

Source: © Graduate Prospects Ltd. Used with kind permission of the Association of Graduate Careers Advisory Services (AGCAS) (http://www.prospects.ac.uk)

Summarizing your knowledge of a particular job/career role

When you start to analyse a particular job or career role there will be a large 'unknown' factor. By using Prospects Planner, asking friends, tutors and your careers advisors and researching information from job adverts, etc. you will start to build up a picture of the job or career role that interests you. You will then be able to compare yourself against the job or career role. Hopefully, you already match some of the skills and knowledge requirements. You may wish to develop some of these at university and include them in your personal development plan for this academic year. However, you will also need to ascertain whether or not the job feels right for you in terms of three other aspects—the job environment, rewards and prospects. You should have identified these in your initial search, but may still feel there are some gaps in your knowledge. Typical aspects to consider are listed in Figure 3.7.

3.2.3 Next stage—the plan

It is usually a good idea for you to take some time alone and jot down some of your own ideas at this point. The sorts of goals you set yourself (typically over the next semester or academic year) will depend upon many factors, but should take into account the skills audit you have recently completed and then be matched to your likely performance against your chosen targets in the absence of any special attention. If you feel confident that you will achieve these goals in the normal course of your further studies and experience, then you can still note them as goals but may not need to take any further action in your plan. However, you will often find a difference between your likely improvement without taking additional deliberate action and the goals you aspire to; in this case, there is a 'performance gap' (Figure 3.8).

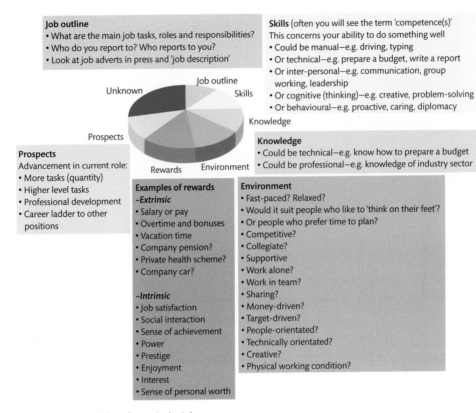

Job outline
• What are the main job tasks, roles and responsibilities?
• Who do you report to? Who reports to you?
• Look at job adverts in press and 'job description'

Skills (often you will see the term 'competence(s)')
This concerns your ability to do something well
• Could be manual—e.g. driving, typing
• Or technical—e.g. prepare a budget, write a report
• Or inter-personal—e.g. communication, group
  working, leadership
• Or cognitive (thinking)—e.g. creative, problem-solving
• Or behavioural—e.g. proactive, caring, diplomacy

Knowledge
• Could be technical—e.g. know how to prepare a budget
• Could be professional—e.g. knowledge of industry sector

Prospects
Advancement in current role:
• More tasks (quantity)
• Higher level tasks
• Professional development
• Career ladder to other
  positions

Examples of rewards
–Extrinsic
• Salary or pay
• Overtime and bonuses
• Vacation time
• Company pension?
• Private health scheme?
• Company car?

–Intrinsic
• Job satisfaction
• Social interaction
• Sense of achievement
• Power
• Prestige
• Enjoyment
• Interest
• Sense of personal worth

Environment
• Fast-paced? Relaxed?
• Would it suit people who like to 'think on their feet'?
• Or people who prefer time to plan?
• Competitive?
• Collegiate?
• Supportive
• Work alone?
• Work in team?
• Sharing?
• Money-driven?
• Target-driven?
• People-orientated?
• Technically orientated?
• Creative?
• Physical working condition?

Fig 3.7 Your knowledge of a particular job

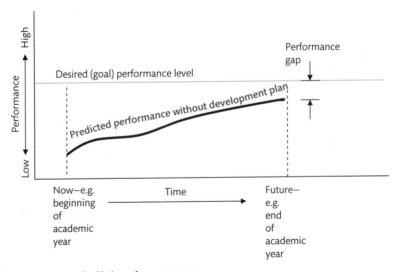

Fig 3.8 Attempting to predict likely performance gaps

Bridging this gap is what you must now consider. How big is the gap? Do you feel that it is possible to bridge (you might have set your sights too high)? Are you unsure of this? This would be a good time to seek further advice from others and your tutor before deciding.

3.2.4 **Goal-setting**

A basic strategy for setting goals: the concept of self-efficacy

Albert Bandura's ideas on self-efficacy were introduced in Chapter 2. However, we are now going to recap and then expand upon his work, as it is very useful when setting personal goals. In his book *Self-efficacy: The Exercise of Control'* (1997, p. 3) Bandura defines self-efficacy as follows: 'Perceived self-efficacy refers to beliefs in one's capabilities to organize and execute the courses of action required to produce given attainments.' This concept is not unknown to us, although we will probably talk of our feeling of 'confidence' about being able to do something. Moreover, we may realize that this confidence in our ability can vary due to a number of factors.

According to Bandura (1997), we can build this self-efficacy from different sources:

- Enactive mastery—if we can become skilled at a task, then we are likely to feel that we can apply it to a new situation.

- Vicarious experience—this means learning by viewing and reflecting upon the experience of others; it is usually easier to accomplish something if we know that it can be done and we have witnessed how it was done.

- Verbal persuasion—perhaps not as powerful as the above, but we all know that words of encouragement from others can be of significant help when we are wavering over whether or not to take action.

- Physiological and affective states—we all know that if we feel tired or sad we are much less likely to take on challenging goals than if we feel energetic and positive.

Integration of efficacy information may occur before a difficult challenge. We will weigh up our perceived skills, our physical and emotional states, words of encouragement from others and then make a decision as to whether or not to 'go for it'. Bandura highlights the implications of self-efficacy in terms which are extremely relevant to goal-setting when he says:

> such beliefs influence the course of action people choose to pursue, how much effort they put forth in given endeavours, how long they will persevere in the face of obstacles and failures, their resilience to adversity, whether their thought patterns are self-hindering or self-aiding, how much stress and depression they experience in coping with taxing environmental demands and the level of accomplishments they realize.
>
> (Bandura, 1997, p. 3)

 Activity 3.5 Confidence

Think of times when you have had to perform a (personally) challenging task. Ideally, think of a task in which you have performed variably in terms of performance due to a variation in your confidence in your ability. Try to think of anything which had happened previous to carrying out the task or your physical and emotional states both prior to and during the task which might have influenced your self-confidence.

Which comes first—interest in goals or ability and self-efficacy?

Or to put it another way—are we interested in the things we are good at, or do we become good at the things we are interested in? Again, Bandura points the way when he writes:

> People display enduring interest in activities at which they feel efficacious and from which they derive self satisfaction. ... Once self involvement in activities gets tied to personal standards, variations in performance attainments activate self satisfying or self dissatisfying reactions.
>
> (Bandura, 1997, p. 219)

SMART goals

Whatever your goals, a simple method for improving your plan is to use the SMART technique, which all goals should adhere to. They should be

- Specific
- Measurable
- Achievable
- Relevant
- Timely.

We will now expand on each of these techniques.

Specific Make sure that you say precisely what it is you are trying to improve. (For instance, if you were just to say 'presentations', this is rather broad. It would be better if you could specify particular aspects such as clarity of slides, audience interaction/rapport, voice levels.) As Bandura explains:

> Explicit standards ... build personal efficacy by furnishing unambiguous signs of personal accomplishments. General intentions, which are indefinite about the level of attainment to be reached provide little basis for regulating one's efforts or for evaluating one's capabilities.
>
> (Bandura, 1997, p. 133)

Measurable You need to measure your present performance and that which you are aspiring to. This will not always be easy! You might have to invent some sort of measure yourself. Also, you may well be advised to break down a difficult task into smaller elements, which you can achieve step by step. (Bandura and Schunk (1981), talk of 'formidable distal goals' being tackled in this way.) These steps themselves must be capable of being measured. Sometimes a learning journal can be used to this effect.

As it is such a tricky part of the SMART technique, let us illustrate it further with an example. Let's say that you decided that your goal was to improve your audience interaction/rapport during presentations. (Last time you did a presentation you noticed that the audience appeared to lose interest halfway through. There were no questions at the end.) Here are some of my thoughts on this—but remember that it is the process that really counts.

Skills Example 3.1 Self-efficacy and goal-setting

One of the examples referred to briefly by Bandura relates to the sport of rock climbing. Let us explore this further. It's interesting to note that writers such as Csikszentmihalyi (1996) write about creativity and the concept of 'flow' (being totally absorbed in what one is doing and feeling that everything is happening in a skilful way) and use rock climbing as an example which embodies both physical and mental skills simultaneously. Picture, then, the rock climber who has halted just before the crux move (the most difficult move on the climb) of what to her is a challenging route. Let's say that this is an overhanging piece of rock; our intrepid climber is leading the climb and roped up to her 'second', whose job it is to manage the rope and (hopefully) hold the leader in the event of a fall. As the leader progresses, she places slings around protruding rocks and jams metal wedges and other devices into cracks in the rock, feeding the rope through attached metal snaplinks (carabiners). The idea is that, should the leader fall, this 'protection' will hold; it does not thus prevent a fall, but should limit the drop experienced by the leader and hopefully she will be left bouncing at the end of the rope, perhaps a little shocked but generally unhurt: or it could all go horribly wrong and the leader could hit the ground ...

It's at this point, poised between action and inaction, that self-efficacy is crystallized in the mind of the climber: enactive mastery—she has practised moves of similar difficulty in the safe environment of the indoor climbing wall and thinks that she is probably technically capable of completing the moves; vicarious experience—she has just witnessed a pair of climbers in front of her successfully complete this part of the climb and she has taken note of the moves the climbers made; verbal persuasion—her second is telling her that she can do it (or maybe just to hurry up and do it because it's getting dark!); physiological and affective states—she knows that she is still fairly fresh and has sufficient energy, providing that she doesn't take too long, and although a little nervous she feels reasonably positive; integration of efficacy information—she weighs up all of the above and makes the final decision to 'go for it', at which point her focus must be solely on each hand and foot placement. She makes it to safety! What a feeling—she knows that she has climbed a difficult piece of rock, near to her physical and mental limit. Her self-efficacy will grow as a result. Later, from the comfort of some local inn over a well-earned beverage, she will recall the event move for move with her climbing partner and she will set herself even more challenging goals for the future.

Let's just imagine, however, that she had failed to get up the overhang at the first attempt—what then comes into play is her persistence to 'give it another go'. It is not uncommon on a difficult (well-protected) move for a climber to have several attempts before actually achieving the move. Alternatively, the climber may decide to leave it for another day but will probably become even more determined to do it and will practise similar moves in the meantime, and will rehearse the moves in her mind's eye. Only when the climber abandons the belief that she is capable of ever succeeding is self-efficacy reduced.

First of all I would try to get other people involved—maybe an observer in the audience, someone I could trust to give truthful but constructive criticism. I would also think about asking the audience for feedback at the end of the session, probably through a questionnaire. However, asking them something like 'What did you think of my attempts to interact with you/our rapport?' is unlikely to be very productive on several fronts:

- the question is probably too broad;
- the audience might not understand what you are asking;
- listeners might think it impolite to give you a low score.

What you will have to do is to break down the concept of 'interaction' into more manageable questions relating to aspects such as:

- level of interest;
- ability to follow the presentation;
- listeners' thoughts on the specific interactive techniques used (e.g. stopping to ask questions of the audience, giving the audience small tasks to perform and then asking for feedback).

In terms of obtaining some sort of level, you could score level of interest from 1 (low) to 5 (high) or signify it in terms which went from 'Bored' to 'Extremely interested'. Be innovative—ask people how they feel.

Achievable A tricky one this! It depends very much upon you and what you think you can achieve and your attitude to failure. Some people believe that we should always have goals that we think are achievable; others believe that we should regard them as inspirational targets to be aimed for but which may be out of reach—but through striving in such a way we will exceed more realistic goals. However, according to Garland (1983) and Locke *et al.* (1984), this may only be the case when the consequence of not achieving the goals carries no cost. What is clear is that when we achieve difficult goals we experience more satisfaction than when we achieve relatively easy goals.

Relevant Put simply, we should seek goals which are relevant to our overall aims and objectives. If we set steps or milestones within a goal, these steps should be relevant to the achievement of that particular goal.

Timely Any good plan has objectives that are defined not just in terms of content, but also in terms of when we want to accomplish them. This is important from a scheduling point of view, as well as offering us the chance to monitor our progress (and perhaps update our plans).

3.2.5 **Format of the plan**

First you should note that the plan is there to help you. There is no single 'right' plan. Your university may already have plan formats for you to follow, or it may encourage you to look at plan formats available from textbooks and websites, or it may allow you to devise your own format. However, plans do tend to follow certain guidelines.
   The plan will usually be in one of two broad formats:

1. The first format will simply consider your goals for the next year/semester in a holistic fashion—that is to say that no distinction will be made between academic, career and personal goals.
2. The second format will seek to make distinctions according to these three headings, and indeed you may have three separate plans (Keynote, 2002 does this).

Both formats have their devotees. The first plan, by its nature, integrates personal, academic and career goals. One argument is that in practice these goals are often interrelated and there may well be transferability of skills between them. On the other hand, the three separate planned headings of personal, academic and career goals lend themselves to a progress files approach; also by focusing upon each element in turn it may assist the learner so that sufficient attention is paid to each area.

Use of skills frameworks

We have already seen that the initial skills audit may use a framework—such as communication, numeracy, IT, learning to learn, working with others—and this may influence the format of the plan, especially if we wish to cover the range of these skills and wish to show this on the plan. To illustrate the process of constructing a personal development plan, consider Skills Example 3.2 and the example personal development plan that follows.

A typical personal development plan, based on the above activity, but this time showing Michael's first goal of improving his presentational skills, is shown in Figure 3.9. (The other

 Skills Example 3.2 Setting goals

Consider Michael, a second year business school student. In his first year, Michael set himself *academic* goals, which improved his basic study skills, *personal* goals, which meant that he made a wide circle of friends and *career* goals, which were focused upon finding out about a range of possible careers. Now, in his second year he has identified three main goals for the year:

1. improve his presentation 'nerves' (this is a big thing for him);

2. run a marathon;

3. obtain a summer vacation job in an area that he might then focus on as a career path.

Breaking the goal into smaller objectives

Let's consider the second of his goals, 'run a marathon'. If Michael has never run more than 3 miles (his baseline) he needs a plan if he hopes to complete all 26 miles of a marathon. He might arrive at the following list of objectives:

- research useful information on marathon training;
- find other(s) to run with/join club;
- devise a training schedule and running log;
- research nutrition requirements;
- complete a 6-mile road race;
- complete a half-marathon race;
- run 20 miles in training;
- complete full marathon.

Measuring success in his objectives

Success in achieving the goal is clear in the above case—Michael crosses the finish line in the marathon. Measuring progress/success in his objectives is also fairly clear if the only measure is to complete the key runs listed; however, he may also have a particular pace in mind. Also, the quality of his training schedule, running log and nutritional requirements are harder to measure; consider the running log—should it be simple or in-depth? Is it there to motivate as well as to record?

GOAL	Improving presentation 'nerves'			
How will I measure goal success?	My own reflection on my feeling of relaxation vs stress—say on a scale of 1 (relaxed)–10 (stressed). Feedback from others on my performance in terms of voice tone, speed and general body language			
Planned activities	Date	Resources required	Evidence to support	Reflections on activities
1. Watch video on presentations	17/10/12	Library DVD	Notes taken while watching video.	Found some useful tips—e.g. rehearse, use prompt cards.
2. Practise with group	20/11/12	Laptop. Prompt cards. Room with projector.	Comments in learning journal.	Other group members said that generally I sounded fine. However, at times I spoke too quickly.
3. Presentation in class	03/12/12	Timetabled presentation slot. Handouts. Memory stick.	Tutor feedback. Audience feedback sheets. Learning journal.	The rehearsals seem to have paid off—felt nervous still but managed to speak quite well.
Unplanned Gave an induction talk (my p/t job) to new starters	25/11/12	Company literature. Flipchart.	Learning journal.	Normally I would have hated this but to my surprise I found this OK.
Reflection on goal attainment (date)	I now feel much more confident/relaxed (was a stressed 7 on my scale, now a more relaxed 3). Feedback from others indicates good voice level and some eye contact. However, still speaking too quickly at times. 10/01/13			
What will I do in future?	Focus upon more eye contact (less looking at screen). Experiment with pauses in speech.			

Fig 3.9 Personal development plan showing a goal broken down into activities (a typical plan will have a number of goals)

two goals—to run a marathon, and to obtain a summer job—would be broken down into smaller objectives and shown in a similar way.) Of particular relevance in the plan are the subheadings. We will discuss these in general in Section 3.3.

3.3 Important subheadings for the plan

Each of the subheadings of the plan is elaborated here.

Goal and steps to achieve (planned/unplanned)

Another word for 'goal' might be 'aim'—this is the overarching end result you wish to achieve. If it is a large goal, you may wish to break it down into further parts—you might call these objectives, targets, milestones, sub-goals or simply *planned activities*. It is useful to show that these are connected with the goal—for example, by the use of a numbering system or by their position on a chart.

Of course, one person's objective might be seen as big enough in itself by another person to be a 'goal'. The advice here is not to get too hung up on the terminology; the principles of tackling them remain the same.

How will I measure success?

Sometimes it is easy to know when we have been successful. At other times we will have to think quite hard about how we will measure our progress. Remember though the old adage that 'what gets done is what we can measure!' It is important that we know when we have achieved success (or a degree of it) in our goals—and also our objectives. This implies, too, that we know our present baseline.

Resources required

Unless we are totally self-sufficient, we will need additional resources to help us to achieve our goals and objectives. At the planning stage we should make a note of these. Resources can include:

- *People*—for example, people we can ask advice from, be part of a team effort.
- *Equipment*—to play the guitar we need a guitar!
- *Materials*—all sorts of consumables.
- *Money*—funding for everything we need to support us in our goal.
- *Time*—yes, we all have the same amount of time, but we may require other activities to be reallocated to give us sufficient time for our goal.

Evidence of goal and objectives achievement

Personal development plans often require verification (by our tutor, for instance) that key goals and objectives have been reached. The learning journal will play a key role in this and will allow you to reflect upon your progress, thoughts and feelings at the time. Other evidence might also be written (e.g. letters, memos, emails, certificates, appraisal forms, feedback sheets). Evidence may be contained in other media—photographs, video recordings—or in the production of some artefact.

Planned and actual dates of activities

As we said previously, objectives need to be timely. Dates are important for scheduling and monitoring purposes. We need to know what will be achieved by when.

Comments upon individual objectives and success in achieving the goal

For a plan to be a working document it needs to be used on an ongoing basis—not just left to gather dust on a shelf. We should review our plan regularly—and update it if necessary. It is useful to have a section on our plan to make brief notes of progress towards our objectives—e.g. under 'Reflections on activities'. Certainly, we need to acknowledge that they are complete (or the extent to which they are complete).

A note on unplanned activities

Let's face it—sometimes we do things which we hadn't planned to do! Or something happens which we hadn't expected. If these affect our plan, then we should note them. Some might have a negative effect—for instance, remembering the previous example, if Michael injures his leg, he will have to re-do his plan. Some might have a positive effect—for instance, a new employer might set up business in Michael's home area, offering summer work experience in exactly the area that interests Michael. So, I like to include 'Unplanned activities' on my plan as well. If you keep a critical incidents journal you can expand on the details of this, along with the planned critical incidents.

Reflection on goal attainment

As the whole point of the plan is to guide you along your path to achieving your goals, a section on your plan to note goal success (or lack of it) is appropriate. This should reflect the success criteria originally identified for the goal.

What will I do in future?

Arriving at the end of the learning cycle, we should ask ourselves if we need or want to develop our goals further. We may then carry them forward to our next plan.

 ## Chapter summary

This chapter has allowed you to get to grips with some of the basic tools of personal development planning. The opening section focused on time management—an essential in any aspect of your life. As mentioned, you will be advised in particular ways by your university/college tutor or work trainer as to the precise form of personal development in use at your university, college or workplace. However, the methods shown are typical: these include the use of initial diagnostic tests, SMART objectives and personal development plans with dates, required evidence and comments. What you may not have come across is Bandura's concept of self-efficacy; although self-belief is not everything (it must not be self-delusion!), it is an important factor in setting personal goals. And, once again, it is often linked to experience—although it may be your observation of others as well as personally experienced activities.

 ## End of chapter exercises

Exercise 1: Activity chart

Refer back to Figure 3.4 'A typical activity (Gantt) chart'. Construct your own activity chart, either on graph paper or using an Excel spreadsheet. Your chart may show your plan for a particular project, or you may wish to use it as an overall view of various activities, as in the example.

Exercise 2: Self-efficacy

Skills Example 3.1 gives a detailed account of how self-efficacy is related to goal-setting. Think of a personal example of attempting a difficult goal, one in which you were ultimately successful, and apply Bandura's theory of self-efficacy (as outlined in the chapter).

Exercise 3: Personal development goal

Refer back to Figure 3.9 'Personal development plan showing a goal broken down into activities'. Select one of your main goals for personal, academic or career development. Next, using Figure 3.9 as a template, decide how you will measure success in achieving this goal and then devise a series of activities which will help you to achieve it. As in the template, you should then add whatever resources you think you will need and what sort of evidence you might provide for each activity.

 ## Further reading

As discussed, there are various ways to document personal development plans. This chapter has presented one method. Your university or college may already have a preferred approach. However, it is worth looking at the following project and website for other authoritative ideas:

Keynote (2002) *The Keynote Project.* Produced by Nottingham Trent University, the London Institute and the University of Leeds funded under the Fund for the Development of Teaching and Learning by the Higher Education Funding Council for England and the Department for Employment and Learning [online]. Available at http://www.leeds.ac.uk/textiles/keynote/main/about.htm (accessed: 19 March 2012).

Albert Bandura's work on self-efficacy has featured in this chapter. To read the original you should refer to:

Bandura, A. (1997) *Self-efficacy: The exercise of control.* New York: W.H. Freeman and Company.

 For further information, please visit the Online Resource Centre at **http://www.oxfordtextbooks.co.uk/orc/gallagher2e/**

4 Communication Skills

 Chapter guide

Student viewpoint

Sarah and Ummar, who had both graduated with business degrees within recent years were asked 'Which communication skills did you develop on your course? Why were these important?'

'Speaking to people from all walks of life and cultures and giving presentations would be the areas I'd choose. These skills have helped me immensely in my job. They have given me a great deal of confidence.'
Sarah

'Developing presentation skills before my placement year gave me increased professional standing during my placement experience. I was not as nervous as I used to be. The other communication skill that I have developed is my ability to empathize with other people—empathy is massive!'
Ummar

 By the end of this chapter you should be able to:

- Outline a basic model of communication
- Show how improvements in your communication skills may be personally beneficial
- Discuss how particular communication techniques can be used to persuade others
- Recognize and address typical barriers to communication

Introduction

You are constantly communicating in all sorts of ways in your daily life. Communication processes are very familiar to you—however, that is not to say that you should not seek improvement. Communication skills help you to express your feelings, emotions, desires and wants to others. The importance of communication for business and management students has already been shown in the opening chapter to be firmly seated amongst the set of essential, key skills for higher education (Dearing, 1997), and foremost amongst the requirements of employers for their business and management graduate recruits.

Chapter outline

The purpose of this chapter is first to explore what is meant by 'communication' and then to introduce general principles. A communication model is outlined that allows you to discuss relevant issues with others. You will see how communication may be used to persuade others through processes of logic, emotion and ethical arguments. The remainder of the chapter is then devoted to an important, practical area—barriers to communication—and how you might overcome them. In summary, this chapter forms the basis for your understanding of communication processes prior to further sections in the book, which consider written and spoken communication skills in more detail.

4.1 A basic model of communication

Let us look at a basic—some would say 'simple'—model of communication, as shown in Figure 4.1.

This is a good model to consider first: it introduces communication terms, with which some of you may already be familiar. It is a relatively easy model to comprehend and allows you to begin your exploration of how people communicate between each other as individuals, groups and within organizations. It is based upon the well-known Shannon and Weaver (1949) model, which is rather mechanistic. In this communication model, there are 'senders' and 'receivers'. Let's say that it is you who are the 'sender' and you wish to communicate some aspect of your thoughts to another, the so-called 'receiver'. The process is rather like sending a radio transmission, in that you have a message which is first of all 'encoded'. Obvious examples of encoding include the dots and dashes of Morse code used by Second World War submarine commanders and bytes of code, used in modern computing applications. However, the most widespread type of encoding occurs when you put your thoughts into everyday speech or writing. After the encoding process, the message is transmitted via some sort of 'channel'. This could be radio waves, satellite, cable, face-to-face communication, audio channel, or some sort of visual method. At the other end of the channel is a 'receiver' (i.e. the person or group you are communicating with), who then 'decodes' this parcel of information and tries to make some sense of it. The above model also shows a feedback loop, which allows the receiver to acknowledge the message and to ask for clarification from the sender—this type of communication is termed 'two-way'. On those occasions where the feedback loop is absent or unused, communication is said to be 'one-way'.

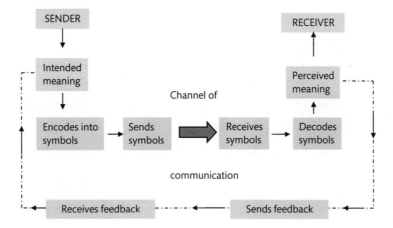

Fig 4.1 The communication process

Source: Based on Shannon and Weaver (1949)

Your natural reaction might have been to think that two-way communication was always 'the best' to use. In many situations you would be correct in thinking this, for it allows for the listener/receiver to question the narrator/sender for any clarification—which is useful for both sender and receiver. Also, if you go one stage further, you can see that the receiver could then become the sender, so that true interaction—a discussion—takes place between the two parties. However, two-way communication may be time-consuming and is not always the most efficient way to convey a lot of information; books are essentially one-way, and yet most people find them useful (providing, of course, that they are well-written and with the appropriate target readers in mind!); plans are another instance of what is essentially one-way information. Of course, it is possible sometimes to use both methods reinforcing each other (someone talking to you through a particular aspect of some computer software, for instance, after which you refer to the software manual for further advice).

Inter- versus intra-communication

You will be aware that you not only communicate with other people—inter-communication—but you also have an 'inner voice', which is sometimes termed 'intra-communication'. Clearly, inter-communication is vital for your inter-personal skills, whilst intra-communication is related to your ability to think things through in your head, to reflect and to plan for the future.

 Activity 4.1 Two-way and one-way communication

Make brief notes of examples of two-way and one-way communication with which you are familiar. Now, can you generalize what you see as the possible advantages of using two-way and one-way communication?

Activity 4.2 Personal benefits

Take a look at Figure 4.2: it shows some possible benefits of better communication for you personally. Can you relate to any of these? Perhaps you can think of others?

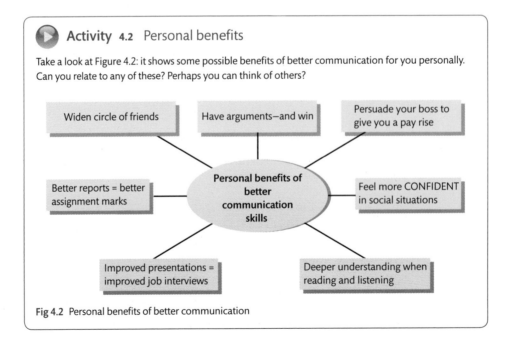

Fig 4.2 Personal benefits of better communication

4.2 Verbal versus non-verbal communication

Verbal communication is communication that uses words—either written or spoken. Non-verbal communication is communication which uses other means.

Figure 4.3 shows some examples of verbal written, verbal spoken and non-verbal communication.

Of course, you may sometimes use all three types of communication at the same time—for instance, when delivering a presentation. Often you will use at least two of the above methods in tandem. For instance, when you are talking to friends a lot of your meaning is conveyed in your facial expressions and body language—perhaps even more so than the words you are using to describe a situation.

A good example of how your appearance can send 'messages' to others is the interview situation. It is often said that interviewers make up their minds about a potential recruit within the first few minutes of meeting, much of their opinion being swayed by physical appearance, manner and style of dress. Whilst this may sound somewhat shallow, there is probably an element of truth in this effect, which was first reported in 1920 by the psychologist Edward Thorndyke (Buchanan and Huczynski, 2004, pp. 226–7).

Again, the old adage that 'the eyes have it' is also true in many cases. (See the work of Argyle and Dean (1965) for original coverage of eye contact and Argyle (1993) for body language.) In many cultures, the eyes are considered to be the windows into the soul, revealing and expressing your true feelings.

Verbal written	Verbal spoken	Non-verbal
Newspapers	News broadcast Chatting with family, friends	Facial expressions—sombre, happy, surprised, angry, disgust, staring, crying, etc.
Posters/advertisements	Spoken adverts/voiceovers	Body language—proud, confident, aggressive, humble, submissive, welcoming, hostile, etc.
Signs	Speeches, discussions, spoken commands, requests, questions	Actions which convey a message—e.g. volunteering, doing nothing.
Books	Books, poems, plays that are read aloud, songs	Style of dress.
Journals	Lectures, presentations, feedback	
Diaries	Audio diary	
Essays	Stories	
Reports	Verbal reports	
Shopping lists	Spoken order	
Instruction manuals	Verbal instructions	
Stories (written)	Narrated stories	
Poetry (written)	Narrated poems	

Fig 4.3 Examples of verbal written, verbal spoken and non-verbal communication

Activity **4.3**   Green Vale'n'Dale opening

To introduce some of the different ways in which you may communicate in a management situation, read through the Green Vale'n'Dale case study below, which has been based on a real-life situation. As you go through the case, note down instances of different types of communication (e.g. written, verbal, non-verbal, etc.) and also the various 'messages' that you are picking up (these messages may be from either the people in the case study or signs you are interpreting from the situation and physical surroundings). Then compare your notes with the commentary in the Online Resource Centre.

 Case Study: The official opening of Green Vale'n'Dale's new recycling centre

Sam was still relatively new to this, his first managerial job, since graduating from university with a 2:1 in Business Studies. He had been recruited just over a year ago as the Business Development Manager for Green Vale'n'Dale Recycling Ltd and reported directly to the Managing Director, Peter Jones, an entrepreneurial extrovert. The company collected and recycled glass, plastic and paper waste products from industrial and retail outlets, as well as making office collections. Sam was one of only a handful of graduates within the company. His job role was quite diverse—the title of 'Business Development Manager' being rather open-ended; in essence he had been employed, according to the Managing Director, to 'bring some professionalism' to the company's expanding operations. In practice, this had included reviewing contracts that the company held with its service customers who supplied the waste material, and assisting in various expansion proposals. The most recent of these had been the acquisition of The Old Brickworks site; an existing factory shed had been converted to accommodate the new recycling machinery and some portable cabins had been installed to act as the site offices. The new factory was to employ 15 new employees—a small but welcome boost for the local economy. Sam had been asked by the Managing Director to work with the new Centre Manager and his boss (the Area Director) in using the opening as a marketing and promotional opportunity.

Today was the day of the official opening. Sam Blixen parked his company car in the unusually tidy area in front of the freshly painted office of Green Vale'n'Dale's newest recycling centre, and wished for a fine day. He noted the banner adorning the top of the entrance doors, proudly proclaiming 'Green Vale'n'Dale welcomes you to the Official Opening of The Old Brickworks Recycling Centre'. The company logo (a green, valley-shaped motif with the words 'Green Vale'n'Dale' and 'Recycle' curving around it) was prominent at each end of the banner, in recognition of the nature of the company's recycling activities. As he walked across the yard to the office, Sam took care not to step into any remaining puddles of fibrous wastepaper waste, lest it marked his black, shined shoes and his best Marks and Spencer Italian wool suit, normally reserved for weddings and christenings.

The plan for the day was for Peter Jones to give an opening speech, quoting some impressive-sounding statistics on the new centre. Sam would then add to this by saying that this was the way forward for the company and served as an excellent example of his brief to expand the company in a way which benefited the local community and provided jobs. The junior Minister for the Environment would then make a speech and declare the centre officially open. There would be several photo opportunities with the minister: in front of the recycling machinery; next to one of the recycling lorries; with a backdrop of a recycling poster display that Sam had organized; and at the wheel of one of the forklift trucks. Guests would include important customers, council members, leaders of local recycling groups and the local press. Everyone would be given a 'welcome' pack of information, with company literature written by Sam, and to round off the event a buffet and drinks would be served.

See the Online Resource Centre for a suggested answer.

The case study displays a variety of communication types:

- the use of words (verbal), most notably in the speeches and the welcome pack;
- images (visual), for instance the photographs;
- face-to-face meetings and the appearance of the Minister for the Environment;
- the poster display and the company logo;
- the body language of the participants;
- messages conveyed by inanimate objects, such as the appearance of the recycling centre itself.

You will note that communication may be used simply to give information, but that it may also be used to persuade, to coordinate activities, to build relationships and to symbolize the importance and nature of events.

4.3 Communication and its use in persuasion

4.3.1 Communication purposes

From the discussion so far in this chapter you may note that there are many reasons why you may want to communicate but, broadly speaking, your reasons might fit into the following categories:

- to convey your feelings to others or to appreciate another's feelings;
- to relay a request or instruction or to receive such an instruction or request;
- to explain something or have something explained to you;
- to persuade or be persuaded;
- to coordinate activities with others for task achievement;
- to collaborate with others;
- to build a relationship with others.

In this section the discussion looks further at the role of communication for those occasions when you are called upon to persuade others in some way.

4.3.2 Using logic to persuade

On business and management courses you are often encouraged to place an emphasis on factual information, to present it in a logical manner and to be rational in your decision-making. This is based on what the ancient Greek scholars referred to as 'logos'—logical argument. To fully understand the grip which logical argument has had in the past, as well as its legacy today in business and management, consider the closing years of the nineteenth century and the 'scientific management' (Taylor, 1911) school of thought. Scientific management, or 'Taylorism' as it is sometimes called, was the foundation of late nineteenth-century and early twentieth-century management thinking. It lay behind the phenomenal growth of industrialization. This approach was based on principles that revered measurement and

Skills Example **4.1**   Gatewell Hospital

This short, fictitious case study is typical of a dilemma that has faced various hospital trusts throughout the country over the past few years—the proposed amalgamation of several hospitals to a single site.

Gatewell Hospital Trust: the proposal—using logic

The senior management team of Gatewell Hospital Trust is in charge of a number of hospitals. Recently it has come to the conclusion that, on grounds of cost, it needs to shut the old, Victorian-built 'Springdene Infirmary' situated on the outskirts of town and to transfer its services to the newer 'Gatewell Royal' in the centre of town. By its calculations this will save £400,000 per year in running costs, increase bed occupancy efficiency rates and improve communication between staff. It will also mean substantial additional savings in the form of staff cuts, particularly support staff (laundry, catering, administration). In line with its policy of consultation with the public, the senior management team has set up a series of meetings open to the general public, at which it will present the change proposal. The team will try to persuade its audience that the proposal is a 'good idea' by pointing out the scale of savings that will be achieved—money that can then be channelled back into the quality of service that can be provided.

experiment, rather than guesswork or rule-of-thumb. It also included the systematic breaking down of whole operations into sub-tasks, which could be measured (the term 'time-and-motion studies' has been used in this context). Taylorism exists today. It is present not just in our car factories but in our shops, our banks and our hospitals. Once again, rational argument tends to be at the forefront of any decision-making.

4.3.3 **Using emotions to persuade**

Communication that appeals to your logic is fine—but you need to be aware that, because people are human beings and not machines, they have individual feelings and personal needs. Because people are essentially social beings, they also associate themselves

 Skills Example **4.2**   Gatewell Hospital Trust: the counter-proposal—using emotion

(This follows on from previous Skills Example 4.1.)

Not everyone is happy with the proposed closing of Springdene Infirmary and the amalgamation of its services with Gatewell Royal Hospital. In particular, a councillor from the Springdene Infirmary's catchment area has received many objections to the scheme from the local residents. At the open meetings held by the Trust's senior management team, she has put forward a strong emotional argument against the closure. She says that local people have told her 'we're losing *our* hospital'. She points out that a lot of 'old folk' rely upon having a hospital that is nearby, as they find travelling any distance difficult. She quotes individual cases to prove her point. She says that 'you cannot put a price on suffering'. She points out that these people have worked hard all of their lives and now, in their 'twilight years', they are being treated with 'little respect'. Also, the hospital employs many local people in the service departments (laundry, catering, administration) and the closure will mean a loss of jobs to many of these people, who will be unable to move to the more expensive centre of town. It will, she says, turn the area into a 'ghost town'.

Student tips on skills and employability

Using logic and emotion to persuade

Nadia is a business student with a part-time job at a reputable hardware store. Here, she outlines how she uses logic and emotion to persuade customers:

> With regards to customer service, the combined use of logic, emotion and persuasive communication can mean the difference between a customer buying products from our store or our partner stores, rather than our competitors. For example, if a customer cannot find a particular product, I give them a variety of options with regards to finding the product, whilst using logic and persuasive communication. These options can range from finding the product in the warehouse if it cannot be found on the shop floor, calling another store to reserve the product, allowing the customer to travel to the other store to pick it up, or ordering the product into the store or to their home. Due to this wide range of options, along with the use of emotional and persuasive communication during this process, I have found that often the customer will not choose to visit our competitor stores, even though they are located only a short distance away.

with group feelings and their needs. And although researchers from the late 1920s have been writing about the importance of individual and group needs, it is surprising how often people seem to forget! People are persuaded not just by logic but by appeals to their individual and group emotions. Indeed, in some cases emotion will overrule logic (Goleman, 1996).

Other than 'logos', the ancient Greeks had two other forms of persuasion—'pathos' and 'ethos'. The great orator Aristotle (384–322 BC), used all three forms in his public speeches and wrote about their use. Pathos (from which we get words such as 'sympathetic', 'pathetic', 'empathy') was originally used to evoke a feeling of pity from the audience, but later became associated with an appeal to people's emotions in general.

4.3.4 **Using an ethical approach to persuade**

The other method of persuasion is that of 'ethos'—used to give the sense of credibility of the speaker or text, particularly through its 'ethical' appeal. Hamilton (2003), states that ethos is:

> enhanced by the reputation of the speaker/writer, the impression the speaker or writer gives in terms of knowing what they are discussing, valid reasoning, good judgement, scrupulous tactics, integrity, reflecting a sincere interest in the audience's welfare, and a willingness for self-sacrifice.

(Hamilton, 2003, p. 701)

In summary, you may note that the use of communication is not just about conveying facts: words have power in themselves to motivate and to persuade. This is a long way from our simple model of communication (Figure 4.1), discussed earlier in the chapter.

Skills Example 4.3 Equality in the NHS

This example uses another illustration from the health service.

A proposal for equality in the National Health Service

In 2000 a government report called 'The Vital Connection' was published. This report looked at equality within the National Health Service. Its purpose was to establish future policy on equality—for instance, the gender balance across various grades of staff. Hamilton (2003) uses this report to illustrate the use of ethos in persuasion. With regard to ethos he has this to say:

> The Minister's foreword therefore, in part appeals through ethos and pathos as a commitment is made to improve the NHS for employees and service users. By stating that the government desires an end to all forms of discrimination this is intended to show the government as worthy. This impression is set at the outset of the document through the deployment of many key words which re-occur throughout the text. Such key words include the following: commitment, equality, diversity, inclusiveness, determined, action, needs, rights, targets, change, and progress.
>
> (Hamilton, 2003, p. 701)

4.4 Barriers to communication

If only communication was easy and straightforward! But, as you will realize from your own experience, this is often not the case. Because effective communication is so important, it is worthwhile to investigate possible barriers. The previous model of communication (Figure 4.1) can be used to illustrate some of these. Through being aware of possible barriers, you may avoid making communication mistakes. If you have already made a mistake, you may be able to analyse what happened and try to avoid repeating it in the future.

4.4.1 Physical barriers

Anything which can physically reduce or distort the message may be a problem. The sound of a road-breaker's drill is an obvious one; someone else talking over a conversation we are trying to listen to is another one. A more subtle one is the perspex screen often found at cashier points in petrol stations and banks. Another one, often found in busy offices or computer classrooms, is the ability to see the other person's eyes but not their mouths—hidden behind the computer screen; this has both the effect of reducing the volume of their voice and also does not allow you to lipread their words.

4.4.2 Language and semantic barriers

It may seem obvious but language differences between people can be a significant impediment—whether in a personal, academic or work situation. The speed at which you speak can be problematic in such situations (rather than your volume). Words need to be spoken clearly. When understanding is difficult between people, there is the need for much patience and tolerance. Sadly, these may be lacking on one or both sides, with the result that conversation ceases as frustration increases. Then, there is what might be termed the 'interpreter syndrome'—found, for instance, when a group of people, with a poor grasp of another group's language, appoint an unofficial 'interpreter' who then translates the message to the rest of his/her group. Whilst this might be useful as a short-term solution, it does little to engender direct communication and understanding between the two groups. Indeed, it may even deepen unnecessarily the feeling of 'them' and 'us'.

Even when the groups speak the same language, strong regional accents or use of local phrases and words can cause confusion. 'Snap' (Yorkshire), 'bait' (north-east England) and 'piece' (strictly speaking, a sandwich—south-west Scotland), all refer to a packed lunch, for instance.

The use of specialized words, adopted within specific industries, for example, can also confuse the casual listener—this is sometimes termed as 'jargon'. When the public does not need to be involved (for instance, over a police radio) this may not matter. However, if the public is the 'client' such as the patient in a hospital, or someone obtaining a bank loan, technical or specialized language may be not be appropriate. The 'Campaign for Plain English' established in 1979 is dedicated to making government and business documents clearer to read and free from such jargon.

Semantic barriers

The *Compact Oxford English Dictionary for Students* (2006) defines 'semantics' as 'the branch of linguistics concerned with meaning'. A semantic barrier arises when people have different understandings of the same word. For instance, the dictionary defines the word 'mean' in two distinct ways: it may be used to convey a sense of someone who is miserly; however, a mathematician will use the word 'mean' to describe a numerical average. Culturally, words

---

 Activity 4.4 When words are not enough...

To do this activity you will need to ask a friend(s) to be your active participant(s). You will also need to provide the relevant articles. Note—if you wish you can swap roles with your friends.

Task

- You are to spend 15 minutes writing instructions for one of the following tasks (you may choose which one):
  - tying a shoelace;
  - knotting a neck tie;
  - re-folding an opened Ordnance Survey map.
- Give the instructions to your friends.
- You must insist that your friends have to obey the instructions exactly as they are written down.
- They are to read the instructions out loud as they perform them.
- They are not allowed to ask you any questions.
- You are not allowed to communicate with them in any way.
- Observe and note what happens.
- Allow a maximum of 5 minutes for them to attempt the task and then terminate the session.
- Now discuss with your friends what you have learnt from the exercise. Focus on communication issues and barriers to successful communication. Compare your notes with the comments in the Online Resource Centre.

Please refer to the Online Resource Centre for a suggested answer.

may also differ. For instance, when someone in the north east of England says that they have 'been bad' it may mean that they have been ill, not wicked!

4.4.3 Message ambiguity

People can talk of 'getting their wires crossed' when they misinterpret a message from someone else. Sometimes this is because they fail to listen carefully enough in the first place. However, at other times it is because the actual message itself may be read in more than one way—it is 'ambiguous'.

 Skills Example 4.4 The loss of a spacecraft: the Mars Climate Orbiter

On 11 December 1998 NASA launched the Mars Climate Orbiter (MCO). The mission of the spacecraft was to orbit Mars and act as the first interplanetary weather satellite. It would also act to relay information from the following spacecraft, the Mars Polar Lander, which was to touch down on the planet. At the end of a 9-month journey, NASA mission control began to realize that something was wrong with the positioning of the spacecraft. It became apparent that it was about 170 km off target. As it entered the Martian atmosphere on 23 September it stopped transmitting its carrier signal. No one knows precisely what happened to the craft, but it was presumed to have been destroyed by hitting the planet's atmosphere at the incorrect angle. A $125-million space project literally went up in smoke.

At the NASA investigation board (NASA, 1999, p. 6) it emerged that 'the root cause for the loss of the MCO spacecraft was the failure to use metric units ... specifically thruster performance data in English units instead of metric units used in the software application'. The *New Scientist* magazine (1999) ran the headline 'Schoolkid blunder brought down Mars probe'. It explained that the spaceprobe was adjusted on its course by small propulsion rockets. A new propulsion supplier had been used for the project—and their engineers used English units, pound force: NASA engineers expected the metric Newton. And 1 pound force = 4.45 Newtons. Quite simply, the two sets of engineers had assumed that the other was using the same units as themselves. All they saw were numbers—but the numbers represented different things in this case. Numbers by themselves are ambiguous—you need to know what they refer to. In layman's terms, this miscommunication is the equivalent of thinking when you've pushed the accelerator of your car that you've just applied the force of an F1 racing car rather than the real force of the average family saloon. Had the size of the difference between the units been larger—say 100 times, the mistake would probably have been picked up sooner; however, because the difference was only 4.5 times it was not so apparent. James Oberg (1999) suggests that a further barrier to communication at the point at which alarm bells should have started to ring at mission control was what he calls the 'assumption of goodness'—in other words, people assumed that something was alright until it could be *proved* otherwise.

This example shows that the consequences of message ambiguity can be extremely costly. In most everyday management and business situations consequences (thankfully!) are rarely as extreme, although mistakes occasionally come to public notice when doctors or medics extract the wrong kidney or misread a drugs prescription. However, even minor ambiguities can be annoying—take, for example, the following phrase, once contained in a (now revised!) exam regulations procedure: 'If the student has not completed any coursework, he/she will not be allowed to do referral work but must re-enrol for the module.' The problem was the word 'any'. Did it mean 'any' in the sense 'in the complete absence of any coursework whatsoever' or did it mean 'any' in the context of 'even in the absence of any one element of coursework, other elements of coursework having been submitted'? The person who wrote the regulation clearly had one or the other in mind. The problem was that either of the above interpretations could be argued as being correct. The message was ambiguous.

Activity **4.5** Barriers

Think of a personal, academic and workplace example where feelings or emotions have been barriers to communication. Make brief notes of the situations.

4.4.4 **Barriers: feelings and emotions**

No matter what type of communication you are using—verbal or non-verbal—you cannot ignore the impact of feelings and emotions.

Liking, disliking and prejudice

You may find that it's hard to listen to or talk to someone you dislike—especially if that person is in one group and you are in another, the typical 'them and us' scenario. And, you may tend to think that their thoughts and ideas are less worthy of attention than your own: in other words, you may tend to pre-judge. Of course, you can be prejudiced *for* something as well as against. The thing is, that if your prejudice is significant, it may stand in the way of your true understanding.

Interest/enthusiasm

Hands up if you have pretended to listen to a conversation with appropriate nods of the head while at the same time being elsewhere in your thoughts. Or how about times when you have looked longingly out of a window while the speaker's voice drones on—or occasions when you have been introduced to someone and cannot wait to get away? Conversely, think of those precious few times when you have held on to every word from a fascinating story, or wanted to know more about someone's life and work. Sometimes you will find that it's easy to listen, but often it's not. As a listener you are in danger of missing out on useful information if you allow yourself to 'tune out'.

Fear/suspicion(!)

Frederick Herzberg (1923–2000) was one of the foremost thinkers of his generation on motivation within the workplace. He had the ability to make the most revealing statements about the state of human relations. In a film clip called *Jumping for the jelly beans* (BBC, 1973) he turns to his audience of industry-hardened managers and warns them of how easily trust can be broken and how difficult it can be to rebuild. He uses the term 'revenge psychology' to describe how people bear grudges over a long time. They think back to what happened to them in the past, of how managers treated them at the time. And they refuse to listen to them now. In such cases, this fear, resentment and suspicion has a root cause. However, many times you may be fearful of change without being able to specify exactly why you should be fearful. At times such as these, imagination and pessimism are a threatening combination to the change agent. What the situation requires, at the very least, is the timely provision of information to individuals and groups and how the changes may affect them.

Other emotions: happiness, sadness, anger

As you've probably come to realize by now, any excess of emotion can have an impact upon communication. Happiness, sadness and anger all fall into this category. For instance, we sometimes say that people are 'on cloud nine' when blissfully happy, 'inconsolable with grief' when a loved one dies or 'blind with rage'.

4.4.5 Barriers: the impact of culture

Cultural differences may be defined in terms of a group's accepted norms (including outward appearances, such as dress), behaviour, values and basic assumptions (Schein, 1985). People tend to use the term 'culture' in everyday speech to describe cultural differences between different nationalities.

At university you are likely to be working with other students and lecturers from all over the world. Sometimes you will find it difficult to understand their behaviours (and vice-versa), so it is useful to be aware of ways in which national characteristics may differ (Hofstede, 2001). You may wonder, for instance, why some students are so polite to their lecturers—to the extent that they do not ask questions in class; this may be due to their respect for the hierarchical difference they perceive between themselves and their lecturer. It might also be because they are used to a memorizing style of learning (Roberston, Line, Jones and Thomas, 2000, p. 93). You may note that sometimes others will tell you what you want to hear, rather than what they really mean—this may be because, in their culture, conflict is to be avoided and harmony encouraged. On other occasions you may observe that other students are reluctant to speak in front of the class, as they do not wish to risk 'losing face' (Eldridge and Cranston, 2009, p. 75). Another aspect may be a group's preference to protect each other as a group (a collective stance) and not to give individuals focus—something which you may or may not do yourself.

However, you should note that the term 'culture' is broader than nationality. Any group may be said to have its own culture. This applies to the work situation too, where even branches of the same organization may operate slightly differently to each other. In organizations that have grown by taking over other companies, the culture of the 'old' companies will often survive for a considerable time.

Thus, cultural differences between people can sometimes be a source of confusion, especially if you do not appreciate their nature, or even, their existence. It is rarely helpful to make a judgement that one culture is somehow 'better' than another. Differences between cultures do exist, and you should aim to take these into account. As we have noted, cultural differences might also directly impact upon what sort of communication is permissible between individuals and groups. However, a warning note here on stereotypes (national and occupational)—these may also be problematic if you assume that *everyone* in that particular group conforms to the stereotype you have in mind.

Language

For all that has been discussed above on culture, we should not forget the more obvious barriers for anyone whose second language is English: speaking, writing and reading the language. According to researchers, 'there is a common acceptance that language comprehension and competence are at the heart of difficulties for international students' (Roberston, Line, Jones and Thomas, 2000, p. 100). One of the main difficulties experienced is that local people speak too fast for those still becoming accustomed to English. If you are finding difficulty understanding your lecturers because of this, you may wish to see them and ask them if they could help you; they may be able to slow down a little (though this is difficult for many people, as we tend to forget), or they may allow you to record their lecture so you can play it back later. Usually lecturers will be willing to help you if they can.

4.4.6 **IT barriers**

Information technology continues to increase at an astonishing rate in terms of its sophistication, availability and ability to connect people with each other and to sources of information. The use of email is widespread for both personal and business users; the

---

 Skills Example 4.5 Cultural barriers to communication

In your studies, you are quite likely to work in groups with other students from a variety of cultural backgrounds. A review of post-graduate, mixed-culture groups of students, engaged with a group-based exercise on a business module (Gallagher and Watson, 2008) revealed the following cultural differences related to communication:

1. *Shyness and reticence to engage*: this applied between students within certain cultural groups who had been taught from an early age not to 'show off'. Sometimes, however, this reticence was present between these students and the tutor; this was often due to ingrained habits to 'respect' the 'teacher' (other members of the group found this rather annoying, as the 'shy' students directed questions to them instead).

2. *Language difficulties*: these were experienced between mixed-language group members. This tended to split the groups by language ability during their whole-group discussions and later by encouraging the emergence of language-based sub-groups working on allocated tasks together. Clearly, this is not a good basis for mutual cooperation.

3. *Face-to-face versus virtual preference*: a further communication barrier related to the difference in preference amongst group members to interact face-to-face or virtually over the Internet (for instance, using MSN). Where this virtual chat facility was used, students would work by themselves in their rooms but be constantly in contact with each other over the Internet. This was fine for those students within the chat network, but not for those left out of it. Also, as the groups later confirmed, this type of communication was quite good for facts dissemination and the coordination of activities but was poor from a creativity point of view.

mobile phone is now a 'must-have' for the majority of people; in the UK, most house-holds have a personal computer and access to the Internet; the virtual learning en-vironment (VLE) is accepted within Higher Education as a standard feature of storing information and as a basis for chat rooms and discussion boards, as well as offering an increasingly interactive means of communication. Electronic databases have revolution-ized the once slow, limited task of research into a fast but seemingly boundless journey. Elsewhere, the 'virtual team' (you will consider the team in Chapter 11)—project work-ers who communicate with each other through the use of IT—as heralded by Lipnack and Stamps in their seminal 1997 text (a long time ago in the IT world!) hardly raises an eyebrow now. By the time you read these words it is inevitable that there will have been further technical advances.

It should be apparent, even from the brief summary given above, that the IT explosion has presented significant improvements in your ability to store, send and receive information. Yet its newness carries with it both benefits and problems. Yes, it's powerful, but you need to recognize that there are limitations to its use. And arguably the biggest of these is in commu-nication that is personal and emotional. Despite (or perhaps because of?) its sophistication, it can lack the vital human nuances of face-to-face communication. You will revisit IT barriers in Chapter 13, which considers the use of email—although it is now an 'everyday' occurrence, it is probably one of the most frequent causes of misunderstanding and needless arguments because of its widespread use.

4.4.7 Other barriers to communication

As you will have noted, there are many barriers to communication—that is one of the reasons why it is so important to be alert and ready to act if you need to improve the situation. This final section looks at other areas that you need to be aware of.

Differing levels of knowledge

This might sound like an obvious barrier: instinctively you will probably not talk to children in the same way as you talk to adults because you suspect that their knowledge is limited. However, it is easy to forget when talking adult to adult that others do not always have the same knowledge base as yourself. At the very least, this can reduce the effectiveness of your communication and, at worst, the other party may simply decide to 'turn off' their reception.

Hierarchy

Do you find it difficult to talk to people in authority? If so, you are not alone. This is an ex-ample of a hierarchical barrier. Again, there may be cultural implications here: for instance, a well-recorded teaching issue is the initial reluctance of some students from particular coun-tries to ask questions of the teacher or lecturer, particularly if they do not understand. This is often not because of an individual difficulty but it is a symptom of a society where teachers are always to be respected as the unquestionable source of knowledge. Linked to this is the concept of 'losing face'. Generally speaking, in this country, lecturers are keen to treat you as adults and encourage you to ask them questions if you do not understand, or indeed, if you hold a different opinion.

Jumping to conclusions

Because we are anxious to make sense of the messages we receive, we sometimes think we know what the message means without waiting to listen to the rest of the facts or asking for clarification on ambiguous points.

Differing values and perceptions

People have different values and perceptions. Take humour, for instance: is it acceptable to make a joke about something terrible that has happened? In the workplace you can contrast the values of managers and staff. For instance, say that there is an urgent customer order: management wants to impress the customer to secure future, profitable contracts and has asked staff to work over the weekend. The Managing Director says he will give staff extra holiday to make up for this, but cannot afford to pay overtime. He says that the firm's future growth depends upon this. However, if staff are not very well paid they may regard their employment as just a job, rather than a career. If this is the case, they may not share the same level of commitment to the company as the Managing Director, who has a high degree of ownership.

Listening

Listening is hard work! How many of us have been accused by our partners of 'not listening', especially if we are tired or in a hurry? You may hear the words but they do not necessarily register in your brain. You may compound the error by not making a note of something important, which you then forget. So, what can you do during lectures or at work to improve your listening skills? Perhaps one of the most effective techniques in a lecture or instructional session is to make your own notes (Di Vesta and Gray, 1972). This forces you to jot down key points as the talk progresses. If you do not understand a point, make a note of it and ask the

---

 Activity 4.6   Listening to a podcast

Oxford University gives you access to a range of interesting podcasts. Go to the following link on 'Building a business: moving your product to the market' and select one of the podcasts that sounds interesting to you. Ideally you can ask a friend(s) to be your active participant(s), but this is not essential.

   http://podcasts.ox.ac.uk/series/building-business-moving-your-product-market (accessed: 31 May 2012). *Note: this link is also given in the Online Resource Centre. Any updates will be given here.*

   Play at least 10 minutes of the podcast, making notes as you go. Now compare your notes with your friend's notes. Did you pick out the same points? Did you give them the same emphasis? What did you miss? If you are on your own, play back the podcast and try to pick up further points you may have missed the first time of playing.

speaker about it at an appropriate point (this may be during or at the end of the session—the speaker may tell you when you may ask questions). Later, while the talk is still fresh in your mind, you may wish to tidy up your notes, add some explanation, or carry out some further research of your own.

 ## Chapter summary

At the beginning of the chapter you explored some of the basic principles of communication. You looked at a simple sender/receiver model. This allowed you to discuss some of the physical and psychological aspects of communication. The power of words as actions was mentioned in Section 4.3 on persuasion using logic, emotions and ethical arguments. The discussion later in the chapter covered some of the more obvious barriers to communication. This might seem a rather negative approach, but first of all you must 'know your enemy', for if you can reduce these barriers you stand a much better chance of being successful in communicating your message.

The chapters which lie ahead, particularly those that focus on reading, writing and speaking, will give advice not just for avoiding the pitfalls but also for enhancing your communication effectiveness.

 ## End of chapter exercises

Exercise 1: Personal appearance

How important do you think your personal appearance is at an interview? You may wish to access one/some of the many self-instructional video clips, easily found on the Internet before answering this question. Discuss your findings with others.

Exercise 2: Ambiguous message

In this chapter, Skills Example 4.4, the Mars Climate Orbiter, was offered to show the result of an ambiguous message. Think of another ambiguous message—either a well-known example or a personal one. Why did it occur? How could it have been avoided?

Exercise 3: A picture...

There's an old saying: 'A picture paints a 1,000 words.' Access a picture or photograph that you think conveys a powerful message. What is the message 'saying' to you? Analyse the picture's effect on your emotions.

Exercise 4: Learning journal

Referring back to your learning journal, or from memory, consider a situation where you experienced, or observed, noticeable communication barriers within a group. This may be a group you worked in at university. Say what these barriers were and how they affected the interaction between people at the time. Give suggestions as to how these barriers might be avoided or addressed in similar situations in the future.

 ## Further reading

As mentioned in the chapter, the Campaign for Plain English produces a useful 'How to write in Plain English' guide. This is downloadable from their website: http://www.plainenglish.org.uk/ (accessed: 19 May 2012).

For some memorable insights on communication barriers between management and workers you can access Frederick Herzberg addressing an audience of managers in the classic recording of *Jumping for the jelly beans* (BBC, 1973). Go to YouTube and search for 'Fred Herzberg'. You will be able to see a series of short clips from this video (accessed: 19 May 2012).

Further information on Hofstede's influential work on how national culture influences people's behaviours is available at http://www.geerthofstede.com/ (accessed: 19 May 2012).

 For further information, please visit the Online Resource Centre at
http://www.oxfordtextbooks.co.uk/orc/gallagher2e/

5 Locating Information and Smart Search Skills

⊙ Chapter guide

Student viewpoint

The ability to search for relevant information is clearly of great benefit to your academic studies. It is also a highly transferable skill that you will use in the work situation. Here are some comments from part-time year 1 management students:

'Information search skills are important—I've been investigating the sort of staff our customers feel give them great service, and what the key drivers of customer service are.'
Kate (Customer Service Leader)

'My research skills have improved [as a result of the course]. An example of this in action is when I looked for different models of training courses, seeing if they would fit with our organization.'
Amanda (Learning Resources Manager)

'I depend upon good information-gathering skills for carrying out audits on deaths of children and mothers during childbirth.'
Zena (Head of Administration: NHS maternity department)

'Knowing where to look for information and knowing which is pertinent helps me appear more knowledgeable and gives me more self-confidence.'
Maureen (Technical Assistant)

⊙ By the end of this chapter you should be able to:

- Locate relevant books, journals and other library information
- Locate relevant electronic sources of information
- Rate the credibility of various sources of information
- Prepare an information search plan
- Reference your sources of information
- Use assignment strategies that help you to avoid plagiarism

Introduction

Locating information for your research and assignments is an essential requirement during your studies. It is a transferable skill that may be invaluable to you within the workplace. Often, you will be faced with a bewildering amount of available information, so the problem is rarely one of being unable to find *any* information. Rather, the skill is one of being proficient in choosing initial sources. This requires a purposeful, intelligent approach. You should then be able to devote your attention to following up these leads in a timely fashion. As you locate relevant information you need to reference your sources for easy retrieval for your assignment writing: good referencing indicates a scholarly, professional approach to your work.

Chapter outline

This chapter gives you some basic but extremely useful ground rules to follow when you are searching for information and referencing your sources. You are encouraged to ask yourself what sorts of journals, books and other information to read and consider the accuracy and credibility of the information. You need to know what information is available and how to look for it. You need to be able to reference your information sources correctly. Also, you need to avoid accidentally (or deliberately) attributing the work of others as your own—the practice of 'plagiarism'. This chapter gives you examples and exercises to embed all of the above skills so that they become part of your everyday work practice.

5.1 Search smart

5.1.1 Before you do anything, make sure you fully understand your assignment brief

No matter how good your research is, it will all be in vain if you have not fully understood your assignment brief. This chapter will go into further detail about your information search. Figure 5.1 illustrates the sources of information discussed in this section.

5.1.2 Initial, readily available information

If you are in the habit of going to a search engine such as Google or a website like Wikipedia to find information at the start of your assignment, it is easy to overlook some of your most useful sources, namely:

- your tutor;
- the relevant module guide and reading list;
- your university's VLE (virtual learning environment—for instance, 'Blackboard', 'WebCT', or your university's own customized site).

Your tutor

As already stated, understanding the assignment question is vital. Also, as your tutor is likely to be the person who will mark your work, it makes sense to ask him or her for clarification.

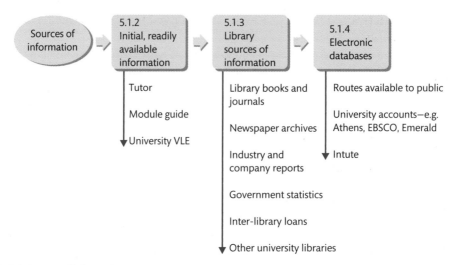

Fig 5.1 Sources of information

Once you are sure about the question, you have the opportunity of asking your tutor for further advice. Tutors are individuals and may vary in the amount of help they think it appropriate to give you (recall the cognitive apprenticeship concept in Chapter 2). It is probably a good idea to give the question some thought and draw up some sort of action plan of key areas, initial thoughts on information sources, which you could then have with you when you approach your tutor. This shows that you have already committed some time and effort to the research process. In this situation, your tutor is more likely to consider that you are requesting assistance with your ideas, rather than asking him to give you his ideas to get started.

Module guide and reading lists

The purpose of a module guide is to give you an overall view of the syllabus and (possibly) a schedule of lectures, workshops and seminar sessions. You will expect to find key words, which you can use in your information search. Often, you will also be given a reading list of relevant books and journal articles. Some textbooks may be listed as 'essential' and you may wish to purchase these, or arrange to share purchases with a friend on the course. Others may be listed as 'recommended reading'. Textbooks are often a good place to start your reading, as they should give you an overview of the main subject themes; they will also have appropriate references in them for further reading. They can form the backbone of your course. However, as a critical reader you need to read additional articles to build up a breadth of information, views and opinions.

Your university's VLE

It is now usual for universities and colleges to provide a VLE (virtual learning environment) with module information available to students on a dedicated website. Information is loaded onto the website by your tutor in most cases. Lecture notes, presentations and other printed information will be available to you. You might also have access to podcasts, videofiles and hyperlinks to other websites. All of these may be used as quoted sources of information, as long as they are suitably referenced.

5.1.3 Library sources of information

University libraries hold a wealth of information. They are also excellent places to visit for advice from knowledgeable staff. Sometimes you will come across additional relevant articles and books. When you consider that often there are areas given over to quiet study or group collaboration, you have an environment that positively assists your research. This section covers a number of relevant library resources.

Library books and journals (hard copy)

It is my experience that library staff are generally extremely happy to help you to locate all sorts of information. No request for information should be thought of as 'wasting their time'. For instance, if you can't find a book on a shelf after spending 10 minutes looking, ask them. Libraries usually have instruction leaflets on how to use all aspects of their provision. Very often you can find instructions on your university site.

Browsing through book shelves can lead to some good finds. Because there is a logic in how books are categorized by your library, there is a good chance that you will find other similar or complementary texts on your subject close to the book you are retrieving. You can browse the hard copies of journals in your library too. It is likely that there are journals located under 'Business' and 'Management' (or whatever your field is). Usually you will see the current journal on display, and several back issues (but not all) may be placed behind these. If you get into the habit of browsing these journals, say once per month, you might only need 15 minutes to keep up to date on the title contents of a number of key journals. If something jumps out at you as relevant, you may wish to take a photocopy of the relevant article.

Library archives—newspapers

Many university libraries will keep either paper or electronic copies of selected newspapers such as *The Times* and *Financial Times* or periodicals such as *The Economist*, on the basis that these are more likely to give credible accounts of events than the 'tabloid' press. They are worth looking at if you wish to get an overall feel for public opinion at the time of the event in question. Another use would be for early discussion of some recent, important event that had impacted upon your field of study. This immediacy is very useful. You should realize, for

---

 Activity 5.1 Journal audit

For this activity you are asked to conduct an audit of journals within your library that are relevant to Business and Management. List the journals available in hard copy, as well as those available electronically. Quickly scan the contents pages to get an overview of the journals you have been recommended. It is also worthwhile browsing through other hard-copy journals in areas such as psychology and sociology for application to organizational behaviour or people management modules, and education for skills development or HRM modules.

instance, that journal articles go through a time-consuming vetting process and often on to a waiting list, that in some cases can take in excess of 18 months, meaning that they were written some time before you get to read them.

Library archives—industry and company reports

Your library may subscribe to marketing information publishers such as Mintel or Keynote. These are useful sources of information on particular industries or sectors of the market. The usual format is that in any particular year the publication will contain a number of reports on selected industrial sectors or markets. You may be fortunate and find that a report has been included in a fairly recent year. Even if the information is rather dated, it may give you some useful background information for your research and some leads to follow up.

'Company reports' usually refer to the reports that by law every limited company must produce every year. At their most basic, these are financial summary accounts that are submitted to Companies House, available for public viewing in the year following their submission. However, many large companies use these reports to communicate their progress to their shareholders and for publicity purposes. In such cases, it is usual to see glossy brochures which begin with a statement from the chairman, reflecting on the previous year and giving their plans for the coming year. The basic financial data is sandwiched within. Sometimes you will be given an overview of the company's operations. Naturally, there will be a tendency for companies to give their brochures a positive 'spin', but you may still wish to use them as a source of information.

Library archives—government statistics and reports

Many different types of survey data may be available in paper format. Increasingly, these will be available through government websites.

Inter-library loans

If the book you want is not located in your library, you will probably be able to get a copy by asking your librarian for an inter-library loan. If you want to locate a paper copy of a particular journal article, you may also consider seeing your librarian for this. These may be available within 24 hours for electronic delivery journals, but for paper copies you may have to wait several weeks for the book or article. Normally you would only ask for an inter-library loan if you thought the text was essential for your assignment. Often, however, you can use a different, more readily available source that provides the same (or similar) information.

Unable to visit your university library?

If you are a part-time student who lives some distance from your university, or if you are a full-time student whose home address is not local and you are at home for, say, the summer holidays, you might struggle to get to your university library. In such cases, you may know of a closer university. You may then wish to check whether they have an agreement with your university whereby you can borrow books from them under what is known as 'SCONUL' access. See http://www.access.sconul.ac.uk for more information on this, or ask your librarian.

5.1.4 **Electronic databases as sources of information**

There are several main routes you may use to access electronic databases. Sometimes these routes will give access to the same databases.

Routes available to the general public

On the basis that we should not ignore a route to information just because it is generally available to anyone with an Internet connection, you may wish to use databases such as Google. An associated database is Google Scholar. These search engines can actually be quite effective at giving you access to topical issues via other websites. However, if you are looking for a specific academic area of study, you will probably find that the databases that your university subscribes to will give you better and quicker results.

Wikipedia—perhaps one of the most popular websites, and yet most academics will advise you not to use it! The reason they give is that the information held on it is not subject to the same expert peer scrutiny as, say, that contained within refereed academic journals. They will point out that the information given may be misleading, and on occasion incorrect, as it does not have these quality checks. It would appear that Wikipedia is attempting to address these quality issues. However, this is currently unlikely to sway the majority of your tutors. The advice here is not to quote from Wikipedia, but to use other sources.

What's available electronically? Using university e-resources

Your university or college will have electronic resources for you to access. These will probably include, as a minimum, access to scholarly databases appropriate to your subject area, as well as individual subscriptions to selected journals, available electronically. It may also have some of your core textbooks available as 'e-textbooks'.

Using Athens accounts/university passwords and usernames

In 1994, the University of Bath established a not-for-profit organization called Eduserv. One of Eduserv's activities is the operation of the Athens service. Athens gives access to online services around the world. Anyone can use Athens, but in practice you will join via your university or college, or one of the organizations signed up to the service. You will be given an Athens ID and password. You may access Athens on your computer browser by going to http://www.athens.ac.uk, or you may go via your university electronic resources site. Your university will subscribe to various educational and professional databases, which will be available through your Athens account. This is one of your main gateways to accessing a wealth of journal articles. Databases that may be available to you include:

- EBSCO;
- Emerald.

Note: technological developments mean that routes to access electronic subscriptions are changing. For instance, your university may use a system where you only need a single password and never see Athens. If in doubt, check with your services provider.

Student tips on skills and employability

Locating/searching for information

Maggie is working in her first full-time job after graduation, as a senior client sales executive for a company that publishes brochures for corporate clients. In this example, she shows that her ability to locate relevant information in a systematic way helps her to do her job and to retain clients.

> If a client is new or inexperienced, it's not unusual for the project to fall behind whilst I am waiting for copy (text and photos) from them to put into the brochure. I've found that, sometimes, the easiest way to avoid this is to be proactive and offer some help in getting the copy together. For instance, in a recent project I broke down what was needed into stages: I estimated what kind of text/images I'd need and a rough word count to stick to. I then looked through all their advertising, such as conference brochures, adverts and flyers, as a lot of the information on these pieces could be repeated and was still relevant to the publication. To fill in the gaps the best place to go to was the corresponding website—this provided me with plenty of copy that I could edit down accordingly. While this initially seemed like more work, I found it to be the best decision in the long run to enable me to hit deadlines. Clients themselves have told me that they find this to be 'very helpful', which can only help in retaining a happy customer.

5.2 Search techniques

It would be comforting to think that there was one 'best way' to locate the information for your assignments and that you could learn this. The reality is that you will develop your own ways to search for material and continue to learn the more that you search. However, that is not to deny that there are certain guidelines that can help you in your search, especially if you are new to this activity. This section will show you approaches that you may wish to consider. Also, being effective in using library systems or electronic databases are particular skills that you can develop as part of your overall search abilities.

Would you give up work if you won the lottery?

To illustrate how you might find relevant information for an assignment, imagine that you have been given the following question by your Organization Studies tutor, 'Would you give up work if you won the lottery? Discuss.' You have just listened to a lecture on 'The meaning of work'. Figure 5.2 shows a range of possible information sources, as outlined in Section 5.1.

What kind of answer do you think is required?

On the face of it, this might be the sort of question asked in a casual chat with friends. The answer might be a simple 'Yes', 'No', or 'Maybe', although most people would seek to qualify their answer to their friends with some sort of explanation for their choice. However, you would realize that this is an academic question, related to your module 'Organization Studies', and may well be related to your recent lecture on the meaning of work. You will, therefore, be

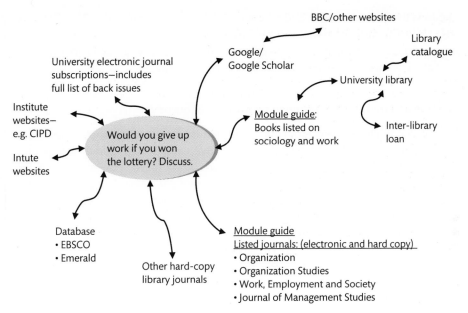

Fig 5.2 Search strategy: initial source investigation

required to carry out some research to answer the question. It is unlikely that you will find a chapter in one of your textbooks that addresses this question directly. But it is likely that such a question has been asked by academics—indeed, you have probably talked about it previously with your friends.

Getting your first good lead

What you really need is to establish that first good lead. Once you have done this, you can begin a detective trail to unearth further information. A good lead will have the following characteristics:

- relevance;
- credibility;
- accuracy;
- give other key information such as names, dates, organizations;
- contain references and websites to follow up;
- be recent (ideally though it may be possible to travel forwards in time, as well as backwards).

Search strategy

You are searching for information, so try to think like a detective! You need to approach your task in a thoughtful way. You need to consider possible sources of information. It makes sense to address the obvious sources and easy sources of information to see if they will throw up a good lead. You may also have the occasional inspired source—this is good, but ensure that you still approach the task in a disciplined way, making notes of your search journey and appropriate references so that you can find your way there again!

On the search trail—what happened on my search journey

I will now tell you how I went about the journey to find my first 'good lead', using the search strategy outlined in Figure 5.2. You should note that every search journey will be unique. Also, I am not saying that my search journey gives the 'best' result, as searching is always rather messy and subject to an element of chance—but it does show a thoughtful process. To illustrate my journey I have overlaid Figure 5.2 with comments—see Figure 5.3, which shows the order in which I addressed the question, from 1–4. For the purpose of this exercise, I have taken the journey as far as finding my first really good lead (Harpaz, 2002) and a secondary useful lead (Morse and Weiss, 1955). From here you would be able to obtain other relevant information by following the references in the articles, and by then comparing these with your course books and journals.

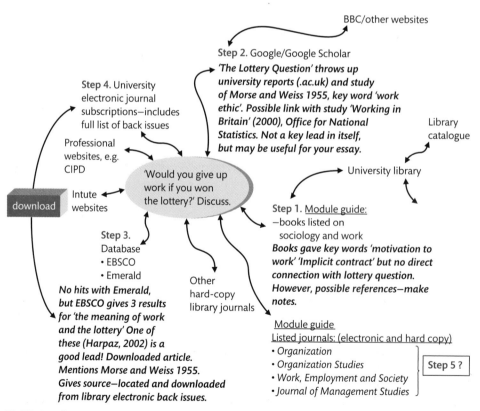

Fig 5.3 Search strategy: initial source investigation results

Skills Example 5.1 Staff well-being strategy

Julie Jennings worked in the human resources department of a medium-sized company that supplied electrical assemblies to a large, established motor manufacturing company. Recently, she had been asked by her manager to set up a staff 'well-being' event in the workplace and to establish guidelines for staff. Her first job had been to gather information. She needed to know what types of employee worked in her organization—numbers, gender, age and occupation; she found that this information was readily available from personnel records. A small number of senior managers and the company's administrative staff were office-based, but most staff worked on the shopfloor and worked a shift system. The production work was semi-skilled in nature and although not particularly physical, was quite repetitive, as well as demanding in terms of deadlines. She decided to research absence and sickness records in the company over the past year to see if there were any trends she could pick out. She discovered that quite a few staff had been absent with repetitive strain injuries and stress-related disorders. This prompted her to seek information from an occupational health specialist, available government publications on the Internet, and to research journal articles about health in the workplace. She soon discovered that other companies were establishing working groups and policies on well-being within the workplace. Armed with all of this information, Julie was then in a good position to invite volunteers to join an initial briefing group, with an agenda that included setting up their first well-being event.

There are several pointers to note from this journey:

- All information is carefully recorded (see Chapter 7 for the benefits of note-taking and the requirements of your note-taking system) and the search route notes—it might be useful to retrace your steps.

- Morse and Weiss (1955) seems to be a 'seminal' article (i.e. an important original idea from which further studies followed) and it appears twice—it is probably worth while locating the original article.

- The Harpaz (2002) article hits all the buttons as a good lead. You may wish to refer to the end-of-chapter activities and follow this one up for yourself.

5.3 Further pointers to the credibility of source information

In your work and leisure time, you are constantly evaluating the messages you receive. Another person's interpretation may well differ from yours. Taking a critical viewpoint, you should aim to be better informed and less biased. You will need validity, relevance and accuracy in your information.

As you have seen, information is available to you from a wide range of sources, which include: newspapers and television, academic textbooks, specialist journal articles, reports and lectures. Increasingly, this information is available from Internet-based sources. Well-informed debate depends upon credible information sources. The argument for credibility extends to your own writing, as your assignments will be judged, partly, on how well you have selected and interpreted your sources of information. You may improve your chances of find-ing credible information if you use:

- 'respected' journals;
- 'respected' textbooks;
- newspapers with a 'good reputation';
- websites established by acknowledged experts in their field;
- multiple sources of information for important points—never rely on a single source.

What is meant by 'respected'?

One way to find out which journal articles and books are 'respected' in the field is to ask your tutor. Their inclusion as essential or recommended reading in module guides should also be a good indication. Also, if they are selected titles in your library or its electronic database sys-tem, they are likely to be credible sources of information. Look for multiple copies of books on library shelves—this shows that the book is probably used as a core reader. Look also for books that have more than one edition; this shows that the original edition was successful enough to have been issued again as a new edition. You should note that these are all signs that the information is of a good quality, but it does not guarantee it. Also, as business and management topics are sometimes complex or controversial, different (respected) authors may hold different views. You should, therefore, always seek other sources of information for important points.

In academic terms, perhaps the most respected source of information is a high-quality journal. The tips just outlined may help you to find these. However, it is interesting to note how academics themselves rate the quality of a particular journal. Consider an article from the *Journal of Business Communication* (Rogers *et al.*, 2007, p. 408), where the authors suggest that the following criteria are among the 'commonly used ways to evaluate journals in various disciplines':

- perception of senior researchers [i.e. what other leading researchers think of it];
- inclusion in major indexes [such as journal lists, book lists, electronic databases];
- acceptance rates [this refers to how difficult it is for a writer to get work accepted—a low acceptance rate suggests that the journal is very selective and of a high standard];
- endorsements by professional associations [for instance, various chartered institutes];
- impact factor [how often do other authors cite a source in their own writing];
- international ranking lists [journals are ranked, often by star rating; an internationally recognized rating is very prestigious];
- journal's longevity [long-established showing success?];
- editor's reputation;
- review board affiliations [for instance, are they experts in this or associated fields? Do they belong to other respected groups or organizations?].

Activity 5.2 Credibility on the web

We looked at the Intute site earlier in Activity 2.1. (Go back and re-do this if you wish, as it gives a most informative overview of relevant business and management databases.) The site features another excellent tutorial, called 'Internet Detective'. Its opening page says it all when it headlines with 'Use this free internet tutorial to discern the good, the bad, the ugly for your online research'.
  This tutorial will show you that not everything on the web is to be trusted!

- On your computer, access the Internet and then go to the address http://www.vtstutorials.co.uk/ (accessed: 9 March 2012), which will take you to the 'Virtual Training Suite', where you will see the 'Internet Detective' tutorial.

Of course, you are a student and not a leading researcher. However, you can still use some of the above indicators yourself. As mentioned previously, the journal may already be a recommended one within your university. The journal will often have an editorial at the front, listing members of its board. You may also see affiliations to leading organizations. In terms of particular articles, you can often get a good idea by reading a typical article and carrying out your own credibility test by observing how it measures up to the following criteria:

- Does it refer to other writers/journal articles and sources of information in its discussion?
- Does it have a comprehensive list of references?
- Does it address the questions raised at the beginning?
- Does it use up-to-date information?
- Does it put forward reasoned arguments, supported by evidence?

5.4 Referencing your information sources

5.4.1 Introduction

As already discussed, you need to make notes on your information search. In particular, you require details of any journal articles, books and other sources of information that you have used in your assignment. You may use some of this information within your assignment, either to make a point or to reinforce your discussion. You should indicate to the reader when you are using this information within your assignment. It will demonstrate to your tutor where you got your information from and it will show that you are researching the area. Also, it means that you cannot be accused of using other writers' words as if they were your own—this is considered to be a form of academic theft and is called 'plagiarism'. Plagiarism is taken very seriously within universities—they don't like it, and they may take disciplinary action against anyone they find guilty of doing it!

You are strongly recommended to obtain a printed booklet showing you how to reference. Your university may have its own. You will probably find that you will need to refer to this booklet throughout your entire programme. You will cover the basic requirements of referencing within this section; however, a dedicated reference booklet will include less-used and more obscure references, and could well run to a 100 pages or more.

5.4.2 **In-text citations**

One half of the 'referencing' process occurs when you mention your sources of information within the article you are writing. Some writers (e.g. Pears and Shields, 2010, p. 4) call the process of including references in your writing 'in-text citations'. We have just used one of these references: 'Pears and Shields 2010, p. 4', which gives the author(s) and date of the reference. This system is one of the most popular ones used and is sometimes called the author/date system; another name for it is the Harvard system. Your university will probably use this system—but you will need to check this.

5.4.3 **Reference list**

The other half of the process, required to accompany your in-text citations, is a list of references which is given at the back of the assignment, report, chapter or book. In this list you will write the full details of the item you referred to in the text. Every in-text citation needs a corresponding full reference. The reference given at the back of this book for the in-text citation just given (Pears and Shields, 2010) is:

> Pears, R. and Shields, G. (2010) *Cite them right: The essential referencing guide*. 8th edn. Basingstoke: Palgrave Macmillan.

Each part of the reference is there for a reason: clearly you are interested in the author, the name of the article or book in which the reference appeared, and the date of its publication. In the above case, the place of publication (Basingstoke) and the publisher (Palgrave Macmillan) will help your readers to locate and possibly purchase the book if they want to.

5.4.4 **Following the same principles**

Using in-text citations with accompanying full references in your reference list is the basis for all of your referencing. Everything else is detail. Different sources of information will require variations in how they are written down, but they all follow the above principles. You can reference any type of communication that occurs or exists, including books, journal articles, electronic information, letters, journals, newspapers, speeches, government papers, meetings, even personal discussions. However, you should note that the Harvard system has been interpreted slightly differently by various respected advisors and publishers. Usually this is a matter of minor differences in style, rather than principle: for instance, you may see the title of a book in bold, underlined, or in italics.

What you need to do is to find a style that is acceptable to your university and stick to it—do not change between styles within the same assignment. You can find full details of how to reference from various places: your university or college may recommend a particular referencing guide; you may select a particular method yourself from a reputable source. A detailed examination of referencing is left for you to carry out yourself. However, some examples of the more common usage of referencing are given below.

5.4.5 **When do I need to reference page numbers in my in-text citations?**

If you give a direct quotation, or use a particular idea, term or model/chart/diagram/figure from your reference source, you should give a page number in your in-text citation. This will help your reader to locate it should they decide to read the original source material. You will often do this for journal articles. It might be argued that as books have an index you do not need to do this for them, but it is probably simplest to apply the same rule. Here is an example:

> Tim Berners-Lee, regarded as the inventor of the web, stated: 'In an extreme view, the world can be seen as only connections, nothing else' (Berners-Lee with Fischetti, 1999, p. 14).

5.4.6 **Examples of referencing**

Example of an in-text citation—book

According to Bryman and Bell (2007, p. 211), one of the most common sources of error in survey research is poorly worded questions.

Another way to write this would be: 'One of the most common sources of error in survey research is poorly worded questions (Bryman and Bell, 2007, p. 211).'

Example of a full reference—book

At the back of your paper or article you would include all of your references (List of References), arranged alphabetically by author's name. Using the example above, the full reference would be:

> Bryman, A. and Bell, E. (2007) *Business research methods*. 2nd edn. Oxford: Oxford University Press.

This follows the general guideline for a book full reference as:

> Author (last name and initials), date (in brackets), title (in italics), edition (if not first), place of publication: publisher.

Example of an in-text citation and full reference—journal article

Journals follow a similar referencing process to books but as they contain distinct, titled articles, you need to include both the title of the article as well as the journal. Your in-text citation may look the same as that of a book (author date), but your full reference will look different: the general guideline for a full journal article is:

> Author, date, title of article (single quotation marks used around this), title of the journal (in italics), volume number of the journal (if volume 3, part 2, 3 (2)), together with the page numbers of the whole article (use pp. and page numbers).

For example, say you are writing an essay about entrepreneurs and write the following in your assignment (in-text citation):

> One of the most well-known entrepreneurs in recent years is James Dyson, who invented a new type of vacuum cleaner (Boyle, 2004).

Activity 5.3 Journal volumes and issues

Using your university or Athens access, observe how the journals *Management Decision* and *Harvard Business Review* are compiled in terms of volumes and issues. If you do not have access to these journals, select several of the journals you do have access to, as recommended in your course.

At the end of your assignment you would include the following full reference:

Boyle, E. (2004) 'Press and publicity management: The Dyson case', *Corporate Communications: An International Journal*, 9(3), pp. 209–222.

Note 1: The above example shows a typical example for a journal which has been issued in a series of volumes and issues. Typically, a volume will represent the journals for a particular year. Within each volume there may be a number of issues (in hard-copy format this may be the journal publication you find on the library shelf). Each issue will contain a number of journal articles, usually written by a number of different authors. Some journals may be issued monthly. Other journals may have issues every quarter (3 months) or twice yearly, or 10 times per year. Some may have issues combined—e.g. issue 1/2 and other issues as normal. Some journals may refer to seasons (Spring, Summer, Autumn, Winter). Some may refer to months instead of issues. You should be aware of these variations and consult your university-approved referencing guide for further details.

Note 2: Page numbers at the end of the journal full reference are included because, unlike books which have an index, and which start at page 1, journals do not have an index and page numbers do not start in each issue at page 1—they continue from the previous issue. If you have not been given the issue in a particular journal you are looking for, but you have the page numbers of the article, you can use this information to find the issue. Page numbers give all pages included in the article.

5.4.7 Articles accessed from Internet sites, journals published online and books available online

Referencing articles from online journals and books and Internet websites follow similar principles to those already mentioned. However, you need to give a web address and also the date on which you accessed the information, as websites are subject to updates. Note: if the journal you have accessed on your search engine is also published in hard-copy format (most are), you may simply use the reference ID of the hard-copy version unless otherwise directed by your tutors. Where possible you should aim to give an in-text citation with an author and date, only giving a URL if this is the only information you have. The following template for the full reference in your reference list is typical of many versions of Harvard style in current use:

- author's title or editor's name;
- date on which the material was created or on which it was published or posted (day, month, year, in round brackets);
- title of the article or other sub-section used (in quotes), as appropriate;
- general title or title of the complete work/website (italic);

- volume or page numbers;
- general information, including type of medium (in square brackets); institution of organization responsible for maintaining or publishing the information, if appropriate;
- Available at:
- page number or online equivalent;
- date accessed.

Tip: as web addresses are usually long and complex, cut and paste from the site into your reference if possible. Here is an example of an in-text citation and reference:

In-text citation

Groups of people who are passionate about learning offer great opportunities for newcomers who wish to communicate with like-minded individuals. Etienne Wenger (2006) refers to these groups as 'communities of practice'.

Reference list

Wenger, E. (2006) *Communities of practice* [online]. Available at: http://www.ewenger. com/theory/ (accessed: 7 February 2012).

The important thing to remember is why you are referencing—ask yourself if someone else could obtain the same information as you.

5.4.8 **Use of referencing software**

Although it is always a good idea to be able to reference manually (so that you understand the underlying principles), you may wish to progress to using commonly available software. This has the advantage of allowing you to build up an expanding database of your references (for all of your work), which you can call up at the click of a button. Bibliographies are generated automatically from your in-text references and updated as you type up your document. Microsoft Word 2010 features a 'References' tab, which is relatively easy to use and which appears in your toolbar as in Figure 5.4.

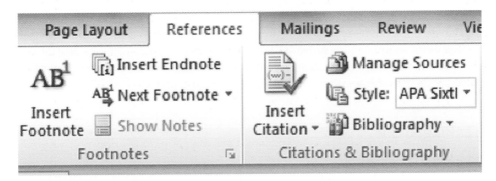

Fig 5.4 Toolbar showing MS References

Source: ©Microsoft. Reproduced with kind permission

You do need to set up the style of referencing you wish to use, as there are many variants, and it may be worthwhile at this point to check with your tutor/organization for a suitable style. You should check available styles against your university recommended style and ask if the style has to be identical or whether or not slight differences might be acceptable. A typical data entry screen is shown in Figure 5.5.

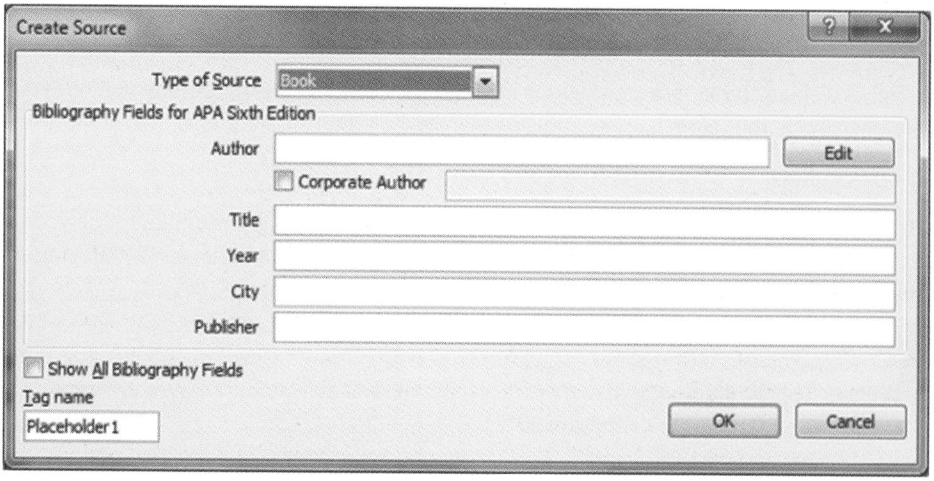

Fig 5.5 Data entry screen: using a series of drop-down menus you should be able to cope with most referencing eventualities

Source: ©Microsoft. Reproduced with kind permission

Another programme you might wish to consider is Zotero (http://www.zotero.org/ (accessed: 6 February 2012)). This is freely available to download, and works with the Firefox web browser. It too acts as a database for your references. It also has the ability to save complete webpages and their weblinks, so is quite powerful. The same note—to check against your university style requirements—applies. Alternatively, you may decide to purchase the referencing programme 'EndNote', which is compatible with Word 2010 to 'search online bibliographic databases, organize their references, images and PDFs in any language, and create bibliographies and figure lists instantly' http://www.adeptscience.co.uk/products/refman/endnote/info.html (accessed: 23 September 2012).

   With any type of referencing software you will need to spend time becoming acquainted with it before you can really reap the benefits. It is quite possible to learn on your own, but perhaps easier—and more enjoyable—to learn with others. You may wish to check for any training that your college or university provides. Alternatively, you may access YouTube tutorials or, in the case of Zotero, instructional videos featured on the website.

5.5 Plagiarism

5.5.1 What is plagiarism?

Plagiarism occurs when you pass someone else's work off as your own without acknowledging them. As mentioned in Section 5.4, universities take a very dim view of this practice. Taken

Activity 5.4 Plagiarism

As plagiarism is such a 'hot' topic in universities, there are three parts to this activity:

- First, go to the following link on the Higher Education Academy website. This is a short video which shows the student viewpoint on plagiarism: http://vimeo.com/channels/154640/9230505 (accessed: 20 May 2012).

- Next, download and familiarize yourself with your university's policy on plagiarism.

- Finally, go to the Turnitin website and watch the demo video(s) on the opening page to see how the system checks your essays for originality: http://turnitin.com/en_us/home (accessed: 31 January 2012).

  For further details, go to the training site for students on: http://turnitin.com/en_us/training/student-training (accessed: 20 May 2012).

at its extreme this view is easy to understand: for instance, say that you find an essay on the Internet and submit it as your own piece of work—then clearly you are not the author and should not be given credit for it. Also, in plagiarism there is the underlying assumption that the accused (yes—students are 'accused'(!) of plagiarism, under university infringement procedures), the student, deliberately knew that he/she was obtaining this unfair advantage and, in many cases, has gone to some lengths to conceal their 'guilt'.

Occasionally, of course, a student might plagiarize something of a lesser nature than the above example (for instance, he gives an end-of-text reference but does not use a corresponding in-text reference) without realizing it. Academic hard-liners might still say 'ignorance of the law is no excuse'. Some universities will take this into account by treating first year students more leniently when they punish them for plagiarism. However, do not take this for granted—you need to check your own university policy on plagiarism.

What other sorts of activities might be regarded as plagiarism? The following list gives some typical examples, and is intended to make you think 'Am I doing that?':

- copying a friend's essay, or parts of it;
- copying sentences, sections, lists or diagrams from books or journals without referencing them or using appropriate quotations;
- cutting and pasting from the Internet or other sources and not acknowledging all sections;
- superficial adaptation of material—for example, using sentences taken directly and 'stitched' to either your own work or other direct 'lifts'.

However, note, this is not an exhaustive list! If in doubt, ask yourself 'Do I wish to hide what I have done?' If the answer is 'yes' or 'maybe', you have probably plagiarized. Many universities are now using plagiarism detection services such as Turnitin, which can screen your essays against a vast databank and produce reports which show how original your work is.

5.5.2 Tips to help you avoid plagiarism

1. When you read a well-written article for your research you may be in the habit of using a highlighter pen or post-it notes for various key words or sentences. This is fine for a first step, but if you write directly from these you are in danger of using the words as they are

written. To avoid using the same words in your report, one technique is to write separate notes, which review your highlights but are written in your own words. However, although this means you are using your own words it does not mean that you are using your own ideas, views or opinions—you still need to reference these along the lines 'Smith (2008) argues that this is the case while Jones (2007) takes a different line'. If you want to quote anything directly, you must reference the words in your text and include an end-of-text reference.

2. Follow the principle given in this chapter of never using a single source for your main arguments. Using various sources lessens your dependence upon any one piece of writing. It allows you to make your own judgement about something (although, of course, you will say that you have based this upon your referred sources).

3. Use a mind map technique (see Chapter 12 for a detailed discussion of this technique) to structure your ideas logically, drawing in various sources. You could use the search strategy mind map (e.g. Figure 5.2) and elaborate on this after you have read various articles. From your mind map draw up a list of headings for your essay, indicating key ideas, articles, quotations, that you will include in each section. This means that when you sit down to write you have a structure to work from that is your own.

4. Do not leave assignments until the last minute. This has two effects: first, it means that you are not tempted to 'cut and paste' something because you are short of time. Secondly, it allows you to 'incubate' the reading in your mind, which then becomes part of your understanding of the subject.

 ## Chapter summary

At its most basic, finding information and using it within your assignments requires you to have an awareness of the resources at your disposal and the ability to use them. This chapter has covered these areas. However, there is no upper limit to how 'smart' you can be in asking the right questions in the first place and providing evidence within your assignment to support your arguments: there is always room for improvement. Techniques such as planning your information search, careful note-taking and referencing do take a deliberate effort to implement at first. However, after a while you should find that you begin to incorporate these methods into your assignment approach naturally.

 ## End of chapter exercises

Exercise 1

Are the so-called 'broadsheet' newspapers such as *The Times* more credible than the 'tabloid press' such as the *Express*? Critically analyse and make notes on this statement, using recent newspaper articles as your evidence.

Exercise 2

'Consuming fish oil is good for you. Discuss.' What would be your approach in tackling this as an assignment?

Exercise 3

In Section 5.2 the Harpaz (2002) article was said to 'hit all the buttons as a good lead'. Find this article and review it in terms of the requirements discussed in the section. The article's reference is:

Harpaz, I. (2002) 'Expressing a wish to continue or stop working as related to the meaning of work', *European Journal of Work and Organizational Psychology*, 11(2), pp. 177–198.

Exercise 4

For this exercise use a 'critical friend'. Print out a copy of one of your recent essays or reports. Ask your friend to:

a. review the information sources in terms of credibility, relevance and sufficiency;

b. assess your approach to answering the question;

c. at the end, show your friend your tutor's comments (if you have them) to compare. Now reverse roles and assess your friend's writing.

 ## Further reading

For further details on referencing you may wish to use either of the following referencing guides:

Pears, R. and Shields, G. (2010) *Cite them right*. 8th edn. Basingstoke: Palgrave Macmillan.

City of Sunderland College, Directorate of Learning Resources (2010) *Harvard referencing: Student style guide*. Sunderland: City of Sunderland College.

 For further information, please visit the Online Resource Centre at **http://www.oxfordtextbooks.co.uk/orc/gallagher2e/**

6 Assignment Research: Developing a Critical Approach

◎ Chapter guide

Student viewpoint

Maggie is working in her first full-time job after graduation, as a senior client sales executive, for a company that publishes brochures for corporate clients. These brochures are used to exhibit their clients' products/services at national trade events and shows. Her comments emphasize how important it is to develop and use skills of enquiry and research in your future career:

'We research after every show—using corresponding statistics and testimonials—and then we decide which articles could be improved/ added to/what new items could be introduced. We use this information to persuade the client to let us make improvements or create additional publications—which, of course, is beneficial to the client but also means more business for us. Being proactive in this way gives us the edge over our competitors because we are seen as more credible; we are able to identify through our research how effectively the client's product (and their USP—unique selling point) is reaching their customers through our brochures, and then how to improve upon this.'

➔ By the end of this chapter you should be able to:

- Understand what is meant by 'criticality' and its importance to employability
- Differentiate between description and criticality
- Analyse assignment briefs in order to identify the scope for criticality
- Assess your need for further criticality development from assignment feedback

Introduction

No matter what your motives are for learning, one thought is likely to be important to you at some stage: 'How can I achieve a good—or a better—assignment grade?' The answer to this lies in a 'smart' approach to how you tackle the whole process. Academics tend to use the word 'critical' for this process. To be 'critical' is to adopt a questioning approach (we shall expand on this shortly). We may adopt a critical approach to whatever we do. It is ideally suited to the problem-solving

Fig 6.1 Achieving a good assignment grade

inherent in the assignments you will tackle at university—and also to those assignments in your future work situations that need a questioning approach. In the previous chapter we did, in fact, adopt a critical approach to finding relevant, credible information, although we did not focus specifically on what 'critical' meant. In this chapter, we are going to start with a more detailed consideration of what criticality entails. Then, we are going to consider how we can combine a critical reading and writing approach to assignments. As some of these assignments may take the form of management reports with conclusions and recommendations, we will also be questioning the practicality and validity of these aspects when applied to real-life situations.

In 'writing' any assignment there is a reflective, continually evolving process going on. In many ways it is a problem-solving process, as much as a writing one; we need to decide what questions to ask ourselves, what to write and how to write it—what to include and what to cut out. Figure 6.1 sums up the relationship between effective information search, effective application to the assignment, and the use of a 'critical' reading and writing approach. It is, perhaps, useful at this point to reiterate the purpose of developing our critical skills: quite simply, employers want people who can ask the right questions and who do not simply accept the status quo—they want innovative thinking.

'Critical'

So, what does 'critical' mean? In fact, it entails a variety of factors that, together, are the basis for an approach. This approach means that you:

- never take things at their face value—you always question;
- ask: who? what? why? where? when? how?;
- seek other views for comparison;
- look for trends and patterns;
- consider not only what happens but what does not happen;
- seek to measure or analyse those aspects that are relevant;
- carefully interpret your findings;
- always give *evidence* to support key statements;
- construct lines of reasoning (arguments) based upon evidence;
- consider the validity and accuracy of your research methods;
- ask if you are asking the 'right' questions in the first place.

It is quite possible for you to spend a lot of time obtaining information on your assignment only to find later that your research was either not relevant or that there was a far more productive way of obtaining your data.

Chapter outline

This chapter gives you some basic but extremely useful ground rules to follow. These help you sharpen your research, reference and assignment skills, using both paper-based and electronic means. In the previous chapter you searched journals, books and other information sources in terms of accuracy and credibility. In this chapter, you will consider how to use a 'critical' approach, which guides you through your research and writing journey. You will arrange your main thoughts into 'arguments', resulting in a thoughtful, balanced assignment that is well supported with appropriate examples and references. Critical writing is a skill you will be expected to develop throughout your degree. This chapter explains various pieces of terminology used by your tutors when they write your assignment briefs. You will be encouraged to think, read and write in a smarter, more 'critical' way.

6.1 Developing a critical approach in everything from basic fact-finding to high-level evaluation

6.1.1 Moving from basic description to higher-level evaluation

In this section, we distinguish between the simple telling of the facts or our basic observations—what we might term as 'description'—to questioning the meaning of what we see or what has occurred—what we might term as 'evaluation'. Let us take, as an example, a newspaper reporter who writes an article about a fire that occurred at a local farm. If the reporter only summarizes where and when the fire occurred and writes a simple statement of the fire damage caused, this might be termed a 'descriptive' account. He may simply state that two people were seen in the vicinity of the fire shortly before the fire started. They were on a public right of way that passed through one of the farmer's fields. He might go on to say that the fire appeared to start amongst the corn stubble in this particular field and that, in due course, a passing motorist alerted the fire brigade. Fire officers arrived 15 minutes later and extinguished the blaze. The reporter would write this as a 'story'—or as academics would prefer to write, a 'narrative', which lists a series of seemingly connected elements of a particular event. So, a descriptive or narrative account provides (perhaps!) the bare bones of something that happened. Is it useful? Yes—it provides some initial background information to what happened. However, it does not necessarily tell us the answers to *why* or *how* the fire happened. (Were the two people responsible for the fire? What had they been doing in the field?) It does not tell us whether there were circumstances that could have been influential to the event occurring. (Had the farmer been in any disputes over the right of way across his land?)

We are interested in the fact that the fire occurred—but we are probably more interested in how and why it occurred, and in this case whether or not it was deliberate. To get the answers to this we (or the Police!) would have to be very critical—i.e. questioning—of the evidence. We would need to do further research if possible, asking further questions. We would have to piece together different pieces of the 'jigsaw' and put together possible scenarios (or, in this case, motives), and then judge which ones seemed to be the most likely. It is possible that we would never know all of the 'facts' and yet still have to make a judgement— or in academic terms an 'evaluation'—as to the likely cause of the fire. In going through these questioning processes to arrive at our final judgement, we would have been following a *critical* line of enquiry. The truth of why the fire happened is more likely to be revealed if we adopt this critical stance, as we will have followed a logical, questioning approach. To summarize: we should have adopted a critical (questioning) approach to all stages of the investigation—from evidence to judgement. However, we might argue that judgement is a higher-order activity (i.e. involving more complex thinking skills) than evidence-gathering of the facts (including the 'story' and other evidence we have managed to find in the course of our investigation).

Importance

When your assignment criteria mentions the need for a 'critical analysis', you should be aware that even if you give the 'correct' answer, you will be expected to justify how you arrived at it. In fact, particularly for contentious issues of judgement, your tutor does not have to agree with your actual 'answer': it is quite possible to get good marks for the 'wrong answer' if you approach it in a critical fashion, providing examples and references to support your statements. It is worth our while at this stage to investigate how our learning may range from a rather basic 'knowledge' stage to the more advanced 'evaluation' stages.

6.1.2 A hierarchy of learning within your degree

If you were to try to describe the learning characteristics of your degree—that 'something' which made your study worthy of something noble enough to be given the title of 'Degree in ...'—what would it be? Would it be the same for year 1, say, as year 3? Surely there would be some progression from your first year to your final year? You would probably conclude that knowledge is important, but so too are skills. But, how much knowledge and which skills, and at what level? And, how do they combine to form this 'degree'? In terms of how we learn through our thinking processes (as opposed to how we learn emotionally or physically), Bloom arrived at the following classification—often referred to as a 'taxonomy':

1. Knowledge
2. Comprehension
3. Application
4. Analysis
5. Synthesis
6. Evaluation

(Bloom 1956, p. 18)

This classification suggests that we learn in a hierarchical fashion; for instance, we need knowledge first before we can proceed to higher levels of learning. No doubt you will recognize these key words from your assignment briefs—proof that the design of your programme of learning has been influenced by the taxonomy. However, it is worthwhile to expand upon each level, relating each to assessment requirements required in your degree.

Knowledge

Knowledge provides the foundations for everything else. In your degree you will need to learn where to access relevant knowledge. You will soon become familiar with how it is signposted and categorized in your university library system. You will start to pick up the terminology for your various business and management subjects. You will become aware that business and management degrees require a mix of factual data and information, which is open to interpretation. In a historical sense you will discover the origins of managerial thinking. And, importantly, you will read about theories and research related to business and management. These theories provide you with tried-and-tested approaches to the many real issues you will face in the business world. You will benefit from the knowledge others have gathered in their research—and you will be able to discuss your own ideas with your class mates and your tutors because you now possess a common 'language'.

Comprehension

Comprehension (which we often refer to as 'understanding') covers three areas—translation, interpretation and extrapolation:

1. *'Translation'*—making sense, word for word, of writing, ideas, symbols, research data and expressions.
2. *'Interpretation'*—this involves a re-ordering or a new view on writing, ideas, symbols and expressions. It would also include your research findings and conclusions.
3. *'Extrapolation'*—means that you infer something further from that which is contained with some writing, ideas, symbols, expressions. It would also include taking your research findings and then predicting what this might mean as an extension of your work.

(Bloom 1956, pp. 204–7)

Application

You might be able to recite what a particular theorist said in his/her theory, but can you actually *use* it? Business and management degrees are essentially practical in ethos, so you will often be asked to apply a particular theory (e.g. leadership) to a given situation. You can do this hypothetically or you could use actual examples. In this way, you begin to internalize the concepts of the theory within your own skills repertoire.

Analysis

Analysis is a key area for any business degree. For instance, you will have to analyse your research findings. This means making sense of the data you have gathered. It may involve breaking something down into its component parts and examining each in detail. You might be interested in a detailed study of each component or your may be interested in how they interrelate.

Skills Example 6.1 The business plan

Gemma and Steve had a business plan to write. They had originally met in the university mountaineering club and now that they had graduated they were keen to establish a business that allowed them to use their knowledge of climbing. Their initial thoughts were to invite a friend who was a qualified climbing instructor to join them (or work for them) in setting up a climbing wall. It soon became apparent that they needed to think very carefully about who their prospective customers might be. Indoor climbing had seen a massive development in popularity in recent years; many of the new 'stars' were in their teens and the once male-dominated sport was now much more gender balanced, with many female lead climbers. A significant number of children's party events were now held at climbing walls. Elsewhere the 'wall' was also becoming a place for climbers to spend time chatting and drinking coffee with their friends. Gemma and Steve knew their task was not as easy as it once might have been: they had competition from other wall providers. They knew that this venture had to be a success as a *business*. It involved time, money and a lot of hard work. They had to think 'Who will our customers be?' and 'What will be different about our wall?', as well as 'Why do we think it will be a successful venture?' There were premises to find, health and safety considerations to satisfy, the technicalities of building the wall and, of course, funding for the set-up. In a nutshell, they had a whole lot of research to carry out and people to network with. Not least of all, they would need money from their bank manager—and she was never going to fund them a single penny without a very well-thought-out business plan, backed up with plenty of evidence of facts, figures and market trends.

Synthesis

In synthesis you are viewing how things build to make a whole. You might, therefore, be interested in creating a generalization, trend or rule from your various findings. From a more practical business point of view, you might be creating a business plan for a new venture.

Evaluation

This involves giving a judgement (or literally a value to) something. On the one hand, it may involve comparing your findings against accepted external theories or standards (for instance, how does a particular company rate in quality terms against a national quality standard); on the other hand, it may involve a comparison against internal evidence (for instance, the percentage in sales figures against previous years).

Following the above discussion, your early assignments might be more concerned with information-gathering and basic understanding of your subject area. Later on, however, your tutors will be pushing you for the higher-order tasks of applying, analysing, synthesizing and evaluating. These tasks increasingly demand a questioning, more critical, approach.

6.2 Critical checklist

Keeping all the requirements of your assessment in your mind at the same time is no easy task!

The acronym WEB-SPUN is offered as a way to remember what may be required in terms of a critical approach to typical business and management assignments (see Figure 6.2). It is a checklist—nothing more (!)—but is likely to be appropriate to many of the types of assessment you are

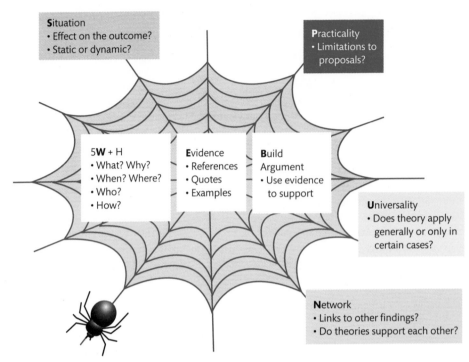

Fig 6.2 WEB-SPUN: a critical checklist to assignments

faced with, as a business or management student. Some people like using acronyms (and you might already have alternative ones favoured by your tutors), others don't, but if the ideas stick in your head after you have worked through this section, the acronym will have achieved its purpose. The first elements of the checklist (WEB) reflect typical advice on investigative assignment writing. The later elements (SPUN) have been included here to make you think, and perhaps spark other thoughts. They are more advanced, so they are likely to be more appropriate for you as you develop your knowledge of your subject. They were derived from critical evaluations during student workshops; see if they work for you. Consider adding other questions of your own and perhaps even making your own acronym! The worked example that follows also shows other important, introductory pointers to different types of research methods and their limitations (typically, you will cover research methods in much greater depth in your later years of university study). A basic information-gathering assignment at the beginning of your studies may call for only a few of the WEB elements to be addressed, whereas a later, advanced, assignment may involve all elements. However, it is worthwhile noting that each element needs to be addressed in a critical fashion. This means that we always need to be 'sceptical of information and knowledge' (Mingers 2000, p. 226).

6.3 WEB-SPUN—a worked example

The following worked example illustrates the use of the WEB-SPUN framework and also gives further tips and advice on how to approach assignments in a critical manner. It introduces some of the types of research methods you will use later in your degree. Remember that the

WEB elements are essential to any assignment and you should use them from the beginning of your course. The SPUN elements are more advanced considerations.

Let's say that you have been given the following (controversial!) assignment:

> 'Great leaders are born, not made.' Write an essay, supported by relevant references, in which you discuss both sides of this statement—i.e. the argument that great leaders are the result of personality traits/physical attributes that are determined genetically, versus the argument that great leaders develop their leadership abilities through their experiences over time. You should not assume that the statement is true. Your role is to be critical and look at the merits and faults of both sides. As part of your answer, you will need to argue what leadership means to you, and in this context how you would define a 'great leader'. You may wish to provide real examples of leaders 'born' or 'made' to illustrate your points.

This is not a straightforward task. To address it you will have to start by asking yourself many questions. There are two approaches to using WEB-SPUN you might wish to try: if you are comfortable with tackling this type of assignment (e.g. drawing up a mind map or making out a list of questions/plan) you might use WEB-SPUN as a checklist after you have drawn up your mind map/plan; alternatively, you could *start* by working your way through WEB-SPUN.

Please note—every time you use WEB-SPUN you are likely to generate different questions, answers and further leads. The purpose of this worked example is not to provide a definitive answer to the 'great leader' debate but to show you how the WEB-SPUN prompts may help you to ask yourself critical questions. (A further worked example is given in Chapter 11 on teamwork skills.)

6.3.1 5W + H and supporting evidence

The 5W + H opening set of questions is usually a good place to start. Used by generations of teachers and philosophers, like all good simple rules, it still applies to problem-solving. The questions are:

1. What?
2. Why?
3. When?
4. Where?
5. Who?
6. How?

So, you could ask yourself the following questions and then note possible answers:

Q1: '**WHAT** is meant by the term "leader"?'

A1: 'Someone who has followers'. You would need to support this with **evidence** from more than one reference—e.g. dictionary, textbook.

Q2: 'What is meant by the term "great leader"?'

A2: 'Someone who influences many people', 'Someone who leads people to great things', 'Visionary', 'Charismatic'. You would need to support all of these answers with **evidence** from more than one reference source. Some of this evidence would be examples of **WHO** these great leaders are/were—for instance, Martin Luther King, Eva Peron, Winston Churchill, Emmeline Pankhurst, Steve Jobs.

As you can see, the great leaders identified lived in different countries at different times, although there is some consistency regarding **WHEN** they lived, to the extent that they were all around in the twentieth century (as opposed to historical figures such as Julius Caesar or Cleopatra). The **WHERE** of their leadership could help focus your discussion; for instance, you could use it in the geographical sense—**WHERE** in the world were they great leaders?—or you could use it in the sense of **WHERE** were they influential (e.g. human rights, humanitarian policies, defending a nation, votes for women, communication technology).

One of the questions of great leadership relates to **HOW**. How did they manage to persuade so many people to follow them, often in quite extreme circumstances? To some extent this will be linked to your definitions of leadership: Steve Jobs was an IT visionary, a creative genius and the ultimate showman, who could tap into the needs of the ordinary individual for both function and beauty in their laptops and iphones; Martin Luther King was a charismatic leader who enthralled his audience through the passion of his speeches, in which he spoke of his 'dream'.

Which leaves us with the '**WHY**'. There are many questions we can ask which start with 'why?'. In this particular case, you may decide to focus on the main topic of debate and ask 'Why are some people good leaders?' You may know what good leadership is and the mechanisms (the '**HOW**') through which people are persuaded to follow. But this does not necessarily mean that you (or others) can lead. Why? Well, as our task implies, perhaps we are simply born as good leaders—or perhaps we learn some sort of trick, some sort of skill that allows us to be good leaders.

6.3.2 **Never rely on a single source!**

This statement bears repetition. Though you might have thought you have arrived at credible information in your 5W + H process, you should always attempt to gather other information that backs up important 'facts' or assertions.

6.3.3 **Build argument**

In addressing the question, you will already see the potential for drifting into a general messy discussion in which we mention many types of leaders and leadership. It is quite common to reach this stage and feel rather overwhelmed by too much information. However, this is normal. Your task is to make some sort of sense of it all. This usually involves linking like things together and discarding information that is not essential to what you now regard as your main **arguments**. Each argument seeks to put forward a case built on a careful examination of the **evidence**. Your argument must be logical, based upon solid foundations—this is sometimes referred to as 'rhetoric' (Mingers, 2000, p. 225). You may seek, through your argument, to explain (as in this case) why one person can lead and another cannot. You may seek to justify some action. Perhaps you wish to group things together. Or, you may be aiming to provide the basis for an analysis or an evaluation.

You will need *sufficient* information to make your claims and build your argument. How do you do this? You have to think like the prosecution in a court of law! Flimsy evidence and insufficient argument will mean that you lose the case. The following list (Figure 6.3) is suggested as a guide:

- Never rely on a single source of information for an essential point—no matter how good!
- Use multiple sources of information to corroborate your main points.
- Ensure your logic is sound—that one point leads to the next.
- Use 'signposts' in your writing to help the reader to follow your logic.
- Consider what is likely to be important, or of interest to your reader.
- Ask yourself whether emotions play an important role in the topic you are researching. Consider how you would counter an emotional challenge to your argument.
- Use examples to *deepen* and *illustrate*/bring to life *carefully selected* important points.
- Examples *may* be from your own experience but are probably better from recent events (e.g. News).
- Include quotations/ideas/theories from your reading of academic journals, books and websites—reference these properly.
- Use established, credible sources of information.
- Consider using some up-to-the-minute sources of information if they can add impact.
- Consider carrying out some quick research of your own—e.g. a focus group or a basic questionnaire—to illustrate a point.
- State any assumptions you have made.

Fig 6.3 A guide to building a better argument

Further questions and further arguments are likely to be formed as we look at the SPUN areas of the WEB-SPUN framework. And, although we are working through WEB-SPUN one element at a time in this example, in reality we are likely to jump from one element to the next as they encourage thoughts in our minds.

6.3.4 **Situation**

Going back to the WEB-SPUN framework, let us consider situation. This is probably very relevant to the main question. Some people would argue that 'being in the right place at the right time' is really a question of a person's ability to grasp an opportunity and then take advantage of it. Luck plays its part. Thus, there may be many potentially great leaders amongst us, but they will only emerge given the right situation. (Of course, you would have to be able to back this view up by referring to the relevant author(s)—Gladwell (2001) in this case.) To some extent this is blurring the original question by saying that it is not just a matter of being born a good leader or being able to be trained to be a good leader; it is a question of the situation being suitable for the individual to use whatever leadership qualities they have. However, questioning the validity of the question is, in itself, consistent with the critical approach.

Looking further we might consider the situation in terms of its dynamic versus static nature. Or, to put it another way, just because a leader is effective in one situation and at one time, will that person be effective at a different time and place? Do things change? Well, we have **evidence** that they do; Winston Churchill, for instance, was the supreme leader in time of war but was voted out of office as soon as peace resumed.

6.3.5 Practicality

Management and business degrees typically aim to inform and help students to be more effective in the workplace. Theory and good practice are used to inform decisions in the workplace, as much as to allow for higher-level academic discussion. It is, therefore, always worthwhile to consider how practical our proposals are to implement—and how practical it is for ourselves, or others, to apply particular theories to real-life situations.

As stated at the beginning, the question of 'Are leaders born or made' is highly controversial. It is one aspect of the more general 'nature versus nurture' debate, which has supporters who believe that our genetics are the dominant factor in our development, and others who advocate that we are born as human 'blank slates' who can be programmed through our experiences. However, even in this highly theoretical discussion, we can still question the practicalities of our arguments. For instance, in the case we are considering, it is theoretically possible that scientists could carry out experiments on people from childhood to adulthood to determine whether or not leaders were born or made through their experiences. However, there would be significant practical difficulties in doing this: on what basis would these children be selected, and more crucially, how ethical would it be to undertake such studies?

Another practical problem arises if we consider that our method of analysis may be flawed or too simplistic. For instance, the way in which most 'scientific' studies are conducted is to freeze as many of the variables as possible so that cause and effect may be determined on the controllable variables. In terms of the notion that leaders are created through their experience—for instance, using adult volunteers and measuring their leadership effectiveness before and after some sort of training—we may be forced to ignore, or be unable to take account of, some of the variables (such as how difficult the task was, who the team members were at the time, how favourable the situation was for the would-be leader). The scientific approach (you may see this termed as 'positivist') may be fine for testing a drug, but does not always hold true for 'real' situations. Nor do we always have the option of comparing an experiment on one group with a 'placebo' group (although behavioural studies of twins attempt to do exactly this). It is probably true to say that in many cases of management research involving human behaviour, we are at best looking for indications and correlations, rather than definitive proof that X has caused Y.

However, you should be aware that there are types of research other than the scientific, rational approach described above. One of these is called 'narrative research'. In this type of study, researchers conduct structured interviews with individuals and attempt to draw meaning from their personal life/work stories. If we now consider the question we have been set, we are aware that many great leaders have had biographies written, and we may consider using these as the basis for a type of narrative research. Perhaps, we might think, this is the way forward. But it does pose the next question—namely, can we generalize (in this case, what makes a good leader) from the stories of a limited number of individuals—and in the case of autobiographies, self-reported ones at that? This is addressed in the next section: Universality.

6.3.6 Universality

What use are theories? Some would argue that they gives us a rough set of rules—approximations that enable us to make decisions that are good enough to help us—or at least give better results than relying purely upon our own judgement. Others would go further and argue that there are certain universal truths in nature and that the point of research is to unearth this knowledge. You might expect in the scientific world of physics that such universal truths could be discovered, but this is not the case. Nothing illustrates this more vividly than two of the most influential theories in physics: one approach attempts to explain the world in very large-scale terms (Einstein's general theory of relativity), and another approach attempts to explain the world in very small-scale terms (quantum mechanics theory)—and they do not agree. According to Professor Julian Barbour (2012, p. 39), 'It is a striking fact that these two theories treat time in ways that are radically inconsistent.' Without pretending to fully understand the complexities of Einstein's theories or quantum physics (!), what we can say is that a particular theory may hold true for a given range of situations but not for all situations (when another theory may be more relevant). Management and leadership theories are just as slippery as physics theories because they are trying to investigate human interactions.

Getting back to the original task of investigating 'whether leaders are born or made', we have already suggested that it may not be possible to form general conclusions from a limited number of personal narratives. What we may be able to do is to gain some understanding of how the various factors interact in those particular cases. Even if we have a large sample of interviewees, they might all come from a relatively similar background, limiting the extent to which we could apply theory. For instance, one of the earliest attempts to formulate a theory of leadership was carried out on US bomber crews. It might be reasonable to assume that this model could be applied militarily to small, tightly knit groups, but it might be more problematic to apply the same theory to civilian situations. In fact, Fiedler (1967, p. 86) asked himself the same question, prompting him to carry out a further two studies in a civilian context.

As a final thought on universality, we should always consider any cultural implications. Many management theories have been derived from a Western perspective. However, the influential theorist Geert Hofstede (see Hofstede (1980) and Hofstede and Bond (1988)) has carried out international studies, which show that different nationalities may have significant differences in leadership and group norms. We might then be prompted to ask whether a great leader in China would be a great leader in the UK. This demonstrates another aspect of the critical approach—that we should be sceptical of one dominant view and also aware of our tendency to take for granted that our cultures and norms apply elsewhere (Mingers, 2000, p. 226).

6.3.7 Network

As a general rule we should never rely on a single source of information, especially for something which is central to our discussion. We should seek to 'triangulate'—i.e. look at the same point from different angles. In this way, we can test the consistency of our information. If our findings are similar, we may be able to draw conclusions; if not, we can say that there are conflicting views. Both outcomes are useful.

Sometimes you might be able to draw parallels with other theories you have studied. In the case of the question 'Are leaders born or made?', this is an aspect of the greater 'nature versus nurture' debate. You could, therefore, investigate this as a more general area. You might already be aware of studies on intelligence (IQ) that have posed the same sort of question. As emotional intelligence (Goleman, 1996) is reported to be a key factor for leadership, you may wish to explore this. In all cases you will be aiming to support your main arguments, so you will need to be selective in your choice of additional material.

6.3.8 **Concluding remarks on the WEB-SPUN approach**

As you will have gathered by now, using WEB-SPUN or any other framework of analysis is all about the *process*. No framework can give you the answers. The clever part still comes from you—your ability to ask the right questions.

 Student tips on skills and employability

Introducing a mobile phone policy—using a critical approach in problem-solving: an example of WEB-SPUN in action (Note that this example shows how the critical approach can be used in situations other than academic report writing)

After graduation, Helen worked in the HR department of a major charity. One of her projects was the introduction of a new policy for the staff use of mobile phones. Until that point the practise had been for staff to make business calls on their personal mobiles and then claim back expenses from the organization. The new policy was to allow certain staff to use mobile phones provided by the organization. Commenting upon the WEB-SPUN framework, Helen said, 'I always used the 5W + H approach—in this case, who would get the mobiles—and, for those who were not given them, what would be a better process for reclaiming business calls on personal phones?'

'Of course', she said, 'I had to persuade our financial manager that this was a good idea, so I carried out a cost–benefit analysis. I researched other companies' practises and policies related to mobile phones. I was conscious that I had to build up an argument and that I had to have evidence to back this up.'

'Practicality was also an issue', she added. 'How easy would it be for existing users to switch their business numbers to the new phones, and would they lose their contacts if they left the organization and had to hand their mobiles back?'

'Universality was relevant too. Would all staff be given the new mobiles? Would all teams? We also had to think about the situation which individuals faced.'

 Activity 6.1 Critical assignment

Read the abridged article below, supposedly written by a student as part of a university assignment (note—reference list not included in this excerpt). The title of the assignment is 'Money as a motivator at Green Vale 'n' Dale Recycling Ltd'. Indicate areas that are weak in terms of a critical approach and suggest improvements. You should be able to relate some (but not all) of your findings to WEB-SPUN*.

Money as a motivator at Green Vale 'n' Dale Recycling Ltd

As part requirement of my degree, an investigation was carried out by the author in March of this year, at Green Vale 'n' Dale Recycling Ltd. I was lucky in being able to easily contact Mr Richards, the General Manager and the fact that I have worked there for the past two summer vacations.

In order to approach the question of money as a motivator in a systematic way, I decided to interview Mr Richards and then also to draw upon my own experience at Green Vale 'n' Dale. I put it to Mr Richards that Frederick Herzberg (1966) said that money was not a motivator. Mr Richards was extremely surprised to hear this; he said that, in his opinion, money was extremely important. He went on to give an example. When he could not offer a better wage rate (he called it 'time-and-a-half') for overtime to be done on a Saturday, two of his staff had refused: this, he said, was irrefutable proof that no one did

Table 6.1 Money and motivation survey

Q1. Do you think money motivates you to work hard?	Y/N
Q2. Do you like working overtime?	Y/N
Q3. How many hours do you work each week?	(Please indicate here)
Q4. Do you sometimes think that other things are more important than money?	Y/N
Q5. If you answered 'yes' to Q4, please indicate in the space below what these other things are:	

Name: Thank you for your time and patience in this survey.

anything unless there was money involved somewhere. Thinking back to my own experience, I tended to agree with him on this.

Some writers have said that money is not that important (Mr Herzberg being one of these), but recent theorists (Smith 1995; Jones 2009) have said that job satisfaction is also very important. I decided that it would be an idea to ask others in the factory what they thought. I devised what I thought was a fairly straightforward questionnaire, with five main questions (see Table 6.1). I gave out the questionnaire during an afternoon break to staff. (Unfortunately, I only received 7 replies back out of the 25 I gave out, but I still think the information is extremely useful, especially as it seems to back up my own original feeling on the subject.)

It was very obvious from my analysis of the completed questionnaires that money was, indeed, the main influence on motivation. Combining what I found here with Mr Richard's interview and my own experience, I think I can say with quite some certainty that Herzberg's theories do not apply at Green Vale 'n' Dale because it is quite clear that money is a motivator here. I would think that it is likely to be the case at other factories similar to Green Vale 'n' Dale, though, of course, I would have to carry out similar surveys there to firmly establish this.

6.4 Assignment improvement and support: feedback from tutors

One of the purposes of this chapter is to encourage you and offer further guidance on how to improve your assignments. In this section, you will consider typical feedback suggestions that tutors might give you on your assignment submissions. Some of these will already have been discussed in Section 6.3 on criticality, but it is useful to see points from your tutor's perspective.

Feedback from tutors falls into two areas: formative, in which your tutor will seek to support/guide your writing as (or before) you engage with it; and summative, where your tutor will mark your work with a recorded grade (e.g. counts towards your module grade) and return it to you with (hopefully!) helpful comments. Summative feedback may be given upon the completion of various stages of your module or maybe upon final completion of your module. It may be tempting to ignore final summative feedback (at the end of the module) if you are no longer going to continue with the subject area, but you can sometimes get useful tips that are relevant to your general study skills. Your choice!

Here is a list of typical, but rather negative comments that tutors might write on your returned work. Some of them make assumptions that you can already understand the difference between words such as 'descriptive' and 'critical'—terms that you should now be aware of, having read this chapter:

a. 'needs more analysis';

b. 'too descriptive' or 'too anecdotal';

c. 'needs more evidence to substantiate statements';

d. 'uses sweeping statements';

e. 'you have assumed this to be the case';

f. 'needs more/better referencing';

g. 'not relevant to answering the question';

h. 'poor structure'.

Criticality

Comments (a), (b) and (c) are telling you that you need to be more critical in your approach. You need to improve your overall approach. Probably what you have written is a rather general discussion. What you will need to do is build more of an argument, adopt a more questioning approach and probably use more examples, theories and references to support your writing. If you receive comments like this, re-read the suggestions given in Sections 6.2 and 6.3 on criticality.

Assumptions

Comments (d) and (e) are sometimes linked. An example of a 'sweeping' statement would be 'It is a well-known fact that women are always better than men at multi-tasking.' Regardless of the truth or otherwise of this statement, the writer should not offer such a contentious, wide-ranging opinion. The critical approach would be to offer a more tentative appraisal based upon the work of various authoritative sources. Rarely are issues such as this so clear cut. To offer such black-and-white images suggests either superb insight and conviction on your part, a lack of research or bias. Although it is probably impossible to eliminate bias, we should at least be aware that we should not offer unsupported statements. You are advised, again, to refer back to the need for evidence—as discussed in Section 6.3.

 Activity 6.2 Feedback

Go to the following link on the Higher Education Academy website. There is a short video showing the student viewpoint on assessment and feedback: http://vimeo.com/channels/154640 (accessed: 31 January 2012)

Referencing

Comment (f) on more and better referencing has two distinct parts. How many references do you have on a typical page of your assignment submission? You should seek advice from individual subject tutors for this. Clearly, you need some to support your arguments and indicate your reading. Does an assignment that has multiple references on every page mean that it is 'better' than one with fewer references? Quite often it does—but not necessarily! You still need to address the main question of the assignment. You still need to use your own powers to select the most appropriate sources (not just as many as you can find). You still need your own creativity and your own originality of thought to construct your answer. And, in an assignment where you need to gather data yourself (primary data), you should be spending time on data analysis as well.

You should also look at your referencing in terms of the credibility of your sources. Expect, also, to be using a range of media—books, journals, e-sources, etc. A tutor will soon comment if your references are only from the web. And a final reminder—have you checked that you have referenced all of your sources? You do not want to be accused of plagiarism! If you are reading comments such as 'Source?' or 'Put this in your own words' against unreferenced writing, treat this as a warning from your tutor that you are in danger of being investigated for plagiarism. At the very least, you need to tighten up on your referencing. For further points you should refer back to Section 5.4 on referencing in Chapter 5.

Not answering the question

Comment (g) (not answering the question) is more likely to occur in examination questions when you are under pressure and genuinely misinterpret the question or have chosen a question that you do not really know that much about. It should not happen in your coursework, but it occasionally does. There are three possible causes here:

1. You have not taken time to read the task and its criteria fully.

    Tasks might be complex. Talk to your colleagues about how they interpret the requirements. Seek advice from your tutor. Prepare an outline of what you are going to do and how you are going to tackle the assignment and discuss this with your tutor. Ask your tutor if you do not understand. It is likely that you are not the only one! Do not think that you are being obtuse or wasting your tutor's time—they would far prefer you to understand the question fully and write a good assignment.

2. You have drifted away from the point.

    It's quite easy to get side-tracked, especially if you know lots of detail on a specific area. To avoid this common trap, keep referring back to the original assignment briefing. Also, if you have prepared a plan for your assignment you should find it easier to avoid this problem.

3. 'Before I answer this question, I must first of all discuss X, Y, Z.'

    This is a less common trap, but it still occurs. Consider the question 'Analyse the leadership style of James Green in the case study. Use appropriate theory to support your answer.' A poor approach to this would be to start your answer by saying 'Before I answer this question, I must first of all discuss various types of leadership style', and then proceed to use (many) precious words giving a book-ish account of leadership styles. This would be fine if the question had been 'Discuss leadership style'—but it is not in this case. Your tutor will assume that you have read the relevant texts on leadership theory; what she now requires you to do is demonstrate the next level of learning—that you can apply your knowledge, in this scenario to a case study. You will be expected to use concepts and terminology from your reading and to quote relevant theories; for instance, saying what aspect of leadership is being used in particular situations. If there is a model, show how your case study applies to it; if there is a leadership diagram, indicate where you would place your leader.

 ## Chapter summary

This chapter has laid the groundwork for you to develop a critical approach to your research, reading and writing. The critical approach is embedded in other chapters in this book, particularly those that deal with presenting information and with creativity and innovation skills. Employers are looking for students who can ask the right questions. There is no upper limit to how 'smart' you can be in asking the right questions in the first place and providing evidence within your assignment to support your arguments: there is always room for improvement.

 ## End of chapter exercises

Exercise 1

Consider the question which a tutor has set for his class of students: 'Consuming fish oil is good for your brain. Discuss.'

What would be your approach in tackling this as an assignment? What questions might you ask yourself?

Exercise 2

Go to http://www.youtube.com and type 'critical thinking' in the search box. You should find in excess of 12,000 videos listed. Select one that you think may be relevant to your study. Watch it and make notes. You may wish to compare your notes with those of a friend who has chosen another video. What are the key learning points? To what extent can you relate these to the contents of this chapter?

 ## Further reading

One really good book to consult is:

Fisher. A. (2001) *Critical thinking: An introduction*. Cambridge: Cambridge University Press.

 For further information, please visit the Online Resource Centre at
http://www.oxfordtextbooks.co.uk/orc/gallagher2e/

7 Reading Skills

Chapter guide

Student viewpoint: Class survey—enjoyable reading

You must read for your degree. However, as this chapter shows, you will generally become a better reader and writer if you read for pleasure as well as for study. I thought you might like to start this chapter with the thought that reading can be immensely satisfying, that reading need not be 'boring'. And, that even in today's world of sound bytes, there is still a place for a good book, the opportunity for your imagination to picture a scene. I asked my class of undergraduate first year management students what they enjoyed reading in their leisure time and would recommend to others. This is a sample of their list:

Other People's Money by Neil Forsyth and Elliot Castro

Harry Potter series by J.K. Rowling

Angels and Demons and *The DaVinci Code* by Dan Brown

The Godfather by Mario Puzo

Autobiographies, real life stories, diaries—e.g. Anne Frank

J.R.R. Tolkien

Twilight by Stephenie Myers

Alan Carr

My Booky Wook by Russell Brand

Lovely Bones by Alice Sebold

PS, I Love You and *Where Rainbows End* by Cecilia Ahern

Arnhem by R.E. Urquhart

Short stories by Stephen King

Band of Brothers by Stephen E. Ambrose

It Never Snows in September by Robert Kershaw

Jodie Picoult

Chocolat by Joanne Harris

Katie Price

My Story by Dave Pelzer

Dean Koontz

Bill Bryson

Now Then Lad ... by PC Mike Pannett

Eden Close by Anita Shreve

Philip Pullman

When the Lions Feed by Wilbur Smith

The list includes suspense, emotion, the supernatural and courage in the face of adversity. It's a modern, contemporary list, rather than a collection of classics of the sort that you might find in a literary critic's recommendations. Each to their own, as they say! What matters is your *engagement* with the written word: to get better at reading, you need to read.

 By the end of this chapter you should be able to:

- Explain the links between effective reading and writing
- Read 'smart'—applying a purposeful reading strategy to your studies
- Apply reading techniques to quickly gain the overall picture from a text
- Review your personal note-taking system to capture key points
- Create ideal conditions for your reading

Introduction

In your studies you will be called upon time and again to read books, journals and reports. At times, you will need to skim large volumes of information to get the overall picture of what is happening. At other times, you will need to dissect the precise meaning from a particular document. This chapter aims to improve your skills in both of these areas.

Chapter outline

The chapter begins by asking the question 'Why read?' and then goes on to show that there is much more to your reading than simply being able to gather facts for an assignment. It emphasizes the importance of building a good vocabulary; it encourages you to read not just for study purposes but also as a leisure interest. The main part of the chapter is then introduced under the heading of 'Read smart'. It uses the 'SQ3R' model as its framework. Under this broad heading various techniques are given that will help you to gain a quick overview of a textbook or investigate a particular section in depth. Finally, the chapter has a section on creating the ideal conditions for your reading which focuses on practical guidance and ideas for you to experiment with.

7.1 Why read?

In the preface to *Book Smart* Jane Mallison (2007, pp. xiii–xiv) talks about 'the joys of being well read' and lists three of these as:

- stimulation of our own thinking;
- gaining of experience—'after you are finished reading one [a good book] you will feel that all that happened to you' (quoting E. Hemingway);
- 'We read to know that we are not alone' (quoting C.S. Lewis).

Activity 7.1 Your experience of reading

Compare your own experience of reading with the three statements above.

The connection between reading and writing skills

Francine Prose (2006) makes a direct connection between reading and writing skills when she says:

> Long before the idea of a writer's conference was a glimmer in anyone's eye, writers learned by reading the work of their predecessors.

> (Prose, 2006, pp. 2–3)

She goes on to say that:

> Though writers have learned from the masters in a formal, methodical way ... the truth is that this sort of education involves a kind of osmosis. After I've written an essay in which I've quoted at length from great writers, ... I've noticed that my own work becomes, however briefly, just a little more fluent.

> (Prose, 2006, p. 3)

If you read a well-written novel, then you may well adopt some of the author's words or grammatical ways of writing in your next essay or report. This would be of general, transferable use. On the other hand, let's say you read a particular article in a marketing journal; this would provide you with specific knowledge or ideas that might be useful in writing a particular marketing assignment.

The building blocks of good communication—the importance of vocabulary

Words are the basis for your reading and writing. The collection of words you have at your disposal is your 'vocabulary'. Rupley (2005, p. 204) defines it in a more precise manner: 'vocabulary is perceived as words and meaning in the shared experiences of the reader and the author'. There is a strong correlation between your ability to comprehend written text and your vocabulary.

Another important point, as Maletsha Joshi (2005, p. 216) notes, is that there is a difference between being able to understand words that you read or hear (your larger, receptive vocabulary) and your ability to use words to write or speak (your expressive vocabulary). You may be more aware of this in situations where you have to converse in a foreign language. For instance, you may be able to grasp what the hotel receptionist is saying to you in French but be very poor at holding a fluent conversation with her. To embed more words from your receptive to your expressive vocabulary requires you to recognize this imbalance and become more proactive in using them in both your written and spoken discussions.

Finally, when you increase your vocabulary you do not just increase the number of words that you know, you also begin to use words that are more precise.

Personal aims/outcomes	Academic aims/outcomes	Career aims/outcomes
Allowing for greater self-expression	Getting better marks in essays and reports	Looking more 'professional'
Greater self-awareness	Passing degree	Writing better CVs
Improving general knowledge	More effective gathering of information	Writing effective business reports, letters and other documentation
Intrinsic enjoyment/satisfaction	Providing an improved basis for comparison and contrasting of various points of view	Ability to sift out pertinent information from masses of data
Adding to personal vocabulary	Improving understanding of subject area	Improved general awareness
Opening up areas of future interest	Improving ability to construct arguments by reading those of others	Better social skills

Fig 7.1 Personal, academic and career aims and outcomes of improving reading (and writing) skills

Figure 7.1 summarizes our discussion so far and adds some additional possibilities. You may be able to think of further benefits.

7.2 Read more

Challenging books and articles

Perhaps the most obvious way to improve your reading is to read more. Of course, what you read is going to be important. If you wish to improve your vocabulary, you could consider subject-specific versus general-use words.

If you want to learn subject-specific words, then you will find these in your textbooks and journal articles. For instance, you may now have an understanding of the phrase 'experiential learning' as you will have read this a number of times within earlier chapters in this book; sometimes there may be a definition in the textbook or a summary of terms/words in the book itself (termed a glossary). Failing this, you can ask your friends, colleagues or your tutors.

If you wish to improve your vocabulary generally, then you should choose to read something which you find challenging but interesting. Perhaps the easiest way to do this is to choose your area of interest first. The next is to find authors who write in a style to which you aspire; ideally, this is mildly challenging in terms of its vocabulary (it will probably also be written in a style that you wish to emulate). You should read one or two pages of the book to get an indication of this. You could also look at the book cover and the endorsements of other readers. Prize-winning or nominated books are sometimes good indicators of 'quality', but be careful because sometimes what the book critics like is not to everyone's taste and vice-versa. The important thing, though, is to get into the habit of reading frequently, ideally on most days, even if this is only for 15 minutes. Have a dictionary to hand for the occasional word you are unsure of.

Skills Example 7.1 Choosing interesting (and educational) books to read

Everyone has their own literary tastes. It's a personal thing and is therefore difficult to provide you with an example that would directly relate to you. The list of books at the front of the chapter illustrates the diversity of choice. One of my own interests is reading about mountaineering adventures—so-called 'armchair reading', as it lets readers experience some of the thrills and spills, yet remain in perfect safety! As far as mountaineering books are concerned, the greatest climbing achievements are not always reflected in the best writing, as great climbers are not necessarily great writers. For this exercise, I performed a mental trawl of my knowledge of some of the 'climbing greats' (if you've got a hobby of any seriousness you will probably be able to do the same for your area of interest). A few names sprang to mind. A quick look at Amazon presented some immediate reviews. Thus, I now know that if I want to read a tense, emotional account I should read Joe Simpson's *Touching the Void* (1998), in which he describes his amazing survival against all the odds after a mountaineering accident in the Peruvian Andes (since made into a film). If I want to stretch my use of descriptive writing I might wish to consider reading one of Jim Perrin's books, such as *The Villain: The Life of Don Whillans* (2006), an autobiography of one of the great characters of post-war climbing.

7.3 Read smart

The rest of this chapter aims to give you advice for improving your reading—and increasing all the associated benefits. I assume that you wish to improve your reading primarily for the purpose of enhancing your understanding of your degree subjects and to improve your writing ability for your assignments. When you read for your degree, what you really need to be able to do is to have a system that allows you to select what to read, to quickly appreciate the key points, to understand and to be able to remember what you have just read. With these requirements in mind, the following (ancient) quotation will be used as a guiding principle:

Tell me and I will forget

Show me and I may remember

Involve me and I will understand.

(Confucius: 551–479BC)

So, the more that you involve yourself with the reading process, the more you are likely to understand. A particularly effective method for doing this is called the SQ3R technique (Robinson, 1970), which stands for:

- Surveying
- Questioning
- Reading
- Recalling
- Reviewing

Fig 7.2 SQ3R sequence

Source: © Pearson. Reproduced with kind permission

This section uses SQ3R as a framework, as shown in Sections 7.4–7.8, to explore the use of various techniques to enhance your reading. Note-taking (included in the framework) will also help you to structure your assignment writing. Figure 7.2 is used to illustrate each stage.

 Skills Example 7.2   Howard Carter—discoverer of the ancient tomb of the boy king, Tutankhamen: a vivid example of SQ3R principles

On Sunday 26 November 1922, Howard Carter, the English archaeologist, made a small hole into the chamber of a hitherto unexplored ancient Egyptian tomb. By the light of a candle he peered in. Lord Carnavon, accompanying him that day into the excavation, asked him the now famous question 'Can you see anything?' Carter, looking through the clearing dust, replied, 'Yes, wonderful things!' The early entries in his excavation diary are limited to comments such as 'Pay men. Fuel. Two donkeys', but here he is unusually expansive in his account: 'Our sensations and astonishment are difficult to describe as the better light [from an electric torch] revealed to us the marvellous collection of treasures' (Carter, 1922). The reason for his enthusiasm was understandable—he had finally found the tomb of the boy king, Tutankhamen, in all its splendour. In archaeological terms this was the find of the decade.

In Section 7.4 you will see that Howard Carter's quest for knowledge followed the same *principles* as those that can be applied to your academic reading strategy—SQ3R. Your quest for knowledge will comprise a number of methods, but an effective reading strategy will lie at its heart. Like you, when you set out on an assignment project, Carter had an initial aim; what he had to do was to approach his task in a logical way. The information existed, but first of all he had to uncover it—just like you will have to do in your reading. Also, like you, he was not sure what he would find, which clues to follow up; all the time he would be building up an overall picture. He had to do this to be able to make sense of his search; he could then take time later to investigate particular artefacts in more detail. His 'reading' was not just of the ancient hieroglyphic writing, but also the paintings on the tomb walls and the artefacts themselves. All the time he made notes and drawings, to capture key findings, and he kept a diary to help him to recall the excavation process. Later he would review his findings and present them to the world.

7.4 Surveying

7.4.1 **The art of surveying**

Howard Carter did not find the tomb of Tutankhamen purely by accident, although 'luck' did play a part in the discovery. He achieved success by a series of surveying steps: first, he had to refer to previous findings by other archaeologists suggesting that the valley in which he was thinking of searching was likely to contain items of interest. This initial phase was crucial; he did not have the time or energy to dig indiscriminately—you face the same limitations in your reading, for what you are attempting do when you are surveying textbooks or journals is to find out their key knowledge or findings as quickly as possible. Use your reading lists, ask your tutors, friends, librarians—anyone who may point you in the right direction. Surveying at this level helps you to select books and journals that will serve as key sources of information; survey the title of the book/journal, the cover introduction and for journal articles the abstract.

Carter then drew up a map of the valley, overlaid it with a grid pattern and systematically began his excavations. Having said this, he had also learnt over the years to follow his intuition, constantly being alert to clues that he might be digging in the right place. You can use this systematic grid approach when searching for books or journals—draw up a systematic search plan, making sure to note what you have already looked at, and what you have still to look at. Keep a journal of your searches. At the book level your 'grid' is provided by the contents page and the index. Journals rely on a standard structure of abstract, introduction, findings and conclusions. Scan these.

When he was successful in breaking into the inner chambers of the tomb, the first thing he did was to make brief notes of the various artefacts, their locations, and then their relationship to the entire scene. In a similar way, the further stages of your surveying will involve a series of steps, from the reading of individual chapters and sections. Gradually you will begin to see how the various pieces of information from your reading fit together. What follows is further advice on reading lists, abstracts and the order of your reading.

7.4.2 **Reading lists and textbooks**

Reading journal articles can be time-consuming. At the beginning of your search a good strategy is to find the most up-to-date, authoritative, but still fairly broad approach to your subject area; this is where good textbooks are very useful. Or you may consider several respected journals. Your module reading list may provide the starting point—or you could ask your tutor for some ideas. If you choose to improve your reading skills as one of your personal development goals, you might wish to talk to your personal tutor for further advice. You could also ask friends and colleagues what they are reading at the moment. Perhaps you could share your reading experience with others in a more structured way, building up a list of useful books, authors and websites.

7.4.3 **Abstracts**

Journal articles often have a brief, overall account, given at the front of the article. This account is usually termed an 'abstract'. Business reports sometimes use a similar device, called

Skills Example 7.3 Abstract

An example of an abstract (Hong, 2012) is given below. Note how the abstract gives you an overall view of the entire article—it is not just an introduction.

The energy factor in the Arctic dispute: a pathway to conflict or cooperation?

Nong Hong*
Author affiliations
* Nong Hong is an associate research professor, Research Center for Oceans Law and Policy, National Institute for South China Sea Studies, China; Adjunct Senior Fellow, China Institute, University of Alberta, Canada.

Abstract

The Arctic has recently witnessed a manifold growth in its geostrategic importance due to the emergence of huge deposits of oil and natural gas, and the potential contribution of northern sea routes for global shipping. As a result of this, northern regions and seas have become a target area for growing economic, political and military interest from the Arctic states major powers outside the region and trans-national companies. This article analyses the perspective of international law on the ownership of non-living resources in the Arctic. It also unfolds the challenges and opportunity in energy development in the north. Joint management of resources is an option that might come into play as countries might see more advantage in approaching the disagreement this way rather than losing a claim in a zero-sum game. The energy factor, rather than a possible curse upon the Arctic, could serve as an opportunity for regional cooperation in the region.

an 'executive summary'. The purpose of an abstract is to allow you to see at a glance whether or not the article is relevant to your reading. In the days before easy electronic access to journals, libraries used to keep drawers of abstracts written out on a card system; you would then either have to find the relevant article in your own library or send off for a photocopy from a centralized source. You may still encounter this system, but many journal articles are now available electronically.

7.4.4 Order of reading

The order in which you read is something you can also consider. You may be used to the idea that you do not have to read every chapter in a textbook—and that you may be able to read a chapter at the rear of the book before you read one near the front (the author will often offer advice on this). But, you may still tend to read a long business report from the beginning to the end. A different method, which you may find more effective, is to read the abstract, introduction and then the conclusion first. This has two main benefits: it prepares your mind for the path the report will take in the main discussion; if you are reading back on your own work you should note that the introduction and conclusion should be linked (often your tutor will read your report's aims and objectives and then check your conclusion to see whether or not you have addressed these within your report).

7.5 Questioning

Before you read an academic textbook or journal article you should be asking yourself the following questions: 'What is it that I want to find? What do I expect to find? What do I already know about the subject?' Have these questions in mind as your read and attempt to answer them as you proceed.

Questions that Howard Carter might have asked himself when he first discovered the tomb of Tutankhamen could have included:

- How important, during his lifetime, was this ancient Egyptian pharaoh?
- How old was he when he died and what was the manner of his death?
- What sort of artefacts would the tomb contain?
- What might these artefacts say about life in the time of the ancient Egyptians?

7.6 Reading

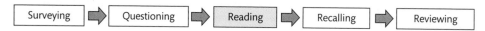

7.6.1 Reading techniques

The act of reading—that is looking at the words on the page—is a skill that can be developed. When you were first taught to read it is likely that you read each and every work out loud to your teacher, perhaps following the words with your finger. Later you would probably have progressed to scanning the words with your eyes only, and reading quietly to yourself in your mind. This approach is probably satisfactory for the majority of your everyday reading of novels and newspapers. However, when you are confronted in your studies by large volumes of information or ideas that are difficult to grasp, you may wish to use additional techniques. Two particular techniques will be outlined here: *skimming*, which gives you an overall picture of a section of writing, and *reading particular sections more than once* if they are important or difficult to understand. These represent opposite ends of the reading techniques spectrum. When you employ them is dependent upon your existing acquaintance with the subject matter and the time available to you.

Using the running SQ3R example, Howard Carter would have used both of these techniques. He had to read a series of signs—ancient hieroglyphic symbols, wall paintings—as well as what the artefacts in the tomb were 'telling' him. He would not have been looking at everything in detail at that point, so what he was doing was trying rapidly to sum up the whole situation: this 'skimming' technique is discussed next, in more detail. *At the same time,* he would also be double-checking certain key points—particularly that this was indeed the tomb of Tutankhamen and not some other king or wealthy person. Later, when he had removed the artefacts to the Egyptian Museum in Cairo, he would spend a great deal of time in very detailed 'reading again' of individual artefacts. The next two subsections on 'skimming' and 'reading more than once' give advice on how to carry out these techniques in your academic studies.

7.6.2 **Skimming**

Do you need to read every single word in a textbook or journal article? This is unlikely to be the best use of your time, as you will have other textbooks and journals to read and only a limited amount of reading time. Of course, the danger is that by reading too little of the book, you might miss some important fact or idea. Clanchy and Ballard (1999) recommend paragraph skimming. Essentially what this consists of is reading the first section in full, but then only the first sentence of each paragraph to gain the overall sense of what the writer is saying. Sounds scary, doesn't it? However, they argue (1999, p. 42) that in good academic writing, the paragraph should contain an 'idea unit', so that by reading the first sentence of each paragraph, you will effectively have a summary of that particular chapter. Of course, you may wish to re-read certain key paragraphs in full—that is another technique; see Section 7.6.3.

7.6.3 **Reading more than once**

Sometimes you will need to read a particular section more than once to fully understand it. This is not a failing on your part. Academic writing can be very precise, providing a lot of information within a typical page—or even a particular paragraph or sentence. Definitions often fall into this category. Consider the example below, given to explain the concept of organizational culture—something that could be summarized much less precisely (but still gives you an idea of what it is) by the phrase 'the way we do things around here':

 Skills Example **7.4**   Edgar Schein's (1984, p. 3) definition of organizational culture

[Culture is] ... a pattern of basic assumptions—invented, discovered or developed by a given group as it learns to cope with its problems of external adaptation and internal integration—that has worked well enough to be considered valuable and, therefore, to be taught to new members as the correct way to perceive, think and feel in relation to those problems.

Every word in this definition is laden with meaning. Consider the first few words (discussion of the entire definition in class can easily take 15 minutes!):

- the word 'pattern' suggests that culture (i.e. 'the way we do things around here') is not the result of one thing alone, it is a range of things which seem to form an overall impression;
- 'basic', meaning that which is an essential foundation;
- 'assumptions'—so deeply hidden that we take them for granted;
- 'invented, discovered or developed'—various means through which this pattern might emerge, suggesting that it might already be there, that somehow it might be in part constructed and also that it is not something that is necessarily static;
- 'given group' suggests that culture will vary from one group to another.

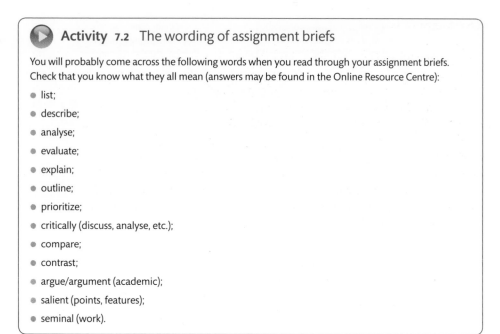

▶ Activity 7.2 The wording of assignment briefs

You will probably come across the following words when you read through your assignment briefs. Check that you know what they all mean (answers may be found in the Online Resource Centre):

- list;
- describe;
- analyse;
- evaluate;
- explain;
- outline;
- prioritize;
- critically (discuss, analyse, etc.);
- compare;
- contrast;
- argue/argument (academic);
- salient (points, features);
- seminal (work).

7.7 Recalling

| Surveying | Questioning | Reading | Recalling | Reviewing |

7.7.1 Benefits of note-taking

Unless you are blessed with a photographic memory, you will need to take notes during lectures and while reading for assignments. The SQ3R example makes direct reference to the excavation diaries of Howard Carter; archaeologists such as Carter take detailed written notes, technical drawings and sketches as they progress in their information searches. Like you, they have to be selective in what they note. These notes are invaluable as evidence of their findings and to guide them in their later interpretation. They may also be available for future investigators to use. In academic terms for your study, the potential benefits of note-taking are shown in Figure 7.3.

- As shown in box (a), taking notes is an active, rather than a passive, activity. You must decide what to write down and you must then attempt to note key points. It has to make sense to you at the time (ideally—if it does not, it gives you a starting point for asking your tutor to explain something further, or for you to find out for yourself).

- Everyone's notes will be unique to them, as shown in box (b), although they will often have similarity in content detail. (This is why if you miss a lecture and ask to see a friend's notes you may find them difficult to follow.)

- Notes should help you to see the 'overall picture', as in box (c), particularly for complex discussions.

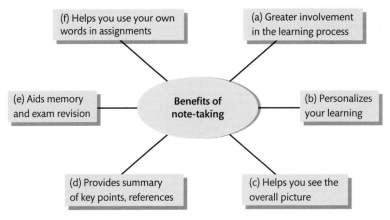

Fig 7.3 The benefits of note-taking

- Box (d) shows that you will often use your notes as the starting point for your assignments and further reading, and you may wish to highlight key facts, names and references.
- Box (e) indicates that producing notes helps you to memorize key facts and figures. If you have to revise for exams, such notes are a good place to begin your reading.
- Finally, as box (f) indicates, when you write notes you begin the process of using your own words in assignments. This helps you to avoid the dangers of plagiarism!

7.7.2 **Requirements of your note-taking system**

Everyone's note-taking will be unique to them. Some people prefer to make notes in a written list or bullet format. Others may prefer to arrange relevant points in some sort of diagrammatic way, often with arrows, connecting lines and symbols. However, there are certain requirements of any system, which will help you to maintain usefulness and accuracy. The following list is suggested:

- *coverage of all key points*—though depth is personal choice;
- *decipherable*—now and in the future;
- *arranged for easy reading*—including use of highlights and colours;
- *flexible* enough to include references, websites, personal comments, further reading or follow-on activities and, ideally, simple diagrams and pictures;
- *retrievable*—there is nothing worse than taking good notes and then not being able to find them later.

These points will apply irrespective of the physical format of your notes, whether they are hand-written, on a computer laptop or in the form of an audio recording.

 Activity **7.3** Review

Review your own note-taking system using the bullet points above as your guidelines.

7.8 Reviewing

Surveying ➡ Questioning ➡ Reading ➡ Recalling ➡ Reviewing

Completing the SQ3R sequence is the review process. In the example, Howard Carter would spend a great deal of time on this. He would go back through his notes and the evidence from the artefacts themselves. Typical questions he could have asked himself at this point might be:

Had he missed anything?

How could he order the information into meaningful parts?

Could he place his findings/reading of the situation within an overall account?

Was there anything that did not seem to fit?

Did he now have the overall picture in his head?

In a similar way, before you write an assignment you will need to review your notes. You may also want to re-read key sections of text that you have highlighted, or specific pages where you have attached post-it stickers in books and journal articles. You may wish to have these close at hand when you begin your writing, in case you need to refresh your memory or use them for quotations.

 Student tips on skills and employability

Using a 'gist' reading strategy

Jen is employed in her first 'real' job after graduation. She teaches English as a second language. Most of her students are adults. Here she relates how anyone can improve their ability to summarize the main or general meaning from whatever it is they are reading:

One of the methods I use is 'gist' reading. I give my students a particular article to read—usually something controversial such as a local authority's decision to construct a wind farm in the countryside. For long articles I might ask students to read one large section at a time. I then ask them to summarize, in a short sentence, the main meaning of each major section. Typically, I will then ask students to say whether they think the writer is for or against the development. I ask them to talk to each other and compare their gist statements before feeding back to the class. This exercise really sharpens up their understanding of what they are reading and writing. The gist sentence is a very useful practice for taking notes when reading a complex article.

Note: further information on gist reading can be found in the Online Resource Centre.

7.9 Creating ideal conditions

There are some basic things you can do to help you to create an environment that will assist you in your reading. Most of these tips are easy in theory but may be difficult to achieve in practice. Thus, a certain amount of thought to build these into your daily routine is likely to yield benefits. You may wish to consider the list of suggestions in Figure 7.4.

 Activity 7.4 Creating ideal conditions for reading

Using Figure 7.4 'Creating ideal conditions for reading', make notes of any ideas that come to mind. You may wish to try out your ideas and/or include them within your personal development plan.

Why don't you try to . . .	Why?	Where?	When?	How?
Make time for your reading?	Because otherwise you may not allow sufficient time for it	Library Your room Train/bus	Between lectures Before/after a workshop Quiet library times Certain times of day—e.g. evening for novels, earlier in the day for more demanding reading	Look at your lecture schedule and create reading/study slots Create routine for novels reading and looking at new journal issues in your library
Take breaks in your reading?	Because your concentration is limited To pace yourself	Wherever you happen to be reading	Ideally at a 'natural break' such as to stretch your legs, have a drink	Get up from your chair Talk to someone Have a drink/meals Do some other non-reading task Listen to some music Go for a walk Telephone a friend
Oxygenate your brain—wake up?	You need to be alert for demanding reading	Walks can be short—take the stairs to the cafe/toilet Some stretching exercises can be desk-based Activities such as swimming need more time and planning	Before you start reading During reading breaks	Get sufficient sleep Go for a walk/swim/cycle Do some yoga/stretching exercises Have a cup of coffee

Fig 7.4 Creating ideal conditions for reading

		Wherever you happen to be reading	During your reading time	Depends upon your personal preference: many people prefer quietness; others prefer to listen to (background) music
Free yourself from distractions?	So you read more easily and comprehend better			
Create the right mood?	Learning is emotional; you'll learn more if you're interested	Various	Before, during, after your reading	Talk to others about your reading and the subject matter Go to the library with friends Go to a quiet 'reading room' Find out about the author's background Visit relevant places where events happened Attend exhibitions, conferences, talks
Just do it?	If you wait for inspiration you may wait a long time Often getting started is the hardest part of any studying	Various	When ever you have the opportunity	Don't say 'Why?'—say 'Why not?'
Take notes?	Our short-term memory is limited We need to keep records and selected information We need to reflect back over our reading Notes help us make sense of our reading	During lectures, workshops, reading books, journals	Certainly when researching, but consider at other times too	Keep a notebook(s) Use your pc

Fig 7.4 Continued

Chapter summary

This chapter has covered some of the fundamental aspects of the reading skills relevant to your study as a student. The important thing is that you involve yourself in the reading process; making time for reading is essential, as it will feed into your writing. It's the sort of activity that you can carry on outside of university, taking an interest in reading novels, browsing through bookshops. It goes to the heart of the learning experience. The guidance on creating the ideal reading conditions for yourself is quite personal, but you may find that small changes have significant benefits to your reading effectiveness—this is an area for experimentation on your part.

The first of the SQ3R techniques—surveying—is essential. You need to maximize the effectiveness of your information search. Some of the SQ3R techniques, such as posing questions before you read a particular book, may seem strange to you at first. However, over time you are likely to begin building the SQ3R approach into your reading, customizing it to suit yourself. Taking notes during your reading is extremely important. This chapter has strong connections with Chapter 8 'Writing Essentials: Preparation, Layout and Structure'. You would expect this, as you will move from one skill to another when you are working on your assignments.

 ## End of chapter exercises

Exercise 1: Fever Pitch

In his million-copy bestseller *Fever Pitch* (1992), Nick Hornby writes about his beloved football team—Arsenal. Its credits include glowing comments from the *Guardian*, the *Independent* and *Elle*. It has established itself as the football book against which other would-be books of the 'beautiful game' are compared. Here is a paragraph (pp. 112–113) to illustrate its style. You are asked to comment upon its:

- vocabulary;
- phrases;
- ability to keep you interested.

(Note: for the non-football acquainted, 'passers' in the first line refers to one footballer's ability to kick the ball to another!)

Extract from Fever Pitch

Liam Brady was one of the best two or three passers of the last twenty years, and this in itself was why he was revered by every single Arsenal fan, but for me there was more to it than that. I worshipped him because he was great, and I worshipped him because, in the parlance, if you cut him he would bleed Arsenal (like Charlie George he was a product of the youth team); but there was a third thing, too. *He was intelligent.* This intelligence manifested itself primarily in his passing, which was incisive and imaginative and constantly surprising. But it showed off the pitch too: he was articulate, and drily funny, and engaged ('Come on David, put it away' he cried from the commentary box when his friend and old Arsenal colleague David O'Leary was about to take the decisive penalty for Ireland in the 1990 World cup-tie against Romania): as I progressed through the academic strata, and more and more people seemed to make a distinction between football on the one hand and the life of the mind on the other, Brady seemed to provide a bridge between the two.

Source: Hornby, N. (1992) *Fever Pitch*. London: Penguin Books, pp. 112–113.

Exercise 2: Journal article critique

1. Select an academic journal article from one of the journals electronically available to you, published within the last 5 years.

Author(s) of journal article	
Year of publication	
Title of article	
Title of journal	
Volume	
Number	
Pages	
MY CRITIQUE	
Usefulness of title of article	(Expand these boxes as necessary)
Usefulness of abstract	
Usefulness of the introduction	
Usefulness of research methods section	
Usefulness of main research findings	
Usefulness of conclusion	
Usefulness of references	
Would I recommend the journal to other students?	
Points of interest to me/things I learned from reading the article (300 words max)	

Fig 7.5 Journal article critique

2. Your journal article should consider **ONE** of the following areas:

   a. skills employers are seeking in today's graduates;

   b. work experience in undergraduate degrees;

   c. The concept of the 'protean' career (this may be a new concept for you).

3. Download the pdf of the article to your own computer/memory stick so that you have a permanent copy.

4. Now prepare a critique of the journal article in the format given in Figure 7.5 (this is also available in the Online Resource Centre as a word document).

 ## Further reading

The advice given in this chapter should give you a sound approach to improving your reading skills. However, if you are looking for ideas as to what to read in your leisure time and to broaden your general knowledge, the following books give recommendations:

The first is a very accessible book, complete with photographs and colour illustrations, giving you an idea of the main storyline and introductions to the authors:

The BBC (2003) *The big read: Book of books: The nation's 100 favourite books*. London: Dorling Kindersley Ltd.

Next is an American book that includes a wide selection of international authors. This publication gives outlines of the recommended books, compartmentalizing them into collections under the headings Biographies, Crimes, On the battlefield, etc. and also by month of the year. It has a more serious feel to it than the BBC's *The Big Read*:

Mallison, J. (2007) *Book Smart: Your essential reading list for becoming a literary genius in 365 days*. New York: McGraw-Hill.

The final suggestion is a work of art in itself! A hefty coffee table style book of stories, lavishly illustrated and arranged in chronological order from pre-1700 to the 2000s. Accessible but extensive in its range of books, the entries have been selected by a host of literary critics, writers, novelists and journalists:

Boxall, P. (ed.) (2006) *1001 books you must read before you die*. London: Quintet Publishing Ltd.

 For further information, please visit the Online Resource Centre at http://www.oxfordtextbooks.co.uk/orc/gallagher2e/

8 Writing Essentials: Preparation, Layout and Structure

 Chapter guide

Student viewpoint

Sarah and Ummar, both recent business graduates, were asked about developing their writing skills during their degrees. The comments below emphasize particular benefits:

'More effective writing skills equipped me to produce much better job applications and boost my confidence.'

Sarah

'I learnt not to "waffle"—to get straight to the point. This has implications for your course grades. You need to stick to word limits for assignments. You want your academic writing to be "bang on the money"—in other words really relevant and concise.'

Ummar

By the end of this chapter you should be able to:

- Match your assignment writing to your assignment tasks
- Focus upon who you are writing for and the purpose of your writing
- Analyse your writing strengths and weaknesses
- Apply various writing formats used for academic purposes (such as short and long reports and essays)

Introduction

In writing you are often trying to communicate your thoughts within a word limit; you are trying to convey these ideas with as much clarity and credibility as you can muster. You are going to use writing throughout your course and in every stage of your work career, so that even small improvements may have a significant impact in terms of extra marks for your assignments. There is always room for improvement in your general technique. Also there are many reasons for writing and many people to write for, so it is likely that you will wish to improve at least one aspect of your writing for specific situations.

Chapter outline

The chapter begins with the tutor's 'insider' view of writing for assignments. Particular attention will be paid to the essentials of correctly interpreting the assignment question and then setting about answering it in a manner that is powerful, direct and convincing in academic terms, supported with appropriate references and examples. You will then consider the importance of ensuring that you keep thinking about who you are writing for and the purpose of your writing. Some time will be spent on discussing the *style* of your writing. You will be shown typical structures for essays and reports, and ways in which to 'signpost' your writing to keep readers fully aware of 'where they are' within your discussion.

8.1 Writing skills

The term 'writing skills' covers a variety of areas. First, there are general writing skills, which include your ability to write coherently, to use correct English, grammar and punctuation. You should note that there may be variation amongst tutors regarding how strict they are on basic errors—the suggestion here is to ask individual tutors for advice. These skills are completely transferable to any writing that you do. Secondly, there are the particular writing requirements for university level work. In particular, these include writing essays and reports in an academic/professional manner, using references and accepted structures.

8.1.1 Preparation for writing

Reading the assignment question (well!)

Why begin this discussion on writing by talking once again about reading? The answer is that it is very easy to make fundamental errors in your writing by not reading the assignment question sufficiently well. The practice of reading the question extremely carefully to begin with, and then of occasionally referring back to the question throughout the writing process is very important. So, no apologies here for having a 'reading' section as part of your guidelines for good writing. Consider the following example of an assignment question (Figure 8.1) of the sort you could now attempt, as the area has been covered earlier in the book.

- The first key word to note would be priority. You are not being asked to think of all your personal development needs. Also, the word 'priority' suggests that you might even attempt to rank those needs you do identify.
- You are also being asked for *specific* development objectives. These will require careful thought if you are not to drift into vague generalities.
- Finally you are being asked to use your knowledge and ability of study and personal skills throughout the exercise—the inference being that without doing so your assignment will not use the learning from your module.

The assignment question in Figure 8.1 is rather brief. Sometimes you are given additional advice. For instance, the text in Figure 8.2 might be added.

Weighting: This assignment is worth 25% of your overall module mark.
Submission Date: 15 March 2013

Task

You should identify what you consider as priority personal development needs as a student and draw up a personal development plan which incorporates specific development objectives as a means of achieving these over the course of the academic year. Your plan must include significant elements of study skills and personal skills, though the bias of these is left for you to decide.

Fig 8.1 Assignment Part One: Setting up a personal development plan

Your assignment should be written as a report using the following key headings:

● Diagnosis of personal current situation and development needs

● Setting goals

● Preparing a personal development plan (action plan)

Fig 8.2 Assignment Part One: Continuation

Diagnosis

Your report should show the methods used in your self-diagnosis and summarize key findings from this part of the exercise. Reference the methods you use.

  Suggested word limit for this Diagnosis section: 1,200 words and a maximum of 1,500 words (note: appendices listed above are not included in the word count).

Setting goals

Goals should include both study skills and personal skills. Please discuss these informally with your tutor and other students before deciding which ones to prioritize. There are not a set number of skills which you should include; however, beware of trying to cover too many (for the sake of this exercise) as what is required is depth of analysis and development.

  Goals should be SMART (see lecture notes).

  This section of your report should show how your goals follow from your self-diagnosis, why you have chosen these particular goals, and how they are SMART. Suggested word limit: a maximum of 1,000 words for this Setting goals section.

Preparing a personal development plan (action plan)

This should describe any relevant factors you took into account in taking your set goals and incorporating them into your personal development plan. The completed personal development plan should be included.

  Suggested word limit: 500 words for discussion and a copy of the personal development plan.

Fig 8.3 Task guidelines

    The reason for giving additional direction on the assignment structure may be to help you if you are new to the subject. Another reason may be that your assignment may be easier to mark. This should help you, your tutor and any other assistant tutors.

    Your tutor may occasionally wish to give you more help and advice under 'task guide-lines' (Figure 8.3). The example shown in Figure 8.3 continues to expand upon what the tutor is asking you to do. It is perhaps a rather extreme example—some tutors would argue that you should be left to ask yourself these questions. Certainly, after year 1 of your degree you would be unlikely to receive such explicit instructions, although you may encounter similar but briefer guidelines. Note that word limits are often used. It is always a good idea to find out how strictly these are adhered to—some tutors may allow plus or minus 10 per cent, others might insist on a maximum and simply stop reading after this is reached!

So is that all there is to read? Well, perhaps for some assignments. However, it is now common for tutors to also include what they call 'assignment criteria'. These are the aspects of your assignment that you will be measured against. They are not the same thing as the tasks themselves; they refer to how well you have carried out the tasks in some way or other. If they are not referred to explicitly they will still be there, but you will have to infer (guess?) from the way the assignment is written: or you could (should?) ask your tutor.

So, ideally you should know what tasks you have to accomplish, how you will be measured against them (the criteria) and the mark allocation for each task. However, you should note that many assignments are not as compartmentalized as the introductory example given here. Some assignments must allow for you to explore and structure the task for yourself; in these cases, the guidance may have to be more general.

Know who you are writing for

If the assignment question has been well written, you will be in a good position to produce a focused piece of work. You know that your reader will be the tutor and you should know to some extent what the tutor is expecting from you. However, if you are writing a business report, then your readership could well be several people: your boss, colleagues and perhaps outsiders. As we discussed in Chapter 4 on communication skills, you would be wise to take into account the experience, abilities and interests of these readers for your report to be effective. If you are working and studying at the same time, you might be asked for a report that analyses some aspect of the organization for whom you are working; in such cases you will have another distinction in your readership: those who might read your report within your organization and those who might read it at your academic institution. Balancing all readership requirements can be difficult at times, but should be borne in mind.

Know why you are writing

What are you trying to accomplish with your writing? Perhaps it is to:

- inform;
- explain;
- investigate;
- analyse;
- persuade;
- tell an existing story;
- create a new story;
- develop an idea;

- express your feelings or those of others;
- coordinate people or activities;
- entertain.

Or perhaps a mix of the above?

Use of 'I' (first person) and third person

Many tutors do not like you to say 'I did this' or 'I think that', as they do not consider it to be very academic. In business circles it would often not be thought of as very professional. It is more usual, therefore, to avoid using 'I' (first person) and to use a different technique; one way of doing this is to use 'the author' or 'the researcher' (third person) but this can sound rather

---

 Activity 8.1 What are you trying to accomplish?

Using the above list as a guide, identify what you might be trying to accomplish (e.g. explain, express your feelings, etc.) in the following documents:

- job advertisement;
- job description;
- company magazine;
- poem;
- customer attitude survey;
- employee performance appraisal;
- advertisement for a second-hand car;
- instruction manual;
- learning diary/journal.

 Student tips on skills and employability

Using persuasive writing

Nadia is a first year full-time business student who works part time for a major fashion retailer. In this example, Nadia shows how she has been promoting sales through persuasive writing on a social networking site:

I was a member of the PR and Events team for the re-launch of a newly extended high street fashion retailer. Our task was to encourage our target market of fellow students and young consumers. To do this we set up a fan page for the store on a popular social networking website. As the page only had very few 'likes' at the beginning of the process, I had to think of ways in which to improve the page—I had to use persuasive language. I included competitions and giveaways, for example 'SHARE this picture to be in with a chance to WIN a place on the GUESTLIST' (in relation to the VIP party that was to be held in honour of the opening of the new store). I also appealed to bargain hunters looking for last minute offers on products left within the store prior to renovation, with comments such as 'Check out our amazing new lines! This is our last delivery until we reopen, so once it's gone it's gone!' When monitoring the social networking page, the team concluded that when persuasive language was used in this way, activity increased significantly.

pompous. Another method is to rephrase your work, saying for instance 'research was conducted' rather than 'I conducted research'. Perhaps the exception to this rule is when you are writing personal statements and reflections, when the use of 'I' sounds much more natural. However, you should always check with your tutor as to their preference.

Diagrams and figures

In the text or in the appendices? This is a tricky question. If you are writing an assignment or academic report, you may wish to check with your tutor first (as either way may be acceptable). If you have a free choice, then you need to decide whether or not the diagram will cut up the flow of the discussion too much if it is inserted in the text and how much access the reader will need to have to it when reading the text, as going backwards and forwards between text and appendices can be disruptive. In all cases, diagrams should always be labelled fully with title and reference number (e.g. Figure 2, often abbreviated to Fig. 2).

8.1.2 **General layout: guidelines**

Style

We all have a natural writing style. Some people may write in rather flowery, long-winded terms, while others might have a very direct way of writing. In general, it is probably best if you aim for a fairly succinct style for your university studies, although it is always a question of balance, deciding which points to elaborate on and which ones to cover briefly.

 Activity 8.2 Writing style

Read the article below, which is a *section* of an essay written by a fictitious first year student. How would you rewrite it in a better style? (Please refer to the Online Resource Centre for a *good* example of student writing.)

Performance appraisals

One of the major problems with conducting performance appraisals is the predilection to link pay directly to performance (Torrington and Hall, 1987). Performance appraisals do not represent the only sort of appraisals that can be undertaken within the workplace, although they tend to be predominantly regarded as the overarching reason for appraisals, often forming the central plank of an organization's appraisal strategy. It is of paramount importance that reward appraisals or appraisals designed to assess future potential of staff are not conducted synchronously with performance appraisals (Fletcher and Williams, 1985). The accusation is that the appraiser assumes the conflicting roles of judge and helper in the event that appraisals for performance, reward and future potential are insufficiently separated. Further studies at this present moment in time back these claims up. Performance appraisals are commonly used in organizations so that managers may carry out formal assessments of their subordinates' effectiveness and efficiency at their work on a regular basis, the standard norm being at least annually.

At the end of the day, it is not a good idea to mix up the different reasons for appraisals. Reward appraisals may be used by managers to discuss the possibility of bonuses and pay increases for staff. During performance appraisals it is usual for the manager and the worker to look back over the previous year at how well the worker has done and then to look forward to the next year. At this point certain performance targets will be set for the coming year and any training that may be necessary to help the worker will be shown on the performance appraisal plan. Sometimes managers have meetings with their employees to discuss their future career path within the organization, including 'fast-tracking' to senior management positions.

Perhaps the most important point to stress is that you should aim to make difficult concepts as easy as possible to understand, without losing any necessary technical or academic detail; key ideas will often need to be emphasized, for instance by using references and/or examples. Positioning of text is also a signpost—your reader will assume, unless you state otherwise, that the first item in a list is the most important one. Also, just because you have mentioned something once, do not think that your reader will think you are being forgetful; repetition (probably rephrased) can be a powerful tactic. Avoid deliberately using words and phrases that make your writing sound difficult and designed to give the impression that you must be a really clever person. For this reason avoid paraphrasing from textbooks and journals: write in your own words.

Bullet points

By all means use bullet points (unless directed otherwise) within your writing, but your writing should not degenerate into a series of them, loosely connected with the occasional sentence. They are useful to introduce an area for further discussion or as a means of summarizing a section. Alternatively, they may be points which you can expand upon a little before continuing with your discussion. One way to introduce a list of bullet points is to use a colon (:)—for instance, let's say that you want to list the key requirements of a good plan. You may introduce your list by saying something along the lines of:

> The following requirements are desirable for a good plan:
>
> - relevant research;
> - careful consideration of the options;
> - flexibility to change, as necessary;

Note that it is not necessary to start each bullet with a capital letter if the bulleted point is not a complete sentence (in which case you would use a capital). However, some people prefer capitals to begin all bullet points—the choice is yours, but be consistent throughout your text. Using the same logic, do not end each bullet with a full stop unless it is a complete sentence.

Use of colons and semi-colons

The most widespread use of colons (shown as :) and semi-colons (shown as ;) when writing business reports is in the use of lists. For instance, the bullet point list given above could be written by using a colon to introduce the list and semi-colons to separate the phrases, like this:

> The following requirements are desirable for a good plan: relevant research; careful consideration of the options; and flexibility to change, as necessary.

Note the use of the insertion of the word 'and' before the final phrase, as well as the final full stop to complete the sentence.

Note that for a simple list of items, or simple phrases, it would be usual to use a comma (shown as,) between the items listed. Here is an example:

> A good plan should be: up-to-date, clear and circulated to all relevant people.

A common mistake when using colons with lists (using bullets or semi-colons, or commas) is to use bullet points or phrases that do not match the form of the introduction to the list. What is wrong with the following list?

A successful plan is one which is used to:

- guide people;
- to monitor progress;
- is useful for reflecting upon improvement.

The way to avoid falling into this trap is to always read the first part (in the above case, 'A successful plan is one which is used to') and then place each of the bullet points at the end of it to see if each individual 'sentence' makes sense. If we do this for the last bullet point shown in the above example, we would have 'A successful plan is one which is used to is useful for reflecting upon improvement', which is incorrect. What could you do to correct this?

Paragraphs

As explained in Section 8.1.1, *Reading the assignment question*, a paragraph should contain a unit of thought. You should, however, generally try to avoid single-sentence paragraphs and very long paragraphs. To start a new paragraph, either indent the first line or leave a line blank between paragraphs (don't do both, and be consistent). Francine Prose (2006, pp. 72–3), quoting the recommendations of Strunk and White on writing style, gives the following two suggestions:

1. As a rule, begin each paragraph with a sentence that suggests the topic or with a sentence that helps the transition [the change from the previous paragraph].
2. Enormous blocks of print look formidable to readers, who are often reluctant to tackle them. Therefore, breaking long paragraphs in two, even if it is not necessary to do so for sense, meaning, or logical development, is often a visual help.

Font

Again, your institution may have a recommended font style and size. Please bear in mind that some of your tutors may not have eyesight as sharp as yours and they will have to do a lot of reading of assignments! Times New Roman size 12, or Arial size 11 should normally be acceptable. Verdana is another possibility.

Line spacing

It's a good idea to use 1.5 (or perhaps 2; again, check with your tutor) line spacing, as it makes your work easier to read and understand. Also, if your tutor is marking your work by hand, he/she can add written comments between the lines.

Activity 8.3 Layout improvement

For this activity you will need a 'critical friend'—someone whose advice you value. Provide your friend with a printed sample of your writing; this might be an assignment you are currently working on, or perhaps some previous work. Your friend should read your work and then comment upon its general layout in terms of its style, and other areas such as bullet points, use of paragraphs, font and line spacing. You can do the same for your friend. Aim to include positive features, saying why you like them, and also areas which you think could be strengthened—perhaps with some suggestions as to how this might be accomplished.

8.1.3 Organizing your writing

Taking notes and keeping relevant information (including references)

As we discussed earlier in Section 7.7, you should keep notes from your reading and lectures. When you are given an assignment these notes may be referred to as a starting point. You will then need to carry out further research with a particular emphasis on your assignment task. It is worthwhile doing this in a systematic manner so that you do not lose the information; also, these notes may be useful for other assignments in the future.

The physical format of your notes can help or detract from this process. Consider using notebooks that will take some rough handling, as you will often be carrying them around from the library to home. Think about keeping dedicated notebooks for your assignments or projects. You can use this technique for research within your work situation after your present studies end—I still have some academic project notebooks from 2000 that I keep on my bookshelf and that still (!) get used occasionally.

Scheduling your writing

In the same manner as reading, you ideally need to allocate time to your writing. You may wish to use a Gantt chart (refer back to Section 3.1 on organization skills) on which you plan for initial reading, outline plan, further reading, draft 1 through to final draft and any other activities (e.g. interviews, visiting places) you need to accomplish.

Use of lists, key headings, mind maps

The initial stages of writing are often very creative. Getting your thoughts written down is part of this creative process. A list of key headings may be useful to give you an overall framework for your reading and subsequent writing; you can add detail to these at a later point. You may also draw a mind map (more detail of this in Chapter 12, 'Creativity and Innovation Skills'), which shows the connections in your mind between various areas that you wish to look at in your assignment. You may decide to draw a more organic mind map before the more sequential list of key headings.

General guidelines on the theory/discussion mix

Although not strictly part of preparation for writing (it's as much to do with the writing itself), you should consider how theory will fit into and reinforce your writing. For instance, your list of headings or mind map can be extended to include an indication of key theorists or theories and examples.

Also, unless you are writing a literature review, you should be wary of compartmentalizing your writing into large sections of theory followed by large discussion sections. There is a danger that if you adopt this approach you will fail to make the necessary links between the theories and your discussion. This is not to say that this approach will not work if done carefully. Although it is harder to organize initially, integrating theory with your discussion is likely to more effective because it forces you into making direct links as you write.

Signposting

By signposting we mean the provision of words, phrases, subheadings, etc. that map out the discussion for the reader. For instance, we might say 'in this section we are first going to consider the proposed project's operational aspects, then we will look at the staffing implications'. It is likely that the signposting you use in your writing will reflect your overall planning for your assignment and your approach to research.

The example shown in Figure 8.4 considers a typical investment appraisal exercise, which you may be asked to do as part of your coursework at university, or in 'real-life' in the work situation: you have been asked to compare three possible sites for a new factory. The diagram suggests that you intend to look at each in turn, using the criteria of access to the site, size

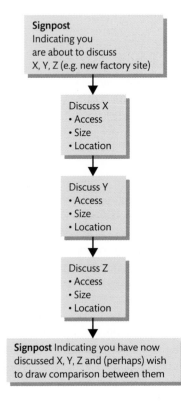

Fig 8.4 Signposting

Activity 8.4 Signposting improvement

For this activity you will again need a 'critical friend'—someone whose advice you value. Provide your friend with a printed sample of your writing. Ideally, this a reasonably substantial piece of work; something in the region of 2,000–3,000 words should be used. Your friend should read your work and then comment upon how well you have signposted. How clear is the flow of information from one section to the next? Are subheaders used appropriately? If a numbering system is used for the paragraphs does this help you to navigate your way through the article? Are there sufficient introductory sections—and are they effective? Are there any summarizing sections—and how effective are these? Are there any sections which seem to emerge too suddenly, or sections which do not seem to be finished by the end of the article? Finally, in general terms, how easy did you find following the article through from beginning to end?. You can do the same for your friend. Aim to include positive features, saying why you like them, and also areas that you think could be strengthened—perhaps with some suggestions as to how this might be accomplished.

of the site and its location. The signposts come at the beginning and end of this discussion, although you should note that you can have signposts wherever you want them. A different approach would be to put the focus on the criteria and use these as subheadings instead of the sites, in which case you would indicate this in your signposting.

Drafts

The first writing in full of your work or assignment is called your first draft. *Inevitably* it will have at least some fairly obvious omissions, mis-spellings and poor grammar. It may need additional information, quotations, references. Perhaps a section(s) may need re-writing. Maybe the order of sections could be revised. It does not matter! The point of a draft is that it captures the essence of what you are trying to write. By producing the draft you have completed a crucial stage in the writing process, but it is not the end process: what it needs is 'polishing' to produce further drafts before the finished draft is ready.

Revising your drafts

Sometimes it is best to leave a draft for a while before reading it through and pencilling in amendments. Or, you may wish to read it through and return to it later to make amendments. You should experiment to find which method works best for you. To test the general readability of the draft, you could consider giving it to a friend to read and asking him or her whether or not it reads clearly and logically; they do not have to be subject experts to do this. If the section is quite technical you might wish to check that you have not made any basic errors in your facts by asking someone with a good knowledge of that subject area to read it and make comments.

Having other people read your draft work is not always easy, especially if the people re-viewing your work are quite critical and not very diplomatic with their comments! It is a natural reaction to be defensive—or even to feel angry with the other person(s) which, of course, is illogical if you think about it, as the purpose of the review is to improve your work. If you find this a problem, one approach is to put the work aside for a few days to allow for a

Skills Example 8.1 The power of writing

Two writers who have influenced management thinking

Here are two writers whose books have impacted directly upon organizational life, the training of managers and strategic thinking.

Gareth Morgan has written a modern-day classic—*Images of Organization* (1986). His writing style is, at the same time, accessible to academics and managers. It is engaging. It is filled with enough references to satisfy the most curious of academic readers. And most importantly it offers a brilliant insight into how organizations may be observed to work from various, very different perspectives. The excellence of the writing complements the creativity of its ideas. Together they have produced a management masterpiece. Here is one of many memorable quotations:

> At first sight, much of what I have tried to say has a great deal in common with the old Indian tale of the six blind men and the elephant. The first man feels a tusk, claiming the animal to be like a spear. The second, feeling the elephant's side, proclaims that it is more like a wall. Feeling a leg, the third describes it as a tree; and a fourth, feeling the elephant's trunk is inclined to think it like a snake. The fifth, who has seized the elephant's ear, thinks it is remarkably like a fan; and the sixth, grabbing the tail, says it is much more like a rope.
>
> (Morgan, 1986, p. 340)

Another author, ground-breaking in his own right, is Daniel Goleman. Like Morgan, his work is read by management academics and managers alike. His book *Emotional Intelligence* is a number one bestseller. His work has sparked much debate about the importance of emotional intelligence; it has certainly popularized its use in many management training initiatives. His writing explores concepts of how the human brain deals with emotional crises; it offers the view that our emotions play a very important role in all of our actions. His later work makes direct links between this and leadership. Here is a short quotation from the first chapter, which demonstrates his ability to encapsulate an idea into a few sentences:

> A view of human nature that ignores the power of emotions is sadly shortsighted. The very nature of homo sapiens, the thinking species, is misleading in light of the new appreciation and vision of the place of emotions in our lives that science now offers. As we all know from experience, when it comes to shaping our decisions and our actions, feeling counts every bit as much—and often more than thought.
>
> (Goleman, 1996, p. 4)

'cooling off' period. When you return to the work you should try to consider the remarks in an objective way. Remember, you do not always have to agree with the comments, but you should recognize that at least one other person thought them and that your tutor may have similar thoughts—how might you handle this?

Checking of first drafts will often improve your writing substantially in both content and style. Even if short of time, you should make every effort to write and correct a first draft. Later drafts will help to polish it further.

8.1.4 Specific structural guidelines for various types of writing

So far you have seen that there are variations in the style of writing you might use. There are also variations in structural requirements depending, to some extent, upon what the purpose

Type of writing	Title	Abstract/summary	Contents list	Introduction	Methodology	Literature review	Main body	Use of subheaders	Numbered sections	Diagrams/figures	Use of 1st person 'I'	Use of 3rd person	Single line spacing	1.5 or 2.0 line spacing	Conclusions	Recommendations/action list	References	Appendices/attachments
Essay	✓			✓			✓	?				✓	✓	?	✓		✓	
Short report	✓			✓	?		✓	?	?	?			✓		✓	?	✓	?
Long report	✓	✓	?	✓	?	?	✓	?	?	?			✓		✓	?	✓	?
CV	✓			?			✓	✓			✓		✓					?
Journal/diary	?			?			✓				✓		✓					
Letter	?			✓			✓	?	?			✓	✓					?
Email	✓			?			✓	?	?									?
Minutes	✓			?			✓	✓	?			✓	✓				✓	
Written task	✓			?	?	?	✓	?	?	?	?	?	?		?	?	?	?

Key: ✓ Recommended

? Possible use

Fig 8.5 Structural guidelines for various types of writing

and format of your writing is (e.g. essay, report, personal journal). For instance, you would not write a contents list for a personal journal but you might do so for a long report. You need to know what is structurally acceptable for these different types of writing. Sometimes your tutor will give clear instructions: at other times you will be assumed to be able to do this for yourself.

In Figure 8.5 you will see various structural elements listed and an indication of whether they are recommended or possible for different types of academic and business writing. You should note that the purpose of the table is to show you that there are structural similarities and differences between different types of writing. We will discuss essays and report writing in the Section 8.1.5, thus covering all of the structural devices shown in the chart. However, it is important to note that these are guidelines only, showing typical structures; 'written task', the last type of writing shown in the chart, could theoretically include any of these structural features, depending upon what the task is.

8.1.5 Essays

A favourite of the traditional examination is the essay question. Here are two typical examples of exam questions requiring an essay answer:

a. Compare and contrast two selection methods used for recruitment purposes. Illustrate your discussion with appropriate examples.
b. Email: friend or foe to communication at work? Discuss.

You may also be asked to write essays within your coursework. As Lea (1997, p. 37) indicates, the traditional essay has three main parts: introduction, main body and conclusion. Referring back to Figure 8.5, you will note that it is usual to write an essay in the third person and to use references to add weight and credibility to your discussion.

The questions posed by your tutor may be very specific (type (a) above) or they may be extremely open (type (b) above). In many essays, what you are being assessed upon is your ability to create an *argument*. An academic argument does not have the same meaning as the sort of argument you might have in everyday life (this is probably better termed as a *disagreement*): an academic argument is a reasoned discussion in which you build a case for a particular point of view (recall our discussion on the use of logos, pathos and ethos in Section 4.3). You will need to support your argument with relevant examples and/or references.

Your ability to reference properly is a generic skill that you will use, particularly in essays and reports. It is very easy for the reader (i.e. your tutor or an external examiner) to assess your referencing skills, so it's extremely worthwhile to spend time getting into the habit of referencing correctly so that it becomes a strength of your writing, rather than something which detracts (and distracts) from it. There are various accepted ways to reference; you should learn the particular style used in your university or college. However, you should be aware that there are variations. The important thing is that you adopt a particular style and are consistent in its use. Having said this, many universities use the Harvard style of referencing and there are generally accepted rules of use. Please refer back to Chapter 5 for further discussion on referencing.

8.1.6 Short reports

Sooner or later your tutor is going to ask you to 'write a report'. Whether or not this actually is a report, as we shall define it, or an essay, or some other written task, is something that you may have to determine further, for occasionally the word 'report' is used in different ways. If you read that your work must be written in 'report format', then this definitely suggests a structure of the type defined in Figure 8.5 with title, introduction, main body, conclusions, possibly recommendations and references. Some tutors may also infer that this means double-line spacing and other page-layout requirements. Taking a different approach entirely, the word 'report' might have been used rather loosely to simply mean 'a written account' of something.

Let us assume that you have been asked to write a 'short report'—say somewhere in the region of 1,500–2,000 words. A typical short report format structure (as defined in Figure 8.5) may be as follows:

- Title
- Introduction
- Main body of report under various headings
- Conclusion
- Recommendations*
- References
- Appendices*.

(* denotes that these may be optional).
Let us consider each of these elements in turn.

Title

Sometimes you will have been given the title by your tutor. At other times you may be expected to devise your own. This is the first thing that the reader sees, and will set a particular picture in her mind. Even the order of wording may be significant (for instance, 'business and computing' may have different overtones to 'computing and business'). Choosing a title that fully reflects the contents of the report can be difficult. One approach is to use a 'working title'—something that seems like a reasonable title at the start—but then be prepared to change it to something more appropriate if need be.

Introduction

As you will see from Figure 8.5, unless the writing is clearly concerned with something of which the reader is well aware, an introduction will be required. Consider the well-used example of the preacher who was asked what it was that made his sermons so successful: 'Well,' he says, 'first of all I tells 'em what I'm gonna tell 'em. Then, I tells 'em what I gotta tell 'em. Then I tells 'em what I've just told 'em!'

The form of the introduction can vary, depending upon what you are trying to achieve. At its simplest the introduction may simply restate a question or offer a basic statement of the contents; it may be then termed 'terms of reference' (for example: 'This report analyses the financial viability of project X. It was requested by the Executive board (see minutes 24/10/09) and is due for discussion at the board meeting 01/02/10').

Sometimes the introduction serves to 'tell 'em what you're gonna tell 'em' by offering an overall signposting to the various sections. For example, 'The report starts by giving an overview of project X, then considers its operation in terms of present benefits and costs, before looking to future possibilities.' At other times, you may wish the introduction to also serve as a means to give some sort of background to your report. This may indicate the environment in which the subject matter is based. It may refer to the historical evolution of events leading up to the present situation. The idea here is to provide some basic information to the reader and put him or her in an appropriate frame of mind so that he or she is then more receptive to the main body of the report. For instance, if your report is a work-based assignment, a paragraph or so about what your organization does, perhaps what the particular department does and some indication of the scale of operation would be very useful to your tutor. But a note here: because of your familiarity with your own organization you may tend to write too much—remember it is only an introduction.

Methodology

Sometimes you may include a methodology, although of course you may use a different heading, depending upon the content of your report. One such heading is 'Research methods', used to provide an outline of how an investigation has been conducted. Let us say that you have carried out an interview survey; the reader needs to know what type of survey, why you chose this method, the basis for choosing the interviewees and the method you used to interpret the data.

Main body of report

If your report is an investigation, you may decide to use the term 'Findings' as a heading. Otherwise you will need to give your own, appropriate headings, to the main body of your report. This is the section where you discuss your subject in depth. You should have a logical structure so that one section fits with another. Paragraphs should be used to convey 'idea units'. In a similar way, you will need to consider using subheadings to break your discussion into bigger sections. The logic of your discussion will often mean that these are quite sufficient to signpost the reader through your writing (recall the discussion in Section 8.1.6, *Methodology*). However, you may wish to number sections, as we have done with the text in this book. The important thing is to ensure that your reader can see where you are in your discussion.

Your report should use appropriate references within the main text body (see Section 8.1.6, *References* for details), which should all be given in full at the end of your report in your references list. It should be clearly presented, spell-checked and you should consider putting it in 1.5 or double spacing. Include page numbers.

Conclusion

This is where you draw together all of the threads of your discussion; where you can link sections, note trends and draw the 'bigger picture'. It is also the point at which you can venture your judgement of the situation (based upon the evidence given within the main body of your discussion), which is especially useful for complex arguments.

Recommendations

You may or may not be asked to provide recommendations—your suggestions for further action. If you do give recommendations, they should clearly follow on from your previous conclusions.

References

You should provide a list of references, which gives full details of any in-text quotations and references used. Further details of referencing are given in Section 5.4.

Appendices

If you decide not to put diagrams, charts, photos, etc. within the main body of your text, then you will need to label them as appendices. You may also put further examples of detailed information in your appendices. The reason for having appendices is to provide a place to include material that either (a) you feel holds information that is vital to your discussion but is too bulky in itself and would break up the flow of your writing; or (b) is relevant but not crucial and the reader may wish to go further in their own reading on the subject area. You should not include appendices because: they bulk out your report; they may possibly have relevant information (but you are not sure); they are not used and referred to in the main body of your discussion. The inclusion of appendices does not replace your need to explain their contents

Activity 8.5 Charts, diagrams and appendices improvement

For this activity you will again need a critical friend whose advice you value. Provide your friend with any appendices from one of your more substantial reports. Your friend should first of all consider whether or not he/she thought that the various inclusions in your appendices were absolutely necessary. This might also relate to the amount of detail given in each inclusion. Next, he/she should comment upon the layout of the appendices—are they clearly labelled, for instance? Finally, your friend could comment upon the clarity and usefulness of any diagrams, tables or charts that you have drawn yourself. You can do the same for your friend. Aim to include positive features, saying why you like them, and also areas which you think could be strengthened—perhaps with some suggestions as to how this might be accomplished.

or how they might be relevant; you must not assume that the reader (who could be your tutor) can mind-read your reasons for their inclusion. Normally speaking, tutors do not include appendices and your reference list *within* your assignment's word count. A typical situation for a research report occurs when your analysis is based upon a particular survey questionnaire—in which case you might decide to include the questionnaire as an appendix item.

8.1.7 Long reports

When does a short report become a long report? The cross-over point is not easy to define and often reports, short or long, are just termed 'reports'. Having said this, writing a report of, say 10,000 words, often requires a different approach to writing one of, say 2,000 words. For one thing, it's clearly a much bigger work in terms of time and effort—for both the writer and the reader. It's probably more important in coursework terms. There is scope for more detailed or additional sections within a long report (such as a literature review). These may include some or all of the following:

Abstract/summary

Abstracts and summaries were discussed in Section 7.4.3. The abstract should be an abbreviated account of the report. If you include an abstract, aim to make it no more than 200 words.

Contents list

If you are writing a report as large as 10,000 words, with appendices, then the need for a contents list becomes apparent. Its purpose is to allow the reader to see at a glance the key headings of your report before they read it in full. It will then serve the speedy location of a section if the reader wishes to go from one part of your report to another. Your contents list should indicate page numbers to facilitate this.

Literature review

As it says, this part of your report concerns a discussion of the available books, articles and other written information pertinent to the content of your report. Some of the reports you write for university will stipulate that you need to write such a review. The review may thus provide a background of the relevant theories and knowledge that already exist, and which you can draw on within your report. Sometimes there may be differences in the opinions of published writers and you may wish to comment upon these here along the lines of 'Smith (1993) says this, but Jones (2002) says that'.

In fact, the literature review can be a very substantial part of your report. Some reports may essentially be desk-based reviews of the available literature. For others, it will be supplementary to the main focus of the report, which may be based on your analysis and evaluation of data. You should seek advice from your tutor on the requirements of the literature review and the approximate proportion you should allocate to it in terms of word length.

 ## Chapter summary

This chapter has covered some of the fundamental aspects of the written skills relevant to your study as a student. As writing skills are so central to everything you do, any improvements that you make could result in significant improvements in your coursework. In this chapter you have addressed the fundamental basis of your assignment writing—what does the assignment question mean? You have tried various writing style techniques in the examples. You have focused on the need to write for particular readers with a specific purpose in mind. In Section 8.1.4 on different types of written assignments you have explored the variety of ways through which essays, reports and other written work may be structured.

 ## End of chapter exercises

Exercise 1: Dello Spring Water

Read the following section of the essay 'Dello Spring Water', which has been written in a rather poor style by a fictitious first year university student. The brief given to our student was for an essay that reported on the recent expansion of the company Dello Spring Water, which bottles and sells spring water from its location in the Cheviot hills. The essay must also outline how Dello's plans are linked to the general market expansion of bottled water. Our student has researched various statements from the company itself (for instance, in the Chairman's Statement in its Annual Report and other information on its website), trade journals and also obtained market statistics and reports on the bottled mineral water market in general. For the purpose of this exercise each sentence has been numbered so that you can easily identify it. Also note that the complete version of the essay would include a list of references at the end that is not included here. You are asked to:

a. correct any obvious spelling mistakes and grammatical errors;

b. restructure the essay into a better format using paragraphs and subheadings as you think appropriate.

Rather than rewriting the sentences in full, you can use the sentence numbers to indicate position. If you join sentences together you can show this using the sentence numbers. If you feel forced to restructure a sentence, identify it by the sentence number and then make your changes next to it, e.g.: Sentence 4 now reads '......'

DELLO SPRING WATER 1{An example of the recent boom in the popularity of bottled water was the recent expansion of Dello Spring Water. 2{At a recent interview Gary Green of the magazine 'Softdrinks Monthly' asked the Managing Director of Dello, Freddie Smithers what had prompted him to open a further bottling operation at his operations plant.

3{Of course he was *delighted* to tell him of all of the new jobs that had been created, especially from the local small town of Wooler. 4{'Its really great' he had said, 'it would of been a shame not to take advantage of the surge in demand for pure water, there's the health lobby to.' 5{Volvic, evian, Pennine Spring are all examples of very strong competetors though not all of them are still, some are fizzy. (Keynote, 2009)

6{According to Keynote's report on soft drinks the expected increase in bottled water rises from 1450 in 2009 to 1900 in 2012 which is quite significant compared to the rest of the drinks market. 7{To promote his range Freddie is offering a set of drinking glasses with the Dello Spring lable etched on them to anyone who finds the lucky spring sign on the back of the bottle label. 8{Mr Smithers made it big in the water industry through his work in one of the major drinks groups and he worked previously in south wales during the 90s before setting up his own business. 9{Market size for soft drinks was £million 9825 in 2007 which includes bottled water, the reason why so many people are turning to bottled water is various. 10{Firstly there are many people who, according to the Keynote report, think that tap water is 'dubious'.

11{Second, there are many people who think that drinking water is healthy. (Allbright, 2003)

12{The thing about Dello Spring water is that it comes from a pure source, straight from a natural spring in the Cheviot hills. 13{Mr Smithers has spent more than £250 000 on the new bottling facility and has employed a further 5 workers. 14{Perhaps his main local rival is 'Evan Better Spring Water' which is established in the nearby Simonside hills. 15{'The taste of the water is superb, so clear and refreshing, because it has been naturely filtered through the rocks' says Mr Smithers. 16{The local news paper has reported, however, that some people have complained, that sometimes the water has an overly peaty taste. 17{Mr Smithers says that this is perfectly natural and part of the charm of the water. 18{The Evan Better company has employed a local sporting celebrity to promote the health-giving properties of it's drink in their promotion campaign. 19{With the prospect of a really hot summer (according to national weather experts) I think its likely that demand for water will sore this year. 20{However recent studies, by experts Brown and Struthers have suggested that the so-called facts about spring water being better for you than tap water water are not true.

Exercise 2: Company brochure for Dello

For this exercise you are asked to draft a mock-up of a company brochure for Dello Spring Water, as discussed in Exercise 1. The brochure is to be A4 size, made of high-quality card that may be printed with text, photographs, diagrams, and any colour you wish. It has a basic format that consists of a front page, two inside pages that face each other and a back page (see Figure 8.6).

a. Your mock-up should focus upon the detail of your printed script, although you should indicate where any photographs, diagrams, etc. would be placed and give an indication of what they would show. Your script therefore needs to be fully written out on each page.

Outside front page	Outside back page
Inside page 1	Inside page 2

Fig 8.6 Brochure for Dello Spring Water

b. To accompany your brochure (for this exercise) you are asked to write a short explanation (200 words maximum) of who you are aiming your brochure at and what your message is attempting to achieve with these reader(s).

Exercise 3: Writing SWOT

Conduct a SWOT (strengths, weaknesses, opportunities, threats) analysis of your writing skills. You may wish to use the diagram in Figure 8.7:

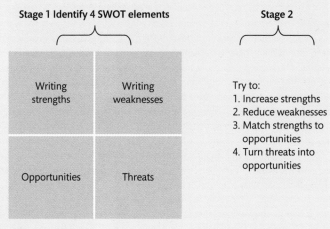

Stage 1 Identify 4 SWOT elements

| Writing strengths | Writing weaknesses |
| Opportunities | Threats |

Stage 2

Try to:
1. Increase strengths
2. Reduce weaknesses
3. Match strengths to opportunities
4. Turn threats into opportunities

Fig 8.7 Writing SWOT analysis

 ## Further reading

You can find the references to this chapter in the bibliography at the back of the book. However, there are many books available that give advice on writing, including study skills texts that consider particular aspects of writing, such as writing essays and dissertations. The following books are recommended.

The first gives sound, practical advice (referred to in this chapter) and includes examples of students' writing:

Lea, M.R. (1997) *Writing at university: A guide for students.* Buckingham: Open University Press.

Another very accessible book (referred to in this chapter) with tips and techniques is the following. It also has good advice on skimming methods in reading:

Clanchy, J. and Ballard, B. (1999) *How to write essays: A practical guide for students.* 3rd edn. Melbourne, Australia: Addison Wesley Longman.

The next book has a unique approach, discussing topics in an encyclopaedic fashion from A to Z. Intended for engineering students, it nevertheless has information applicable to management students. It is clearly written and contains interesting snippets of information; for example, the derivation of Internet terminology has a list of commonly mis-spelt words, and grammatical sections:

Young, T. (2005) *Technical writing A–Z: A commonsense guide to engineering reports and theses.* New York: ASME Press.

This book is a modern classic—this bestseller by Lynne Truss gives excellent advice on punctuation in a humorous fashion:

Truss, L. (2003) *Eats, shoots & leaves: The zero tolerance approach to punctuation.* London: Profile Books.

If you're interested in 'how babies babble, words change meaning and languages live or die' (front cover), then this is the book for you. Written by a professor of English language, this book is still accessible by the non-expert:

Crystal, D. (2006) *How language works*. London: Penguin Books.

 For further information, please visit the Online Resource Centre at **http://www.oxfordtextbooks.co.uk/orc/gallagher2e/**

Presentation Skills

 Chapter guide

Student viewpoint

At the start of a presentation skills workshop a group of first year management students were asked the following question: 'What makes a good TV news presenter?' They said that good presenters could read out loud fluently, but in addition had:

'become aware of and understood the issues'

'prepared for their presenting by becoming used to using the equipment'

'practised (ideally) reading the news item'

'used the appropriate tone of voice'

'used appropriate facial expressions, eye contact and body language'

'the ability to remain calm and carry on in the face of technical difficulties'.

In this chapter you will see that these are all valid points for your own academic presentations.

 By the end of this chapter you should be able to:

- Identify various presentation purposes
- Use various methods to capture your audience's interest
- Devise effective presentational formats
- Use various presentation props
- Use various methods to improve your delivery
- Apply knowledge and skills to handle presentation nerves

Introduction

Sooner or later you will be called upon to give a presentation. This may be as part of your course or it may be in a work situation. It might be to secure that next job during your interview. The aim of this chapter is to give you some practical advice on how to perform well in such situations. If you feel uncomfortable now with the thought of 'doing presentations' you should realize that this is quite a common feeling. However, after you have read this chapter and tried out the various techniques for yourself, you should begin to feel more relaxed about them.

Chapter outline

The chapter begins by taking a slightly unusual approach. It considers those presentations that we watch every day—news broadcasts on the television. Here are people who work for a living by giving presentations. Their jobs have various aspects: to communicate serious messages; to inform and explain; to involve you in the community.

The main sections of the chapter are grouped into presentation design, presentation delivery and building confidence in presentations. Presentation design covers areas from thinking about the purpose of your presentation to ways of designing your slides for maximum impact. Presentation delivery focuses upon your personal performance in terms of practice, voice techniques and body language. The final section, building confidence in presentations, is more psychological in nature; it shows how you can influence your confidence through how you think and behave.

9.1 Anyone can read the news ... can't they?

Prompted by the workshop referred to at the beginning of this chapter in the 'Student Viewpoint', an interview was arranged with Colin Briggs from BBC Look North. The aim was to ask Colin for his views and tips for successful presentations. Skills Example 9.1 is the result.

 Skills Example 9.1 An interview with Colin Briggs, presenter for BBC Look North

'If you'd heard the introduction, would you be interested in hearing any more?' were Colin's opening words of advice. It was, he said, essential to find something interesting in a topic which, on the face of it, may seem rather dull; the skill was in finding some 'nugget', some fascinating fact, memorable quote or a different approach that would 'shake people up'. However, he said to be wary of slipping into the use of cliched phrases and those overworked and somewhat indulgent phrases that you would never actually use in everyday speech (at this point I reflected upon some of the more commonly overused management cliches: 'outside-the-box thinking', etc.)

His advice on delivering the presentation centred around three aspects: inflection—the way that we emphasize certain words and how we can turn a phrase into a question by raising the pitch of our voice at the end of a sentence; tone—for instance, sombre, serious, cheerful; and pace—the speed at which we talk (typically, newsreaders speak at about 180 words per minute). Linked to the above is something else: the pause. It takes confidence to use pauses in presentations. They should not be overused, but if used correctly they can have great effect. Often the pause is there to give listeners time to reflect briefly on a key point; it may be there as a substitute for the unsaid conclusion, hanging in the air; similarly it may be there to allow the humour of a phrase or the situation to develop. Colin's advice was to listen to presenters on both TV and radio, and to good public speakers who could 'work' their audience.

I asked 'Do you ever get nerves, and if so, what do you do about them?' Colin said that, yes, he did occasionally experience such occasions. He said that it did help if you knew overall where you were going with the presentation; there were times to gloss over minor hitches and times to be frank about others, such as technical difficulties. However, what impressed most was his advice that it was very useful not to take things too seriously, even when mistakes were made. As he said, 'Nothing lasts forever!'

The example gives a clear indication of what good news presenters do. It is very clear that reading the news—that is, *presenting*—is a skilled activity. You may wish to use some of Colin's advice in your next presentation. The example does not go into detail about the presentation design, but you should note that many of the principles (for instance, choosing the content, thinking about the intended audience and aiming for maximum impact) apply both to TV presentations and to your own academic presentations. Also, as the design work actually occurs *before* the presentation, the rest of this chapter is structured to consider presentation design first in Section 9.2, before looking at aspects concerned with the actual delivery in Section 9.3. Finally, Section 9.4 deals with anxiety and how to build confidence in giving presentations, which gets right to the heart of the most emotional part of presenting.

9.2 Presentation design

You should consider a number of factors in your academic presentation design. Figure 9.1 shows headings for these factors as they appear in this chapter.

9.2.1 Words versus images

Perhaps the most important thing to bear in mind when preparing a presentation is that it is not a written report that you are reading to an audience. It is very different in its depth and its impact. It can only be selective. Also, it appeals much more readily to people's feelings.

One reason for the emotional effect of presentations is that they often make powerful use of images, for, as Branthwaite (2002, p. 177) tells us, 'images have a more direct connection to feelings and unconscious ideas'. Goleman (1996) shows how your brain can be 'hijacked' by the immediacy of images that are linked to your past experiences, triggering the more

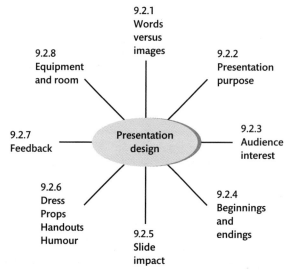

Fig 9.1 Presentation design

Activity 9.1 Presentation purposes

Think of examples of presentations, or typical situations where presentations may be used, which correspond to each of the purposes shown in Figure 9.2.

primitive parts of your brain that are connected to fight/flight processes—the ones that kick in before the thinking (cognitive) processes can make sense of the situation (consider your own 'instinctive' reactions to avoid something thrown at you). People also tend to regard images in an overall, holistic and more intuitive way (Branthwaite, 2002, p. 167). Many artists, photographers and movie makers use the image to evoke deep feelings in us; for instance, to inspire, to shock and to elicit compassion.

You may also recall from Section 1.5 what Howard Gardner (1993) had to say about multiple intelligences; in presentations you have a much greater opportunity to use a greater number of such intelligences. The result of doing this successfully is to enhance the intended outcomes of your message. However, you should not forget the emotional power of words themselves to create a mental image in your mind, sometimes every bit as powerful as a picture on a screen (think of those stand-up comedians who make us laugh by creating often preposterous and surreal images within our minds).

So, does all of this mean that presentations are only concerned with your emotions? No. It simply means that they are an excellent medium for conveying and eliciting emotion in others. You can convey information, explain plans logically and present business cases in your presentations. However, you can only convey a limited amount of information: time, concentration and the ability to listen to the spoken word are limiting factors. If you want to convey a lot of information to someone, give them an instruction manual, a computer disk or a book: if you wish to give them key facts or an important message with high impact, go for the presentation.

9.2.2 Be clear about your presentation's purpose

Presentations may have one or more main aims or purposes. You need to be sure about what you are trying to achieve. Figure 9.2 shows typical purposes—to inform, persuade, motivate, educate and entertain.

9.2.3 Capture your audience's interest

The first thing you should think about after the purpose of your presentation is how you are going to 'connect' with your intended audience. There are three basic considerations: their background knowledge; their interest in your subject area; and their level of involvement in your presentation.

Background knowledge

It is not necessary for your audience to have the same knowledge of the subject as you (if the purpose of your presentation is to educate them, this will clearly not be the case).

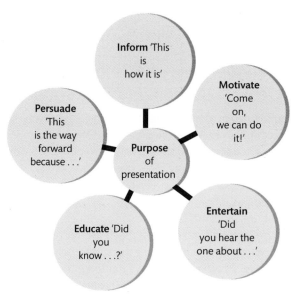

Fig 9.2 Typical purposes of presentations

However, you should have an idea of what level of understanding they do have. Sometimes, if you suspect that there will be a wide variance in levels of knowledge in your audience, you may decide to pitch your discussion at a relatively low level of knowledge. You may wish to tell your audience this in advance of your talk, saying that you do not wish to leave anyone behind in your presentation. Perhaps you might add that going over some of the basic areas will serve as a reminder to those who have previous knowledge of the area; this might also be a diplomatic tactic to use if you suspect that some of your audience do not want to admit to having little knowledge of the subject area. You might be able to cover some basic details and then launch into a more complex discussion, which will satisfy the more knowledgeable members of your audience.

Link to their interests

On some occasions it will be easy to ascertain the interests of an audience. For instance, if you are going to give a presentation to a group of fellow students who have come along voluntarily to a lunch-time talk you are giving on digital photography, it's a fairly safe bet that they already have some experience of digital photography and want to learn more about it. However, if you were asked to give a presentation to fellow students on an unannounced subject of your choice during a scheduled class time, this might not be as easy. You may have some idea of their interests if you have shared a class with them, talked to them at work or socially and know something of their personal, work or career background. You might also get some clues from the ways in which they have previously received other presentations and the questions they have asked. You should recall the ways of appealing to others that we covered in Section 4.3, *Communication and its use in persuasion*: using logical argument, connecting with people's emotions, and reminding them that you speak as one of them (or one who can relate to them).

Student tips on skills and employability

Presentation design for a video website

Wojciech is a second year business student. Given complete freedom to create a group learning experience, he decided to establish a video website with his friends. Here he describes the purpose of the website, how he marketed it to his prospective audience and how he designed the layout and content of the site:

The purpose of the site was to create an informative video website on career opportunities for current and future graduates, with information arranged in sections, as follows:

- Learning skills (CV examples, advice on CV writing, graduates' expectations, etc.)
- Videos (section full of videos on interview and CV advice, as well as employers' requirements)
- Video interviews (pack of videos conducted by me and other students with real-time employers).

The title chosen for the site was http://www.sungradsopps.wordpress.com, which was derived from Sunderland Graduates Opportunities. Our first design had a palette of green, orange and yellow colours so it would not only attract viewers visually but also, we thought, ignite a spark of 'hope'. Video material was added and developed to allow students a choice of what they wanted to do; read or watch and listen. In terms of marketing the site—i.e. the question of how to reach students—we used the following methods:

- Posters displayed around the University
- Our lecturer kindly promoted it on the University VLE
- We left business cards at key points and in the Student Union building
- We advertised through wordpress.com (by posting information and links, i.e. soft spam) on global overseas blogs and websites.

To date our website has had over 6,500 visits, with a number of comments from satisfied students, not only from Sunderland University but also from various parts of the world such as the USA, South America and Asia.

Get them involved

Your level of audience involvement will vary, depending on the purpose of your presentation, their knowledge and interests and your preferred presentation style and ability. At the very least you want to engage their minds so that they listen, rather than think about what they are going to do after this boring presentation! The more you can achieve this, the greater will be your audience's retention of your message and sense of meaning. Some of the techniques that follow (such as attention to beginnings and endings) will help generally in this respect. However, you may wish to use more active methods of engagement. Here are some possibilities:

- Ask them a question.
- Write their answers on a flip chart/white board.
- Ask people what they want to get from your presentation.
- Ask people to introduce themselves (perhaps just to the person next to them).
- Ask for a show of hands (for instance, in a training session on presentations ask 'Hands up if you actually like giving presentations').

- Walk amongst your audience.
- Ask for a volunteer to try out an activity.
- Tell them they will be asked to write a yellow post-it with comments/what they have learnt/ questions on the presentation, which will be put onto a board at the end of the session.

9.2.4 Think about beginnings and endings

Getting the beginning and ending of your presentation right will have a noticeable improvement on your presentation's effectiveness. Figure 9.3 shows a typical presentation and the level of interest shown by the audience. You will note that initially interest is high: the audience is keen to find out what the presentation will be like. However, as the talk continues, interest inevitably declines. Then, with the end in sight, attention levels typically pick up again. Your job is to use these natural attention tendencies to your advantage. The audience's attention span is something you should be aware of. Somewhere in the region of 15–20 minutes is alright, but after that you are really going to have to introduce special interest points or changes of pace to keep your audience with you. You should aim to make your beginning and closing elements of your presentation full of impact and meaning. You will require clarity and creativity in your design. You will need preparation and rehearsal for a polished delivery.

Beginnings

No matter how well you know the people at your presentation, it's always a good idea to introduce yourself and welcome your audience to your talk. You should briefly tell your audience what the topic of your presentation is. You may then start with some sort of introduction. The nature of this introduction is up to you to decide. Some approaches you could use are:

- Give a route map along the lines of 'We will start by looking at A, move on to B, and then conclude with C'. This is fine for a systematic approach.
- Give a controversial statement, then disprove it in the rest of your presentation. For instance, 'Learning skills are a waste of time in the modern workplace! Let's examine this assertion ...'.

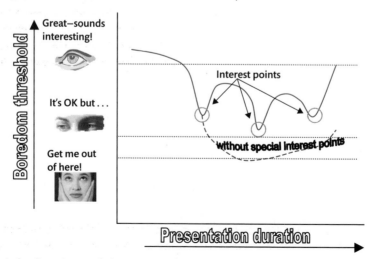

Fig 9.3 Typical audience interest during a presentation

- Show an emotional image. For example, you might show a happy, smiling group of people associated with the message of your presentation. This could easily be seen as too manipulative or sugar-coated, so be careful if using this approach.

- Give a thought-provoking quotation. It must not be too well-known or over-used; it must be appropriate for people to make the connection between it and your presentation. For instance, if your presentation concerns strategy, you might use the following: 'To win without fighting is best' (Sun Tzu *circa* 400BC, *The Art of War: Sun Tzu*, p. 34).

Endings

Constructing a powerful ending to your presentation is a real challenge. Yet all the great speeches you have heard will finish on a memorable note. As an absolute minimum your audience should know that your presentation is complete. Don't fall into the trap of announcing something like 'Well, I guess that's about it, really. Thanks for listening.' This suggests that you haven't rehearsed properly. It's also a weak ending. Here are a few suggestions as to how you might devise suitable endings:

- If using the route-map approach, summarize the key points. You may wish to add conclusions. Perhaps you will pose further questions for future investigation.

- Use a 'book-end' approach. For instance, if you started with an image, end with an image; if your first words were those of a quotation, return to it or use a suitable one in reply.

- Memorize your last few sentences so that you are word perfect (have a flash card as a back-up reminder).

- Remember to thank your audience for listening. Then ask if there are any questions.

9.2.5 Create maximum impact with your slides

There are many advanced techniques you can use if you use a slideshow. However, there's little point in using these if you do not cater for the essential needs of your audience—their ability to clearly understand your message. The current standard Microsoft package is PowerPoint®, so we will discuss this one in particular, although the principles discussed will apply to other packages. See the Further reading section at the end of this chapter for advice on PowerPoint® tutorials. This section is based on advice given by the leading educational advisory service in the UK, known as JISC TechDis. JISC is the Joint Information Systems Committee, a government-funded body. JISC TechDis aims to assist the education sector by providing expert advice on disability and technology. (See Further reading at the end of the chapter for more details of the website.) So, the advice that follows is consistent with allowing for maximum clarity of your message to a wide audience with varying sight and hearing abilities.

Tips for slide appearance

- Write no more on a slide than you would on a postcard.
- Use font size 24 as a minimum on PowerPoint®.

Writing too much on a slide is counterproductive. Your audience will spend too much time trying to read directly from it, rather than listening to you. Also, slides soon appear cluttered. It is far better if you use short phrases or bullet points and then talk around them. You should resist the urge to simply read everything word for word from your slide—if your audience wanted this they could simply read your presentation from a hand-out. Also, as we can generally read about three times as fast as we can talk, your audience will have reached the end of your slide and be waiting for you to read out what they have just read. Font sizes will appear larger or smaller, depending upon the projector you are using, and its distance from the screen. Using size 24 should mean that your script is usually large enough. Reading a slide should not be like trying to read the bottom line of an optician's chart! The following are useful points to bear in mind when trying to obtain an effective contrast between words and background:

- In a light room use dark-coloured text against a light background.
- In a dark room use light-coloured text against a dark background.
- Dark blues and creams are particularly effective.

Example 9.1 shows a poor example of a PowerPoint® slide, which has too many words. The font size is too small—Arial 10. The author was trying to show a whole document. One way

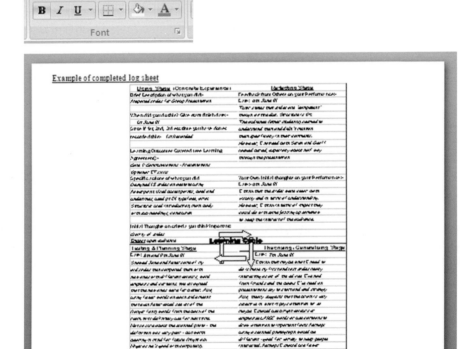

Example 9.1 Too many words!

Further referencing tips—ordering your references alphabetically

- Create a table (1 column wide by say 20 rows) in word for your reference list
- Enter references as you go along, author first
- When you have finished your essay, do a data sort in ascending alphabetical order to re-arrange your references correctly
- Erase the table border (no border) if you wish

Example 9.2 Readable size font

to solve this problem would be to show the box outline below with headings; a further four slides could then show the detail of each box in larger font size.

In the next example (Example 9.2) you will see a typical bullet-pointed slide. You will see that the 28 pt size gives a very readable appearance and is not too cluttered. It is very simple. Each bullet point would be revealed by a mouse click, giving the speaker full control. The speaker would say a few words in an informal manner for each line of bullets. The font choice

Activity 9.2 Slide readability

Experiment with different sizes of font, background colour and font colour. Ideally, you should try this in the sort of room that you would normally hold your presentation. View your slides from a distance and determine what you regard as effective formats based upon your observations and the advice in this section.

is Arial which, along with the simple background, gives the clean, uncluttered appearance the author was looking for.

What about references in presentations?

Showing that you have referred to theoretical models, textbooks and journal articles raises questions for academic presentations. Presentations are concerned with impact rather than detail, so it is not usual for detailed 'end-of-text' references to be given, although sometimes you may wish to include an in-text reference if you really think it is essential. However, there is often someone in the audience who is keen to know where you obtained your information. One way to address this is to print separate Word hand-outs with references included and give these at the end of the presentation (so as not to disturb your flow). Another possibility is to include the references on an addendum slide after your 'ending' slide, but not to show this in your presentation. You can then print out hand-outs from PowerPoint® showing all the slides with this included. It has the advantage of tying your references to your presentation so you will not lose them should you require to use them in future. Example 9.3 shows a slide produced in this way.

References

- AllinsonCW and Hayes, J (1996) The Cognitive Style Index: A measure of intuition-analysis for organizational research, Journal of Management Studies, 33:119–135
- Amabile, TM (1995) KEYS: Assessing the climate for creativity: Instrument published for the Center for Creative Leadership, Greensboro, NC
- Amabile, TM (1997) Motivating creativity in Organizations: On doing what you love and loving what you do. California Management Review, Vol 40, No 1, Fall 1997 pp 39–58
- Balchin, T and Jackson, N (2005) Developing Student's Creativity: Importance of creativity Styles as given in http://www.heacademy.ac.uk
- Bleakley, Alan (2004) Your creativity or mine?: a typology of creativities in higher education and the value of a pluralistic approach, Teaching in Higher Education, Vol 9, No 4 pp 463–475
- Brophy, DR (1998), Understanding, measuring and enhancing individual problem-solving efforts, Creativity Research Journal 11, pp 1230–50
- Cropley, AJ (2003) Creativity in education and learning, London, Kogan Page
- Drucker, PF (1985) Innovation and Entrepreneurship, London, Heinemann
- Gardner, Howard, (1983) Frames of mind: The theory of Multiple Intelligences. New York: Basic Books, Inc.
- Gardner, Howard, (1993) Multiple Intelligences: Theory into Practice. New York: Basic Books.
- Guilford, JP (1950) Creativity, American Psychologist, 5: 444–54
- Kirton, MJ (1989), Adaptors and Innovators: Styles of Creativity and Problem Solving, London, Routledge
- Knight, P (2002) Notes on a Creative Curriculum, prepared for the Higher Education Academy's Imaginative Curriculum Project
- Shaw, M (2005) Indicators of Creativity in 18 QAA Subject Benchmark Statements as given in http://www.heacademy.ac.uk
- Sternberg, RJ & Lubart, TI (1999) The concept of creativity: prospects and paradigms, in : RJ Sternberg (Ed) (1999) Handbook of Creativity,Cambridge, Cambridge University Press

Example 9.3   Slide showing references

Example 9.4 Photos and cartoons

Reinforcing your slides with what you say

You should always tell your audience what your slides are showing—they should not be left just to view them without any commentary. People with hearing difficulties will also appreciate it if you:

- face forward at all times so that lip readers may see you speaking;
- use microphones connected to an induction loop, if provided in (for instance) a lecture theatre;
- when taking questions from the audience repeat the question before answering it (this is a good technique in any case, as some questions may be asked in a quiet voice).

Going beyond the basics

Having mastered the basics, you may wish to add a few special effects. A word of caution here, though; don't get carried away with the technical wizardry at the expense of addressing your prime message. A pretty presentation will not make up for serious deficiencies in your content. You may wish to use hyperlinks to connect to websites or other presentations; perhaps you want to link to a video clip, or embed a clip in your presentation. If so, please refer to the Further reading at the end of this chapter for advice on how you might do this. Example 9.4 shows what you can do with a simple photograph—in this case, even a collection of books is more interesting with a photo! Photos are good for giving a reality dimension to your slides. They can be used to convey emotions too. The writer with the pen in Example 9.4 is a customized cartoon—appropriate, perhaps, for this type of presentation—but always think of your purpose and your audience.

9.2.6 To use or not: dress, props, hand-outs and humour

Dress

The question of whether or not you 'dress for the occasion' is one which may well cross your mind. It is one of those issues that seems to divide people. On the one hand, some will argue that it's the presentational content that is important, not the dress sense of the presenters; on the other hand, some people will argue, with equal vigour, that the presenter is part of the presentation and should dress accordingly. Ask yourself 'Does the way I dress affect the way I feel about myself and how I behave?' If you know in advance that you are essentially presenting to one person (for instance, your tutor), it should be a fairly simple case of asking that person for their views. If your audience consists of a variety of people, you will be unable to do this. Like it or not, as you will recall from Section 4.2, *Verbal versus non-verbal communication*, what we wear is likely to send some sort of message to those around us. So whether or not you dress to suit the convention of the situation (and a business presentation norm will differ from, say, an art presentation) or choose to make the statement that it's your content that matters and not your appearance, you will still be communicating a message to your audience. Quite simply, it's not possible to not communicate. Be aware of your dress message. Is it adding to the impact of your presentation? Or will it be a distraction?

Props

You are probably quite prepared to use PowerPoint® and flipcharts in your presentation, but have you thought about using other devices or 'props'? Props are often physical—things we can see or feel. An example in a presentation about chocolate production would be to hand out chocolate bars (in which case, the audience could smell and taste the chocolate as well). Props bring the message to us with added impact by using our various senses (recall Gardner's Intelligences from Section 1.5). Props also add an element of variety to your presentation, and they can offer an element of realism: I recall attending a talk at a gold mine; at the end of the presentation, each member of the audience was invited to pick up a gold bar single-handedly, with the promise that if they could do so they could keep it. Needless to say, we all tried but all failed, our fingers slipping off the smooth inclines of the bar. The message? Gold is extremely heavy!

Remember too that props can include the careful use of sound. One benefit of using music, for instance, is that it can set the mood at the beginning of a presentation. Natural sounds, such as the call of birds, the waters of a stream or the wind can also be used to effect. However, be careful not to overdo it and bear in mind that people can be quite particular about the sorts of music they like. This is probably an area where you should experiment in less important presentations until you build up an idea of what works for you.

Hand-outs

Do you give hand-outs to your audience? And if so, at what point—before, during, or after your presentation? And do you give hand-outs providing an outline only or full notes?

 Activity 9.3 Music tracks

Select music tracks suitable for background 'mood' music, to be played in the lead-up to presentations concerned with the following:

1. industrialization of the workplace;
2. the production of cocoa in Nigeria;
3. protecting the environment.

Make your own notes of how you think the music might influence a potential audience.

The next stage is to play your music track and show the title slide of each presentation to 'critical friends'. Ask them for their comments upon the suitability of your musical tracks and compare these with your previous notes.

Hand-outs are not essential, but you might decide that they can help you, particularly if your talk is instructional. The following advice is suggested:

- If giving hand-outs to your audience means that they choose to read what is there rather than listen to you, then you should hand them out at the end of the session. If this is the case, tell your audience at the beginning of your presentation that you will be giving them hand-outs at the end for detailed notes. This also allows you to avoid having to wait on slides for audience members who wish to take detailed notes as you proceed.

- If you are using your hand-outs as a framework—for instance, with some parts completed but other areas left blank for them to complete during the course of the presentation— then you would distribute the hand-outs at the beginning.

- If your presentation is humorous rather than instructional (for instance), then hand-outs are not required at all.

Using humour

Telling jokes is extremely hard to do well. A selected few professionals can do it and earn a living from it. But even then, tastes vary from person to person. The advice here is, unless you are very confident, do not attempt to tell jokes. However, that is not to say that you cannot and should not use humour. Humour may be present in the absurdities of everyday things and thus occur naturally within the content of your presentation. Or it may occur when you inadvertently say something that others find funny; it may occur when someone in the audience asks an unusual question or makes an unexpected remark. Humour can thus serve to 'break the ice' and enliven your presentation. Try to welcome it if it occurs. Certain activities for audience participation may be fertile grounds for humour to emerge naturally. Finally, be prepared not to take yourself too seriously and simply try to be yourself.

9.2.7 **Get useful feedback**

If you are serious about improving your presentations you need feedback. There are two ways to achieve this.

Own interpretation

At the end of every presentation get into the habit of reflecting upon those areas you did well at and those you could improve upon. If you have listed presentations as an area for skills development in your personal development, you may choose to record these in a learning journal or critical incident sheet. You thus also have a record to compare your progress against over time.

From your audience

If you are giving your presentation as part of your course of study, you may receive verbal and written feedback from your course tutor. Ideally, this should also give some suggestions as to how you might improve—if it does not, you may wish to ask for further advice. The other way you can gather feedback is to ask for it from your audience. The simplest way to do this is to distribute a feedback sheet to people at the end and ask them to complete it. This works best if you can do the same for other class members when they do their presentation, as it does require some effort to complete and there is sometimes the issue of 'questionnaire fatigue'. Make it easier for your audience to answer: design your questionnaire with some closed questions (e.g. yes/no or graded from, say, 1 to 5) and some open ones (for instance, 'What did you like about this presentation?; What could have improved it?').

9.2.8 Equipment and room layout

It sounds simple—and it is—but make sure that you check out all your equipment and your room layout before your presentation. It is easy to be complacent, even for experienced presenters. The best way to do this is to try out your slides, sound system, lights, etc. before your presentation so you know that they work and that you know which buttons to press. Go to the back of the room and check that your slides can be easily read. Think of where you are going to stand to operate any equipment, taking care not to obscure the projection screen and trying to maintain eye contact with your audience. On the actual day of the presentation, ensure that you always have back-up materials in case your main slideshow (or whatever) fails.

9.3 Delivering your presentation

If you wish to improve your presentational skills as part of your personal development, it is a good idea to establish a baseline of your present skill level and then monitor your future performances for improvement. Activity 9.4 describes how you might do this.

The remainder of this section will show that you can often make very marked improvements to your final presentation by ensuring that you make a real effort to practise, work on your voice and your body language. Figure 9.4 shows how Section 9.3 on delivery is closely related to Section 9.4 on building confidence.

Fig 9.4 Presentation delivery (Section 9.3) showing links to confidence (Section 9.4)

Activity 9.4 Analysis of your current presentation skills

You may approach this exercise in one of two ways: analyse a presentation that you are soon to do as part of your course, or prepare a 10-minute presentation on an interesting area—for instance, someone you admire as a business entrepreneur. Next, complete a critical incident sheet (see Chapter 2, Figure 2.2). You may add to this by asking for someone to video your presentation. This will act as a baseline record of your performance. You might also ask for your audience's comments. After reading through this chapter and involving yourself with the various activities, you should try this exercise again (a reminder will be given at the end of the chapter) to identify improvements as well as any ongoing areas for development.

9.3.1 Practise

Practise reading out the various sections of your presentation. Time them. When you have a rough draft try it out in front of an audience—a friend, for instance. Ask them for honest feedback; the accent should be upon improvement. Run a time check again. You may find that in front of your audience your timings are different to when you practise by yourself.

Decide upon whether or not you will use a script of some sort. You may wish to use a series of cards with key headings on them ('flash cards'). However, although you may decide to memorize key sections, you should not read word for word either from your script or the presentation screen, as this will probably sound very artificial.

Be prepared to change the order of your slides. Be ruthless in cutting out slides that are not up to standard. Beware of having too many slides. Finally, don't rush it!

9.3.2 Voice tips

- The first requirement is that people can hear you. You may naturally speak in a fairly quiet voice. If so, a good idea is to practise with a friend sitting at the back of the room and ask your friend to comment upon how easily they can hear you.

- Speed is important too. You will usually find that you need to speak slightly more slowly than you would in a conversation. Remember too what Colin Briggs said in Skills Example 9.1 about using appropriate pauses; you may use these for effect, to emphasize ideas or simply to give time for your words to sink in fully.

- Finally, try to vary your tone now and then. Again, advice from a friend can be very useful.

9.3.3 Body language

If you want to really connect with your audience you should try to remove any physical barriers between you and them. Try to eradicate any annoying physical habits you have, such as constantly pacing up and down or jingling the change in your pocket. The best way to become aware of these is to practise (again) in front of a critical friend. Another way is to watch a video recording of yourself. You may read about various body language tips, including how to stand and what to do with your arms (don't fold them defensively, for example). Two suggestions of particular note are:

- Eye contact: even if you a giving a presentation to a large group of people, try to establish some sort of eye contact. However, avoid focusing for too long on any one person as this may make them feel uncomfortable. Try to involve all of your audience in your gaze.

- Try to make your audience feel comfortable. Yes! Focus on them, rather than yourself. Usually they will want you to give a good presentation. Feed them a smile or two and often they will respond accordingly.

9.4 Building confidence in presentations

For some fortunate individuals, the thought of having to give a presentation is of no great consequence: for a significant number of people, however, the prospect of having to stand up in front of others can be quite daunting. We will incorporate two approaches that go beyond the usual anecdotal advice to be found on settling your 'nerves'. The first of these is directly based upon the 'Five areas approach' to overcoming anxiety, designed by Dr Chris Williams. The second approach, that of improving confidence, applies Alfred Bandura's advice on self-efficacy to the specific situation of giving presentations.

9.4.1 Anxiety in presentations—unhelpful behaviour

It is quite normal for us to be frightened or to worry from time to time. It is part of being human. Psychologists remind us that we all have a 'flight or fight' response to real or imagined dangers. In past times this served well to protect us from predators by either running away from them, or by preparing our bodies to be on maximum alert and poised to fight the threat that faced us. These reactions are still triggered in our present-day lives. Presentation nerves are an example of our minds and bodies reacting to what we (perhaps unconsciously) regard as a threat. Up to a point a certain amount of nerves is to be expected and, indeed, can be positive if experienced in a mild form, which is just sufficient to sharpen our senses for the talk. However, more extreme reactions may lead to us underperform and make the experience a negative one, rather than the constructive outcome desired.

So, what can you do to prepare yourself for your presentations? Well, perhaps the first thing is to be aware of how your body and mind interact in such situations. Then you can make efforts to influence this situation. What you must realize is that there are a number of factors that can influence the amount of anxiety you experience before and during presentations. These factors (Padesky and Greenberg, 1995) can be considered in the following areas:

- how you think;
- your emotional mood;
- how you feel physically;
- how you behave.

In themselves, these factors can have a tremendous impact upon how you perform in a given presentation. However, you should also recognize that as your mind and body are linked, then so too are all of the above factors: change one of them and you are likely to change the others. It makes sense to try to improve each factor, even if only a little, as the overall effect will still be noticeable. Figure 9.5 shows a 'worst case' scenario in which each of the factors has been given a negative interpretation. Consider the worst case scenario represented by Figure 9.5.

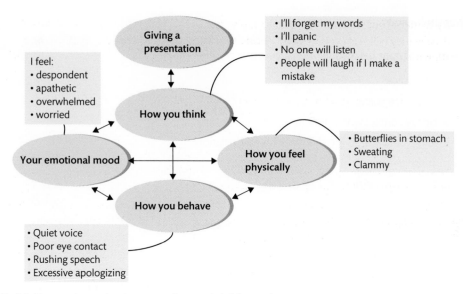

Fig 9.5 Overcoming anxiety in presentations—unhelpful scenario

Source: C. Williams (2003) *Overcoming anxiety: A five areas approach.* London: Hodder Arnold. Reproduced by permission of Hodder Education

How you feel physically

You might experience some—or all—of the following:

- butterflies in stomach;
- sweating;
- clamminess.

How you think

Here are some typical negative thoughts concerning presentations:

- I'll forget my words!
- I'll panic!
- No one will listen!
- People will laugh if I make a mistake!

Your emotional mood

Emotional moods that are unhelpful include the following:

- despondency;
- feeling apathetic;
- feeling overwhelmed;
- feeling worried.

Your behaviour

Examples of poor behaviour when giving presentations are:

- a quiet voice;
- a monotone voice;
- poor eye contact with listeners;
- reading (detailed) scripted notes with no deviation;
- rushing speech;
- excessive apologizing.

9.4.2 Anxiety in presentations—helpful behaviour

By reflecting upon your experience of presentations in your learning log and from the comments from your listeners, you should be able to identify your strengths and weaknesses. You may also wish to ask someone to video your presentation so that you can play it back later, to observe yourself. You should be able to categorize strengths and weaknesses under each of the areas of thinking, physical feelings, emotional mood and behaviours. The next stage is to identify areas for improvement. This will mean replacing your unhelpful feelings, thoughts, emotions and behaviours with more helpful ones. Figure 9.6 summarizes possible improvements.

Consider each area in turn, although of course in practice you may well be trying to improve several areas at once.

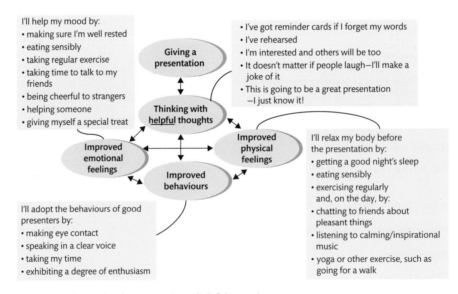

Fig 9.6 Overcoming anxiety in presentations—helpful scenario

Source: Based on Williams (2003)

Improving your thoughts

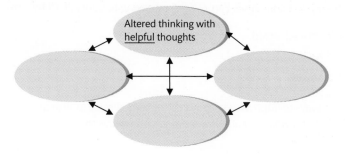

You need to replace unhelpful thoughts with more helpful ones such as:

- I've got reminder cards if I forget my words.
- I've rehearsed.
- I'm interested and others will be too.
- It doesn't matter if people laugh—I'll make a joke of it.
- This is going to be a great presentation—I just know it!

At first this will seem strange. If you have spent years thinking in a negative way you cannot expect miracle results overnight. You might reason that thinking positive thoughts is unrealistic. But consider this: your negative thoughts are definitely unrealistic—most of the bad things you imagine as possibilities never actually happen! What you are doing by constantly replaying the worst possible situations in your head is setting yourself up for failure. It is a form of destructive self-hypnosis. By immediately thinking of a positive counter-thought to a particular negative thought, you can help to create a more balanced outlook. At first you may not believe your counter-positive thoughts; that does not matter. Just as you have come to accept your negative thoughts as 'real' over time, so you will gradually come to accept your more positive thoughts after many repetitions. But of course, reading this will not be enough—you will have to try it repeatedly!

Improving your mood

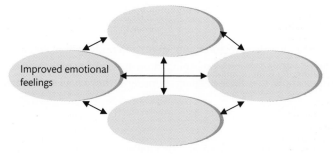

Ideally you want to feel in a confident, up-beat mood. There is strong evidence (Padesky and Greenberg, 1995) that thinking in a more positive way can improve our mood—as indicated in Figure 9.6. However, there are other ways to help your mood. Some of these may have an immediate effect, whilst others will become increasingly powerful over time. Look at improving your mood (Henderson, 2008; Parry, 2008) by saying to yourself: I'll help my mood by:

- making sure I'm well rested;
- eating sensibly;
- taking regular exercise.

As these are also ways to improve your physical feelings, we will look at these in more detail in the next section, *Improving your physical feelings*. Other ways to improve your mood include:

- taking time to talk to my friends;
- being cheerful to strangers;
- helping someone;
- giving yourself a special treat;
- getting some fresh air.

Illnesses such as the 'flu can also leave you feeling rather 'down'. The tips suggested above will help, as will accepting that as you recover more fully you will naturally begin to feel brighter in your mood.

Improving your physical feelings

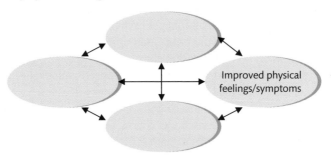

You will also improve your physical feelings by doing many of the things listed to improve your mood, for instance by:

- getting a good night's sleep.

Of course, you know that sleep restores your mind and body so that you may cope with the demands of the day ahead, but it's one thing knowing and another thing doing! However, top athletes, for example, take their sleeping seriously as they know how much it affects their performance.

- Eating sensibly.

Your body works best when it is given regular intakes of nutrients. Think of your body as a machine which needs a fairly constant level of blood sugar; this means not skipping meals or bingeing on sugar-rich snacks, which send your blood sugar levels into a series of peaks and troughs. One other thing to note is caffeine. Caffeine (particularly coffee, some colas and energy drinks, although tea also contains caffeine) can make some people alert, but others jittery.

There are other ways to calm any jittery feelings down. Here are a few, which you might wish to try on the day of your presentation:

- chatting to friends about pleasant things;
- listening to calming or inspirational music.

Music has a way of getting straight to your emotional and physical receptors. Yet the choice of the track is highly personal. Build up your own personal library of tracks; some you may play to help you to relax, others to energize you, others to cheer you up and maybe some to play when you just want to blast everything else out of your head!

- Yoga or other exercise such as going for a walk.

Exercise such as yoga and tai-chi encourage correct, deep, slow breathing whilst focusing your mind on what you are doing in the exercise. Even five minutes of well-practised exercises can significantly reduce your stress levels, calming your body and your mind. You do not have to change your clothes, although you may wish to find a quiet spot, if you feel uncomfortable knowing that others can see you. Simple breathing exercises may be performed without most people knowing. Ideally, learn the techniques from an expert. Videos are useful if you can't do this. An alternative, easily accessible, calming exercise is walking, which may be brisk or more leisurely. A brisk walk of say 15–20 minutes allows your body to use up some of the excess adrenalin that it has been producing, and this will help you feel calmer but still alert.

Improving your presentational behaviour

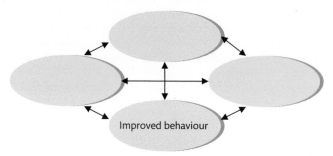

Improved behaviour

By observing and then copying the behaviour of good presenters you will improve your own performance. There is some truth in the saying 'Fake it till you make it'. In other words, you do not have to believe wholeheartedly in your new behaviours at first. However, over time you will begin to use them naturally. Tell yourself to adopt the behaviour of good presenters by:

- making eye contact;
- speaking in a clear voice;
- taking your time;
- exhibiting a degree of enthusiasm.

Activity **9.5**   Preparing for a job interview

Consider the various travel options open to Sarah in the case study 'The job interview', and the likely effects upon her physical and emotional response during her interview; you should focus on her presentation. You should state any assumptions you make about Sarah's personal preferences and her strengths and weaknesses. If you wish, you could imagine yourself in Sarah's position.

 Case Study: The job interview

Sarah worked as a team leader in the call centre of a national insurance group in the north of England. She was effective and well-liked. Recently, she had been looking for a promotion but she soon realized that the prospects of advancement from her current employer were limited. She had subsequently answered an advert for a call centre manager vacancy in a communications group and had been successful in securing an interview. As a call centre manager she would be in charge of a section of team leaders and their staff. She would not have to relocate, as the office she would work in was close to her home.

The interview was to be held in two weeks' time at the company's head office; this was located in the Midlands area of England—some 200 miles away. The interview was scheduled for 10.30 a.m. As part of the interview she had been asked to prepare a 10-minute PowerPoint® presentation outlining what she regarded as the key challenges of leading a team in a call centre environment, and how she was suited to tackling them.

Sarah quickly found the company's head office location using a route-planner package on her computer. The company would provide reasonable interview expenses by rail or road and was prepared to pay for one night's bed and breakfast accommodation. She owned a car, which gave her several travel options. One option was to travel to the interview on the day. If travelling by train, this would mean an early start—taking a 20-minute taxi ride to her local rail station for the 6.45 a.m. train, arriving at her destination station at 9.45 a.m. This left 45 minutes to catch a taxi from the station for the short (10–15 minutes?) ride to the company's head office. Travelling by car on the day was a possible option, but she suspected that she would hit early morning rush hour traffic so it was difficult to be precise about how long the journey would take, although her route planner gave a time of 3 hours and 35 minutes. Her other options involved travelling down to the Midlands on the previous evening (either by car or by train) and spending the night at a bed and breakfast guest house.

 Chapter summary

This chapter has covered a range of presentational techniques which experienced presenters have found useful in most situations. As discussed, many people would single out presentations as the area of communication that they are most uncomfortable with—and also the area they would like to improve the most.

By following the guidelines in this chapter you should be able to avoid some of the more common difficulties that face you, especially if you are relatively new to giving presentations. Good preparation and design will show in your slides. Rehearsing in front of your friends will hone your speaking skills. However, the chapter has gone further by giving you some tools and techniques for helping you to relax more during your delivery, so that you perform better and, with practice, feel more confident. You are encouraged to try out a variety of techniques to see what works best for you.

 ## End of chapter exercises

Exercise 1: Presentational pointers

Re-read Skills Example 9.1—*An interview with Colin Briggs, presenter for BBC Look North*—and make notes on any points which you think might provide useful pointers to your own presentational skills.

Exercise 2: Analysis of your updated presentation skills

To do this exercise you should first have completed the presentation skills in Activity 9.4, and then worked your way through the chapter. The exercise is to repeat the previous activity and to compare your two performances. The activity is shown again, for your convenience below.

 ### Activity 9.4 Analysis of your current presentation skills

You may approach this exercise in one of two ways: analyse a presentation that you are soon to do as part of your course, or prepare a 10-minute presentation on an interesting area—for instance, someone you admire as a business entrepreneur. Next, complete a critical incident sheet (see Chapter 2, Figure 2.2). You may add to this by asking for someone to video your presentation. This will act as a baseline record of your performance. You might also ask for your audience's comments. After reading through this chapter and involving yourself with the various activities, you should try this exercise again (a reminder will be given at the end of the chapter) to identify improvements as well as any ongoing areas for development.

Exercise 3: Voice and body language

For this exercise recruit the services of a 'critical friend'. This is a good activity to do if you are due to give an important presentation. What you are going to do is to give your presentation in full (say 15 minutes) and ask your friend to pay particular attention to how you use your voice and your body language. Your friend should note things they like about your voice and body language, as well as areas they think you might improve. These are areas for you to consider. How, or if, you alter them is your decision.

Exercise 4: Dealing with anxiety

For this activity refresh your memory by re-reading through Section 9.4.2, *Anxiety in presentations— helpful behaviour*. For each section—improving your thoughts, mood, physical feelings and presentation behaviours—draw up a plan of action for your next presentation. After the presentation has taken place, make notes on any improvements that you or others notice.

 ## Further reading/work

PowerPoint® tutorials

You should be able to use an appropriate graphics package to create your slides. One of the most widely used is Microsoft PowerPoint®. There is a range of free materials for you to use. A good site to use is the official Microsoft site, which gives free tutorials on how to use the various components of Microsoft Office (e.g. PowerPoint®, Word®, Excel®). Also, you may wish to buy one of the various Microsoft or independent booklet guides. These cover basic to advanced levels. Some of them have

accompanying CDs. Some are in colour, others black and white:
http://office.microsoft.com/en-us/training/default.aspx.

To try out the JISC Techdis website, which considers how to use PowerPoint® for multimedia purposes,
go to the following address:
http://www.techdis.ac.uk/resources/sites/accessibilityessentials3/index.html.

For some classic reading on body language, you could read:

Pease, A. and Pease, B. (2004) *The definitive book of body language: How to read others' attitudes by
their gestures.* London: Orion Books Ltd.

 For further information, please visit the Online Resource Centre at
http://www.oxfordtextbooks.co.uk/orc/gallagher2e/

10 Quantitative Data Presentation

 Chapter guide

Student viewpoint

There are few, if any, occupations where a prospective employee will not, as a minimum requirement, be expected to demonstrate competence in numeracy. An increasing number of organizations now assess competence as part of the employment interview process. Below are comments from three of my former students who, as you can see, are in posts with management responsibility in different industries but all require a level of numeric competence.

'Businesses are managed by Key Performance Indicators and budgets which both require numeric capability. As a technical specialist, numeracy is also critical in terms of monitoring trends and corrective action effectiveness. If something can't be measured then it can't be controlled—without the data, all you have is an opinion.'

Denise (Technical Manager)

'In my current role of Contracts Manager, monitoring performance of contracts is essential to ensure that public money is spent wisely. Without this information [data] it would be very difficult to assess if the local population is receiving good quality services and value for money.'

Trish (Contracts Manager)

'In my role we collect data to use in:
- the statistical analysis, monitoring and benchmarking performance of suppliers;
- trend analysis and quality issues relating to supplied products;
- determining depot layouts.'

Andrew (Warehouse and Distribution Manager)

 By the end of this chapter you should be able to:

- Define the key stages in presenting data
- Outline and explain the importance of collecting accurate data
- Understand some of the basic tools in drafting tables, charts, graphs and diagrams

Introduction

To compete in the fierce commercial markets that typify the working environments of modern-day businesses, skills in numeracy are essential for an increasing number of workers. It is therefore rather worrying to note that the UK does not currently enjoy a good track record in numeracy skills, a top newspaper recently stating, 'Half of adults have maths skills of a primary pupil' (Woolcock, 2012, p. 5). However, the UK government has taken steps to redress the situation. It acknowledges the need for skilled workers and is striving to promote the nation's ability to produce and trade in the world markets. The Department for Business Innovation & Skills, the government department charged with the task of its 'key deliverables' (which include Innovation, Skills, Enterprise, Trade and Markets), emphasizes its commitment to investing in skills as it faces what it terms 'new challenges, new chances' (BIS: Department for Business Innovation & Skills, 2011). But what exactly are the numerical skills that are so much in demand from employers and so key to business competitiveness? Perhaps the answer to this is suggested by an article some years ago in *The Times*: 'Most employers would not understand A-level further maths and are far from convinced that it has any relevance to their workplace. What was once known as *arithmetic* (author italics) is a different matter entirely. Basic numeracy skills are essential' (Hames, 2007, p. 35). The new organization *National Numeracy* gives an even clearer picture when it states that 'Numeracy means many different things to different people' (National Numeracy, 2012) and that some see numeracy as:

- the foundation of mathematics, the concepts learnt in school ... such as quadratic equations, statistical analysis and calculus
- the ability to perform simple number calculations
- skills ... you need to do a job (for example, using spreadsheets, calculating invoices) or to be an engaged citizen (for example, making sense of statistics reported in the media).

(National Numeracy, 2012)

Putting this into context for you as business and management students, this means you need to be comfortable with handling numbers and basic statistics. It is essential that you can do this to create meaning for what is happening in your business/market and thus to make informed decisions. You need to be able to do the following, as a minimum:

- carry out basic arithmetical operations (e.g. add, subtract, multiply, divide, work out percentages and fractions, squares and square roots);
- collect data, order it into tables and interpret tables created by others;
- create basic charts from data, which explain the meaning of what lie behind the figures and interpret charts created by others;
- have a grasp of basic statistical measures (such as average, range, spread);
- have an awareness of how statistics can be used to inform decisions correctly, as well as how they may be used in misleading ways.

This chapter does not cover basic arithmetical operations, so if you have a need to improve in this area you should seek advice—many universities now provide support. However, the chapter does give essential guidance on the use of data, tables and charts. Even if you feel familiar with these, you may pick up further pointers from the examples and the directed reading on accepted forms of data presentation.

Chapter outline

The chapter opens with a review of the key stages involved in the collection, analysis and presentation of data. The stages are developed using the critical questioning technique.

The data you will use throughout most of this chapter relates to that collected from a fictitious group of 60 students who are following the first year of a BA Business and Management (BABM) degree programme. The students have now completed the first semester of their course and have also completed the first three units of their course. As part of the ongoing quality assurance programme within the university, a range of surveys are carried out over the first year to ascertain student opinion and seek suggestions for improvement of college facilities. At the end of semester 1 all students within the BABM degree programme are asked to rate their experiences of the facilities and give their overall rating of their experience at the university to date.

The file BMSurvey (available in the online resource centre) contains details relating to the students in three sections. Part one details the basic student data, part two lists examination results of subjects studied from semester 1, and part three shows individual responses to the facilities services.

Further detail on the data held in the file is shown in Figure 10.1.

Section 10.1 deals with how the data is collected in a range of business and management situations. Please note that all the examples are based on Excel® spreadsheets.

10.1 Key stages in presenting data

Let us assume that you have been given the task of collating and presenting data for a department (this could be any—Operations, Finance, Human Resources or Sales/Marketing) within your organization.

You could ask the following questions (5W + H, as given in Section 6.3):

- What data is required to prepare the report/presentation?
  It is essential, before you begin to prepare data for presentation, to clarify what the questions are that need to be answered, such as, 'Is the data readily available?', 'What resources do you need to access the data?' For example, if you are required to access data outside your organization, is it generally available? Will there be a cost involved? Also, if the data is to be collected within the organization, do you have the relevant level of approval to access the data?

- Why are you preparing the report/presentation?
  There could be a variety of reasons for reporting the data:
  1. There could be a requirement in the organization for data that monitors progress of a particular process. This could involve areas such as food production, where there is a need to monitor both production output and quality on a regular basis.

Part One	General information about the student
Group	There are three groups—A, B and C
Name	This required the students to give their first name
Nationality	Country of origin
Gender	Male or female
Accommodation	Is the student living at home (1), in a single flat (2), sharing a house (3), in lodgings (4) or something else (5)?
Part Two	Results of each of the subjects studied in semester 1 with an overall average
Law	Examination result
Marketing	Coursework assessment
Finance	Case study analysis and report
Average	*A mean of the above three results*
Dist	*The number of subjects where the student achieved distinction*
Part Three	Ratings of five key areas of university provision
Refectory	The students were requested to consider within their rating a range of factors including opening hours, comfort, service and quality of meals
Teaching	The students were requested to consider within their rating the quality of the teaching and the support facilities
S. Union	The students were asked to consider within their rating only the quality of the accommodation provided
Sports	The students were asked to consider the quality of the sports provision available to students
Overall	This rating required students to rate their experience so far against their expectations before enrolment; 5 and 4 would be above expectations; 3 would be as expected; and 2 and 1 would be below expectations

Fig 10.1   Detailed comments on BA Business and Management Survey

Note: BM Survey available from the Online Resource Centre.

2. There may be a need to report on changes taking place in the organization. This could involve a weekly/monthly status report on a major development that includes reporting on building progress, financial and staffing issues.

3. The report may be of a long-term nature in that it involves a review of issues that may impact on the future direction of the organization. This is clearly the most complex type of report/analysis and involves making use of both internal and external sources of data.

- When is the report required?
  In preparing any report, particularly where you are reliant upon data from other sources, it is important to plan effectively so that you are able to complete within the given

timescale. You will therefore need to ensure that within the timescale you have sufficient time to collect, analyse and prepare the data for presentation. An important aspect for any business is meeting the time constraints. As with your assignment work at college, missing the deadline is not really an option.

- How will the data be collected and analysed?
  There will be a need to ensure that the information you use is suitable for purpose, is valid, up to date and accurate. Where data is available from within the organization (internal sources of data) you can be clear about the validity and accuracy and so you should be confident of using this in your report. However, you need to be more cautious when using data from external sources. This will be discussed in more detail later in the chapter.

  (Note: The examples given in this book are all based on data analysed using Microsoft Excel®.)

- Where will the report be presented?
  The report could be made in a range of situations. You may need to present the detail to a small group of colleagues in a small conference room, to a large group in a conference situation or, as is becoming increasingly popular, to people via video conferencing. Each method will require a different range of skills and techniques.

- Who is the intended audience?
  By clarifying who the recipients of the report are, you will be able to ascertain the type of presentation that is required and how much information is needed. For example, if the report/presentation will be provided to the public at large, what do they already know? This will influence the type of charts and diagrams that are used. If, on the other hand, the audience does not have any prior knowledge, you will probably be required to make the presentation simple to understand.

  However, where the audience is more sophisticated, such as a group of managers/peers with whom you are familiar, you may need to present the report at a higher level of detail, as you have a clearer understanding of the statistical knowledge of the group.

 Activity 10.1 Key questions

The BMSurvey file (available in the Online Resource Centre), shown in brief in Figure 10.1, contains a range of data collected from 60 students following a BA Business and Management course. The information collected may be useful to a wide range of people within the university. Using the critical questions below, draft a table to identify four groups/departments that may use the data:

Who needs it?

Why do they want it?

What might they do with it?

Are there any ethical issues involved with passing this information to other departments?

Skills Example 10.1   The 'top 10' and Pareto analysis

James had been recruited to a wastepaper recycling company as their new business development manager. He was the company's first business graduate—the other managers had all worked their way up to their present positions and had few formal qualifications. He reported directly to the managing director. The MD asked James to present his findings (at the next board meeting) on the company's 'top 10' customers. James quickly collected the sales data relevant to the past 12 months. He arranged sales in priority (largest first) by different categories: sales income against customer; sales tonnage against customer; estimated annual contribution to profit against customer; customer with greatest increase in sales rate over the 12 months. He knew these were measures that the managers at the board meeting would readily understand. He presented the data in bar chart format, showing the highest bar first, followed by the rest in order of reducing size. He commented at the meeting that sales seemed to follow an 80/20 distribution—i.e. 80 per cent of sales could be attributed to 20 per cent of their customers—and that established management thinking was that it made sense for companies to focus their sales efforts accordingly. He said that this approach was sometimes referred to as either the '80/20' rule or the 'Pareto' effect (after the person who popularized its use). The managers at the board meeting agreed that it was a useful method to show how customer sales compared against each other and they would be starting to include their own Pareto analysis in their own monthly reports.

10.2 Collecting the data

10.2.1 Sources

Before you start any analysis of data you should decide where you can source the information you need. This section covers the different types of data you can collect in preparing reports and presentations. Data is available from a range of sources, classified as primary or secondary data.

Primary data refers to data collected specifically to satisfy the current investigation. The data is therefore collected to satisfy a particular requirement and can involve a combination of direct observation, questionnaires and direct interviewing. This could range from a small, internal observation exercise within an organization to collect data from a production process to a large-scale national research programme. The defining characteristic of this data is that it has not existed before and directly meets the need of the investigation. However, the collection can be both expensive and time-consuming.

Secondary data can often be a less expensive option because it is data that has already been collected or published by another organization. There is a wealth of external data available today via the Internet from government sources, media and other organizations. A major issue with this data is the question of validity. You should therefore be careful that the data is satisfactory for your needs. Data will also be available from within your own organization, and here you will be in a better position to check the validity of the data.

As you can see in this chapter, the collection of the data from BM students will have involved a mixture of primary and secondary data. The secondary data, such as name and age, will have already been collected and will be available from original enrolment forms, and examination results will be in the records supplied by module tutors. Primary data collection methods have been used to collect the ratings of facilities.

10.2.2 **Types of data**

The two main types of data in the data set are *qualitative* data (sometimes referred to as *categorical data*) and *quantitative* data.

   Qualitative data deal with descriptions, attitudes and opinions. These can be collected from verbal data, such as questionnaires, interviews or transcripts of conversations, and from non-verbal data, such as observation or videotape that will need to be interpreted. For example, in the survey for BMSurvey we could have asked the students to write a statement on their opinions of the facilities offered in the categories of refectory, teaching, students union and sports. Giving each student freedom of expression can result in a very broad range of subjective open-ended answers, but can also result in the responses being very difficult to analyse and measure.

   Galileo said 'Measure what is measurable, and make measurable what is not so.' This will help the readers of any report to make sense of the data. You will see later in this chapter that instead of asking students to write a statement, which would involve a great deal of analysis, we instead asked them to rate the facilities by allocating a score on a scale of 1–5. By doing this we make the information measurable.

   Quantitative data are data that by measurement or counting can be divided into groupings or categories. These can then be represented pictorially by table, chart or graph. Quantitative data can be described by the following four sub-divisions:

- nominal;
- ordinal;
- discrete;
- continuous.

   Nominal data come in a variety of named categories with no particular order attached to them. We might collect data in the university by type of accommodation or gender. In our database we have nominal data in the form of gender (male or female) and country of origin, which in this example are China, England, Finland, Lithuania, Greece, India, Nigeria and Sri Lanka.

   The table in Figure 10.2 shows the gender of students. In the data set being used in this chapter there are 25 male and 35 females.

   As you will agree, I hope, although the table in Figure 10.2 is clear and useful, you will see during the analysis developed in the chapter that it is not worth committing this table to a chart. In fact, this is something you must keep in mind for the future. Not all data needs to be represented by a table, chart, graph or diagram if it can be made clear in one sentence—for example, 'the student group consisted of 25 males and 35 females' is easily understood. Save your charts for giving better and more useful information. There is such a thing as 'chart overload', or providing too much information.

Male	Female
25	35

Fig 10.2 Gender of students on BA Business and Management, first year

Country of origin	Number of students
China	14
England	19
Finland	3
Greece	6
India	10
Lithuania	2
Nigeria	5
Sri Lanka	1
Total	**60**

Fig 10.3 Country of origin of students on BA Business and Management, first year

Nationality	Male	Female	Total
China	6	8	14
England	4	15	19
Finland	2	1	3
Greece	2	4	6
India	6	4	10
Lithuania	2	0	2
Nigeria	2	3	5
Sri Lanka	1	0	1
Total	**25**	**35**	**60**

Fig 10.4 Gender of students on BA Business and Management, first year (by country of origin)

The table in Figure 10.3 shows more detailed nominal data in the form of the country of origin for the students in Year 1 of the BABM programme. Whilst the data can again be regarded as useful, it does not give us the detail of gender within each national group.

In Figure 10.4 we can see that by combining some of the nominal data we can include all the information from Figures 10.2 and 10.3, as well as providing more detail in the form of a breakdown of male and female for all students by country of origin. It is still a simple table and it is easy to understand, clear and useful.

When you develop a table that includes a range of numbers, take care not to include too much information. If the table contains too many numbers, rows and columns it becomes difficult to understand.

Ordinal data is the term for data that are ranked in order. Collection of the data involved the surveyed person making a qualitative judgement as to a particular aspect under review. For example, in our database we have ordinal data from our survey in the form of assessments of the quality of the services provided to students by the refectory, teaching staff,

	Refectory	Teaching	Students Union	Sports	Overall
Very poor (1)	3	1	14	16	0
Poor (2)	34	5	11	10	4
Fair (3)	23	20	19	18	30
Good (4)	0	20	10	10	17
Excellent (5)	0	14	6	6	9

Fig 10.5 Facilities rating scores by students on BA Business and Management programme, 2009

students union, sports facilities and their overall experience. The level of service could be rated as:

Very poor (1)

Poor (2)

Fair (3)

Good (4)

Excellent (5).

Figure 10.5 shows a count of the students' ratings of each of the five aspects surveyed, assembled into an order by rating.

Once again, this table is easy to understand and clear and useful. Both of the tables in Figures 10.4 and 10.5 would normally be supplemented by a diagram or chart. We will be returning to the charts to support tables later in the chapter.

Discrete data is the term used when only certain values can be recorded. These are usually whole numbers, such as the number of children in a family, the number of rooms in a hotel or the number of students attending a class meeting. Within the BABM data set the examination results are an example of discrete data, as they can only be whole numbers.

Continuous data are data that, in theory, can take any value within the range of data. This will normally apply to such areas of measurement as weight and height. Within the BABM data set the *arithmetic mean* of the three examination results is an example of continuous data.

10.2.3 Averages

There are many occasions where the distribution of values is widespread, as you can see from the data collected in the student survey and shown in Figure 10.5. To make for improved understanding you may need to describe the data with one figure. This is called a measure of average or a measure of location. Mean, mode and median are the three measures of average you will consider in this chapter.

Mean

The most familiar measure of average, which you will have already come across and use in everyday life is the mean (arithmetic mean). This is calculated by adding up all the values in the distribution and dividing the total by the number of values. For example, Sarah had the following results in her semester 1 exams: 66 per cent, 45 per cent and 54 per cent. The mean result is:

$$\frac{66 + 45 + 54}{3} = \frac{165}{3} = 55\%$$

The major advantage of using the mean is that the calculation uses every value in the distribution and therefore it can be used for further mathematical calculations (not covered in this book).

Mode

The mode is simply the value that occurs most frequently (the most often) in the distribution and represents the typical item. For example, if you reviewed the length of the longest holiday break (in weeks) chosen by 15 staff you see the following:

1,2,1,2,2,3,2,1,3,1,2,2,1,3,2

By analysing the data further, you can see that 5 chose one-week breaks, 7 chose two-week breaks and 3 chose three-week breaks. The mode was therefore two weeks.

Median

The median is defined as the middle value occurring in the data. If you use the same holiday example above, you need to rank the data from lowest to highest:

1,1,1,1,1,2,2,2,2,2,2,2,3,3,3

You then pick the middle value of the distribution. In this case, the middle value is the eighth value, which gives a median of 2 weeks.

When would we use the different measures of average? We need to think carefully about what the result means and whether it is of value to use this figure as representative of the whole data set. If we examine the mean, mode and median scores for the Law results in the table of semester assessments in Figure 10.6, we can see that the measures of average are different. Why is this?

- The mean score of 52 per cent has been calculated using all 60 results. By using all the results we have a measure of average that included every result in the calculation.
- The mode of 48 per cent represents the result that occurred most often. There were nine students who achieved a result of 48 per cent and in fact these are the only figures that are used in the calculation.
- The median gives a score of 51.5 per cent, which is the middle point in the data. This means that half of the students scored less than 51.5 per cent and the other half scored more than 51.5 per cent. Again, this would not give us enough information on its own about the results to be of value in this instance.

In this situation, the lecturer would probably use the mean, not just because it is the highest of the three but because it uses all the results in the calculation and best represents the whole data set.

There are other parts of the database where the best measure of average could be different. For example, in the database, the facility survey of the refectory showed that 34 out of 60 students said the facilities were poor. This is a key cause for concern. The mode would therefore be the best measure of average in this instance.

Another aspect you will be concerned with in collecting data is the spread. There is a number of measures of dispersion that are of value to a person analysing data. The only measure you will be concerned with at this stage is the range. To calculate this value, you need to subtract the highest value (maximum) in the distribution from the lowest value (minimum) in the distribution. Using the figures above this is very simple, in that the highest was 3 weeks and the lowest was 1 week. The range is therefore:

$$\text{Maximum} - \text{Minimum} = 3 \text{ weeks} - 1 \text{ week} = 2 \text{ weeks}.$$

When analysing large amounts of data, it would clearly be very time-consuming to carry out any of the calculations as shown above. Where the data is entered into an Excel® spreadsheet the task is very simple. Figure 10.6 shows a summary of the measures of location and dispersion of the student examination results from semester 1.

The results from the three semester assessments, in Figure 10.6, are also examples of discrete data, as the results are only expressed in whole numbers. This, however, would be of limited value presented pictorially. You can see in Figure 10.7 the range of results achieved by students in the Law examination and you could link the student number to the spreadsheet, but that is the limit of its value.

Similarly, the individual average of each student will only give us a general picture of the highest and lowest results and therefore the range.

The chart in Figure 10.7 has limited meaning unless you bring some order to the data. You can do this by grouping the data. The table in Figure 10.8 shows the data grouped in sets of 0 to less than 10, 10 to less than 20 ... up to 90+. For example, if the overall pass mark required was an average of 40 or more, you can see that 5 students have not met the pass grade.

You can then show the table of results as a chart, as illustrated in Figure 10.9. Note that in this example the bars are joined together. This is because the data is continuous in that the scores of any student could have been any value in the table. We call this type of chart a histogram.

		Semester assessments			
		Law	Marketing	Finance	Average
Summary statistics of semester 1 assessments	Mean	52.0	50.7	52.9	51.9
	Mode	48	40	44	48.3
	Median	51.5	51.0	47.5	50.0
	Maximum	72	76	82	76.7
	Minimum	28	28	34	37.3
	Range	44	48	48	39.3

Fig 10.6 Summary statistics of semester 1 assessments and facilities survey

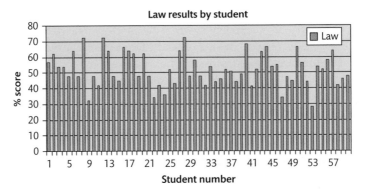

Fig 10.7 A chart of Law results by student

Average result	Frequency
Less than 10	0
10 less than 20	0
20 less than 30	0
30 less than 40	5
40 less than 50	25
50 less than 60	18
60 less than 70	8
70 less than 80	4
80 less than 90	0
90+	0

Fig 10.8 Table of average scores for BABM students, semester 1

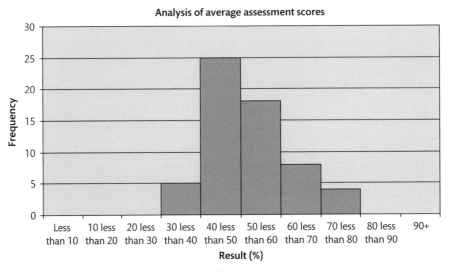

Fig 10.9 Average scores of BABM students, semester 1

Activity 10.2   What does it mean?

If you were presenting the information in Figure 10.9, you would need to put the chart into words. What is it telling you? Make relevant notes on the following:

- How many students achieved a distinction (70 and above)?
- Which group contained most students? How many?
- What you can conclude from the chart?
- What changes can be made to improve the chart?

 Student tips on skills and employability

Getting financial facts/figures/stats across to managers/staff/others

Maggie is working in her first full-time job after graduation, as a senior client sales executive, for a company that publishes brochures for corporate clients. In this example, she explains how statistical data is used to inform future publications:

> We measure various outputs after every show and use these statistics to decide what publications could be improved/added to, what new publications could be introduced, etc. We then use the research and corresponding statistics and testimonials to persuade clients to let us make changes and to create additional publications (more business).
> The sales team also utilize this research every day, using the stats to persuade exhibitors to buy advertising, e.g. 'we know for a fact that over 83 per cent of visitors say it is very important to have a guide at the show', 'we know from over 75 per cent of visitors that they class the guide as an excellent reference tool—the guide keeps on working for you after the show has been and gone.'

10.3 The basic tools for presenting data

There is a saying that 'a picture is worth a thousand words'. When applied to presenting data this may well be true in some situations, but there are still times when the tables, charts, graphs and diagrams are not of any use on their own unless there is some explanation of what the picture is trying to show the reader. There will always be a need to have a balance between the narrative explanation of the data and the tables, charts, graphs and diagrams that are chosen.

Whichever mode of presentation you decide to use, you will need to use a mix of narrative, tables, charts, graphs and diagrams. There is a number of general factors that are common to all and need to be borne in mind when drafting your presentation. These are worth listing as a checklist, which can be constructed and used to assist you in all your future presentations. Some of the basic rules that apply to all tables, charts, graphs and diagrams, for example, are:

1. Ensure that the report concentrates on the issue under investigation. Do not lose track of the fact that you are there to report the facts.

Activity 10.3 Using a narrative approach

To continue our journey, I want you to read the narrative report below, which is a short summary of the data held in the appendix of BMSurvey:

Narrative report

At the end of semester 1 a questionnaire was issued to all first year students of the BA Business and Management programme. The survey was completed by all 60 students from three groups. The students, 25 male and 35 female, come from 8 countries across the world. The breakdown of students from each country is: China (14), England (19), Finland (3), Greece (6), India (10), Lithuania (2), Nigeria (5) and Sri Lanka (1). The gender breakdown of each national group is China (6 male/8 female), England (4 male/15 female), Finland (2 male/1 female), Greece (2 male/4 female), India (6 male/4 female), Lithuania (2 male), Nigeria (2 male/3 female) and Sri Lanka (1 male).

   The students were asked to rate four aspects of the provision they had experienced in the first semester, namely: the refectory, the teaching, the students union and the sports facilities. For each of the facilities they were asked to rate their experiences on a 5-point scale. The ratings are 5 (very good), 4 (good), 3 (as expected), 2 (poor), and 1 (very poor). As some of the students may not have made use of all facilities, they were also asked to provide an 'overall' rating of their experiences at the university in their first semester. Again, they were asked to rate this on the same scale of 1–5.

   All students completed the questionnaire and the mean, mode and median ratings were calculated. The students' rating of the refectory gave an average score of 2.3. The ratings ranged from 3 (as expected) to 1 (very poor). The students' rating of the teaching gave a mean score of 3.7. The ratings ranged from 5 (very good) to 1 (very poor). The students' rating of the sports facilities gave a mean score of 2.7. The ratings ranged from 5 (very good) to 1 (very poor). The students' overall rating gave a mean score of 3.5. The ratings ranged from 5 (very good) to 1 (very poor).

   Note: This is not a complete summary of the data. It is only 340 words long. The report could go on well beyond 1,000 words in describing the database, but I think this section will be sufficient to prove my point.
   Now carry out the four tasks shown below:

1. Describe the database that is outlined above in a short paragraph.

2. Next, write down what you consider are the three key points of interest in the passage.

3. Now compare your conclusions with the points made by some of your colleagues or ask a colleague to read the narrative and compare it with your notes. Are they exactly the same?

4. What does this show you about presenting the data in narrative form?

There is a discussion of some of the above four points in the Online Resource Centre.

2. Do not get distracted by presenting complicated or elaborate charts. Keep it simple.

3. Avoid ambiguity by ensuring that you have clearly defined what the data represents. The title of the chart is very important.

4. Avoid distorting the data by careless presentation. Note that there are some examples of distortion in this chapter in presenting the data in tables, charts, graphs and diagrams.

5. Be consistent in design, in particular in the choice of typeface and labelling.

6. Where necessary, explain the data and draw attention to the key issues.

7. Always quote the sources of your data.

The (UK) Parliamentary House of Commons Library has identified a number of key principles for tables, charts, graphs and diagrams in a series of 'Standard Notes'. Some of the key points below are derived from these:

Principles for tables

1. Table number—if there is more than one reference table at the end of a paper then they must be numbered

2. Title—this should tell the reader what data the table contains and the date or time period

3. Ordering—time series data must be ordered earliest to latest from top to bottom or from left to right

4. Alignment—everything bottom aligned. Numbers right aligned, column headings right aligned, row titles left aligned. If column sub-headings are used these should also be right aligned but the main heading can be centred

5. Column width—try to keep them as even as possible. Wrapping column titles can save a table looking lopsided

6. Row/ height spacing—for long runs of data increase the row height (by half a line) every five lines to help the user read across. (Note—lines are not used to separate data)

7. Rounding decimals—be consistent. Number of decimal places depends on context and how robust the data are. Units (thousands, millions etc) in titles will help

8. Long/wide tables—if the table needs to wrap over one or more pages then repeat the column headings/row titles as appropriate.

Source: Guide to Statistical Tables—Commons Library Standard Note (Bolton, 2009)

Principles for charts, graphs and diagrams

Another good source of statistical advice is the Data Unit of Wales. The following recommendations are derived from 'A guide to presenting data' (2009):

1. Never use three dimensions.

2. Do not overlap bars in bar charts (this distorts the visual comparison).

3. Use colour sparingly: shades of a colour are often more effective; bold colours may draw attention away from the main purpose.

4. Always put the zero point on the scales when graphing absolute numbers or preparing standard bar charts.

5. Always label the diagram effectively.

6. Always show gridlines to aid interpretation.

7. Always use appropriate rounding of numbers on the axes.

8. When using pictograms, remember these are usually one dimensional in measurement— the number is represented by one or more pictures of the same size.

Source: Local Government Data Unit—Wales (2009)

Chapter summary

You should now be familiar with some of the requirements of collecting data in order to present information in a meaningful way as part of your studies, and indeed in preparation for your future career. There are many pitfalls in collecting data and you must ensure that the data you are working with is accurate and will enable you to focus on users' needs. There is a saying that I first came across when working in computing: 'garbage in, garbage out'. If the data you use at the early stages of an investigation is not accurate, then the results on completion will be of little value, so always ensure that the data is fit for purpose.

You will now be aware of the various formats that are available to present the data, helping users to get what they want simply and quickly. The careful choice of pictures and words is essential to make the statistics clear and useful.

Having completed this chapter, bear in mind that your numeracy skills development has only begun. You will now need to:

- Develop a plan of action to enhance your skills. There is a number of introductory texts that will explain the range of statistical techniques that will assist you in your course, such as *Business Data Analysis Using Excel* by David Whigham (2007).

- Work through the use of Microsoft Excel® to support you in your analysis and presentation of data in the form of tables, charts, graphs and diagrams. There are many online support websites, which supply simple step-by-step tutorials.

- Explore the range of other spreadsheet software for analysis/reports that can be developed to support your studies or can be used in future work situations, such as financial planning, budgeting and database applications.

- Prepare yourself for the interview process, which will include, in many instances, numerical competence testing procedures.

 End of chapter exercises

Exercise 1

In the data shown in the survey (BMSurvey available from the Online Resource Centre) there is a column that gives the type of accommodation currently being used by each student. The categories are as follows:

- 1 Single flat
- 2 Parents/home
- 3 Shared
- 4 Own home
- 5 Lodgings

1. Draft a table layout and complete the table by simply counting the numbers of each from the spreadsheet.

2. Represent the table, again by hand, in the form of a bar chart.

3. Represent the table, again by hand, in the form of a pie chart.

4. Which, of the three forms you have drafted would you choose to use in a report? Why?

5. Explain the figures in the form of a narrative to accompany your choice of presentation, drawing attention to the points you think are of particular relevance.

6. Are there any points you feel may need further investigation? Give examples.

Exercise 2

Produce the tables you drafted at points 1, 2 and 3 in Exercise 1 using Microsoft Excel®. The answers in the online resources have been done using Excel®.

 ## Further reading

A number of useful guides on numeracy and the use of statistics may be found online on the http://www.parliament.uk website. As the name indicates, this is an official (Great Britain) Parliamentary website. Individual authors have published guides. You may find the following relevant to your studies:

Anseau, J. (2007) *Rounding and significant figures—Commons Library standard note*. Available at: http://www.parliament.uk/briefing-papers/SN04443 (accessed: 24 July 2012).

Bolton, P. (2009) *Guide to statistical tables* [online]. Available at: http://www.parliament.uk/briefing-papers/SN05072 (accessed: 24 July 2012).

Bolton, P. (2010a) *How to spot spin and inappropriate use of statistics—Commons Library standard note* [online]. Available at: http://www.parliament.uk/briefing-papers/SN04446 (accessed: 24 July 2012).

Bolton, P. (2010b) *How to understand and calculate percentages* [online]. Available at: http://www.parliament.uk/briefing-papers/SN04441 (accessed: 24 July 2012).

Cracknell, R. (2007) *Measures of average and spread—Commons Library standard note* [online]. Available at: http://www.parliament.uk/briefing-papers/SN04444 (accessed: 24 July 2012).

Young, R. (2007) *A basic outline of samples and sampling* [online]. Available at: http://www. parliament.uk/briefing-papers/SN04447 (accessed: 24 July 2012).

The Local Government Data Unit—Wales also produces useful guidelines. The following link is recommended:

Local Government Data Unit—Wales (2009). *A guide to presenting data* [online]. Available at: http://www.dataunitwales.gov.uk/presentingdata (accessed: 24 July 2012).

Yet another website to publish a useful guideline is http://www.straightstatistics.org, with the following link:

Hawkes, N. and Sierra, L. (2010) *Making sense of statistics* [online]. Available at: http://www.straightstatistics.org/resources/making-sense-statistics (accessed: 24 July 2012).

You can find more information on the Pareto principle in many textbooks on quantitative methods. The following link provides a useful overview: http://management.about.com/cs/generalmanagement/a/Pareto081202.htm (accessed: 8 October 2012).

 For further information, please visit the Online Resource Centre at
http://www.oxfordtextbooks.co.uk/orc/gallagher2e/

Teamwork Skills

 Chapter guide

Student viewpoint

In many situations the rewards of working in a successful team are won only after a challenging learning process. An essential part of this process is to experience working with others—hence the inclusion of team exercises in many degree programmes. Here are some comments from a group of multinational students, reflecting back upon the 'hard lessons' they learnt from working in teams at university.

On acting as individuals before starting to work as a team:

'Everyone thought they were right.'

Omar

On the shyness of some team members when contributing to group discussions:

'I was surprised at the other group members' inhibition and different attitudes.'

Dirk

On individuals analysing their own team orientation:

'The profiling exercise in terms of team roles was good—but should have been done earlier.'

Katerina

On building trust:

'Perhaps it would be a good idea to socialize more.'

Dirk

 By the end of this chapter you should be able to:

- Analyse your own team's stage of development
- Direct your team's approach to project work
- Write a Team Agreement detailing how you will work together
- Write a summary ('minutes') of each team meeting
- Identify social skills that you can develop through working in your team
- Examine your own role(s) within your team
- Select and apply an appropriate strategy for conflict resolution within your team
- Outline a range of helpful team behaviours (COACH)
- Adopt a more considered approach to cultural issues within your team

Introduction

When you write your CV, whether it is for a vacation job or that career post you have been dreaming of, it is quite likely that you will describe yourself as 'a good team player' or as having 'good teamworking skills'. In other words, you do not need this book to tell you that employers are definitely looking for staff who can work well in teams. If you did need proof of this, you would only need to conduct a quick search on a government website or one of the leading employment bodies, to see teamworking prominently listed. The management researchers Stevens and Campion (1999) provide us with a good idea of what employers mean when they talk about 'good teamwork': they mean knowledge, skills and abilities (KSA) in five areas—conflict resolution, collaborative problem-solving, listening to one another, goal-setting and planning and task coordination.

It follows, therefore, that teamworking skills development should also feature strongly in your business or management programme as one of the key employability requirements to prepare you for the world of work. This further suggests that such skills may be developed during your time at university (Chen, Donahue and Klimoski, 2004), and that they are capable of being transferred to your future career and work situation. However, worthy as these career and work motives are, the development of team skills at university also helps you to fully engage and develop in social, personal and academic ways while you are at university.

Chapter outline

This chapter takes a structured approach. It answers the question 'What is a team?' and 'Why work in teams at university?' The initial discussion introduces the concept of teams and then considers how teams develop. The purpose of this is to show you how effective teams work, so that you may seek to incorporate this knowledge in your future team experience within the university and later in your career. Some of the theory regarding teams is given in this section—you will perhaps cover more of this in other modules, such as people management or organizational behaviour. In Section 11.3, you will consider how working as a team at university improves your specific subject knowledge and skills. Further sections then show how you develop your social and personal skills by working in teams.

Having answered the question 'Why work in teams at university?', the chapter then addresses two particular aspects of teamwork that will be relevant to you both at university and later in your career: conflict resolution in teams and cultural issues. You will be presented with various strategies for handling differences between team members; these will help you to work more productively at university as well as being transferable to the work environment.

11.1 What is a team? Why work in teams at university?

What is a team?

For the purposes of this chapter a team is defined as:

A group of people who work together to achieve a particular task(s).

To elaborate upon this, consider a class of 25 students. This may be a convenient group size for workshops or seminars, as the seminar tutor is capable of directing this number of students and still having some interaction with individuals. However, it would probably be ineffective to give such a group a common task each week in class where they had to work cooperatively together. It is much more usual for the tutor to break the class into smaller groups of say, four to six students, and ask these groups to work on the task. This is almost an instinctive reaction. However, if you were to analyse the advantages of doing this you might arrive at the following list:

- The group size allows each student to have some role to play.
- Decisions may be reached within a reasonable timespan.
- Over time the group will get to know each other—and may then work better.
- There are sufficient people to share knowledge, advice and opinions.

In textbooks on organizational theory you will read of the academic debate between groups and teams (see the Further reading at the end of this chapter) and that some writers use the terms rather loosely. To summarize, however, a team is considered either to be a group that performs (well), or it represents someone's wishes for how that group *should* perform. So, a *group* of 11 football players that does not perform well as a collective body may not be considered to be working as a *team*.

Why work in teams at university?

As mentioned in the introduction, there are various reasons and benefits of working in teams while you are at university. Figure 11.1 gives an overview of five key areas, which will be

Fig 11.1 Working in teams at university: skills

further detailed in Sections 11.2 to 11.6. The five key areas required for team skills at work are given by Stevens and Campion (1994, 1999) as:

- collaborative problem-solving;
- communication—listening effectively;
- conflict resolution;
- goal-setting and performance management;
- planning and task coordination.

One of the aims of teamwork at university is the transfer of generic team skills to the work situation, shown in Figure 11.1.

11.2 Team skills development

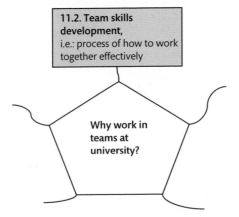

The process through which teams form and develop has been rigorously tested in practice. By learning how this process happens, you will be more able to work with the dynamics of any group or team that you find yourself in. It allows you to discuss the health of your team with other team members using a common 'language'. Also, it tells you that teams often go through a particular sort of learning curve before they become effective. The model of team development that we are going to use, introduced by Bruce Tuckman (1965) and developed in his later work with Ann Jensen (1977), is now well established in education and training. The model shows that teams go through a series of stages in their development—forming, storming, norming, performing and adjourning. It is only by going through the stages of forming, storming and norming that the group can actually begin its work in the performing stage. Further detail is shown below.

Forming

This is the stage at which the group is brought together. It is a time of 'orientation', when the group discuss their purpose as a group and their general direction. Alternatively, the group may be set up by a consultant (or at university, by your tutor) and be given a brief that says how you are to work together on a particular task. Some members may feel that the group offers them a safe environment, while others will wish to use the group to push forward their own ideas. Little work is done at this stage.

Storming

This stage is characterized by the airing of the various opinions of group members. It is a time when the emotions of group members appear—ranging from mild anxiety to inter-personal conflict—as members seek to establish their own position and, related to this, how the task should be tackled.

Norming

During this stage, resistance to working together as a group is overcome and the group decides how it is going to go about its job. It is a time of agreeing a range of 'group norms': ways of working and behaviour that are generally acceptable to the group.

Typical group norms for a group of students who have been given a project to work on might include:

- acceptable levels of work input;
- degree of trust and openness expected;
- ways of allocating tasks;
- how decisions will be approved;
- deadline expectations;
- attendance at group meetings.

Performing

As the term suggests, now that the group has sorted out how it is going to work, it can begin to be a functional unit. If the group has got 'stuck' at any of the previous stages, it may not begin its work. Alternatively, if it has managed to somehow struggle through the stages but in an unsatisfactory manner, it may not perform particularly well.

Adjourning

The group disbands at this stage. This may simply be because the task is complete and the reason for the group's being together no longer exists. Perhaps the task is no longer considered important, or another has replaced it as the focus of attention. Another reason may be that group members move on to other areas of interest.

 Activity 11.1 Storming

Think of a time when a group you were in became 'stuck' at the storming stage. What happened? What did you learn from this?

11.3 Group assignments: developing subject knowledge and skills

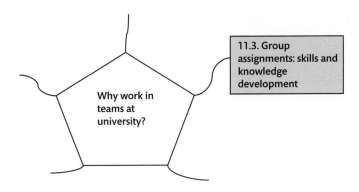

It is perfectly true that you can learn on your own. You can research and be creative, have experiences and reflect upon them. However, at some point you will feel the urge to talk to someone about those experiences, your ideas and the questions that remain unanswered in your mind. In a similar fashion, you can tackle certain tasks yourself—but larger, more complex ones will be beyond your capability as an individual. So, sooner or later, you will reach the limitations of what you can achieve in terms of your ability to learn and do on your own: this is where working with others—teams in particular—has its benefits. It is quite likely that you will spend a significant part of your working life in teams—this is one of the main reasons why you are asked to work in teams at university. For some of your work you will be involved with large, complex projects that require a coordinated effort for their completion. Project work at university gives you the opportunity to engage with this process. For now we will focus on some of the benefits associated with teamwork that emerge from the bullet list below:

- large, complex projects possible;
- greater range of information available;
- more ideas generated;
- collaboration can lead to even better ideas;
- motivational aspects of teamwork.

Tackling large, complex projects

You can achieve so much with your team—but the way in which you tackle a project is one of the determining factors for your success. A systematic approach will help you to control your project; if you also allow the team to have time to be creative, you will have a winning formula! To illustrate a project approach that satisfies both requirements, you are asked to consider the group presentation Skills Example 11.1, which outlines an assignment brief given to year 1 management students.

Skills Example 11.1 The great speechmaker

The following extract is part of a first year group assignment brief (other details not shown).

Group presentation: A great speechmaker

GROUP GUIDELINES

- This is a group assignment.
- You will be assigned to a group by your seminar tutor with a view to getting a mix of different personal backgrounds to assist your inter-personal learning.
- Groups will normally consist of 4 to 5 students.

TASK: research and presentation

Your group is to choose someone (living or dead) whom you regard as a great speechmaker. Your group should research this person in terms of one or more of his/her speeches and the skills and qualities that this person demonstrated in making this speech. Your group is to present its findings by means of a 15-minute presentation.

Now consider the flow chart in Figure 11.2, 'Teamworking in action'. This shows a systematic way of tackling a project. As it stands, it is a general process that you can follow. We will apply the steps of the flow chart to the skills example above (Great Speechmaker).

Step 1: Team gets together

You will note that the group has agreed how they are going to work together, as shown in their 'team agreement' in Figure 11.3. In the case shown, the format for this agreement was drawn up by their tutor as part of the formal process for groups working within their class. You would probably do this in any case, in a more informal way, if your group was working effectively. However, it is something that you may wish to consider, as people sometimes make incorrect assumptions about what is expected of them and others. Note that in the example the group is multicultural; it is not always obvious that everyone knows what is expected of them, so an explicit team agreement such as this may be useful. Research by Akkerman, Petter and de Laat (2008, pp. 385-6) supports this approach—see the Further reading.

Step 2: Brainstorm/idea generation

This is a very creative step. You are looking for a free-wheeling approach to getting as many ideas as you can, no matter how improbable—you feel that you can really let your imagination go at this point. You then sort through the ideas and select some to take forward to the next step. For further discussion of creativity, mind maps, etc. see Chapter 12 on Creativity and Innovation. Make sure that you retain copies of any documentation you use—it does

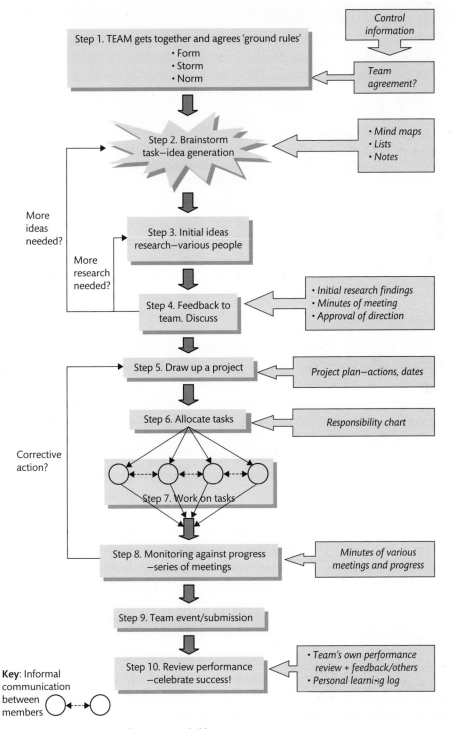

Fig 11.2 Teamworking in action showing steps 1–10

TEAM AGREEMENT FOR TEAM 'X'–[Date:]		
Team members (full names)	**Contact details—e.g. mobile, email**	
Anna ARISTOPOULOS	e.g. 0789 123456	e.g.:ann.aristo@cloud.com
Dong ZHOU	[number]	[email]
Lorna SMITH	[number]	[email]
David BROWN	[number]	[email]
WEI Jin (Mary)	[number]	[email]

INFORMAL COMMUNICATION

We have decided:

1. to use English whenever we are in group discussions and for emailing each other;

2. to be available on Thursday evenings for a weekly MSN chat;

3. to use our university VLE group discussion board.

MEETINGS

We have decided:

1. to hold a weekly meeting after our Marketing lecture on Tuesday morning, meeting up in the Library discussion area;

2. that everyone must be present at the meeting—if they can not be there they should inform us in advance if possible;

3. that we will take notes (minutes) of each meeting.

MAKING DECISIONS

We have agreed:

- If a decision goes to a vote, the majority view will be taken.
- We will give everyone a go at chairing our meetings.
- We will choose a group spokesperson.
- We will choose someone to edit our individual contributions.

SANCTIONS

We hope to all work in harmony together. We all have different strengths. We accept that this is a group piece of work and we are all responsible for doing our best. However, we agree now that:

- if individuals have problems in working in the group or on the task, we will try to sort them out promptly by talking to each other;
- we will seek advice—as soon as possible—from our tutor for those serious problems we cannot resolve ourselves.

SIGNED: Anna Aristopoulos, Dong Zhou, D Brown, Lorna Smith, Mary Wei

Fig 11.3 Team agreement

not matter if it looks 'messy'. In the minutes from the teamworking example, three possible speechmakers are listed: Winston Churchill, Nelson Mandela and the Greek philosopher, Aristotle (Figure 11.4).

Step 3: Initial ideas research

You now need to carry out some initial research on your ideas. It should enable you to go to the next stage. In the example, this research would be to gather more facts about the three speechmakers.

EXAMPLE OF MEETING MINUTES			
Team Meeting Minutes *Meeting No. 2*			
Subject *'Great Speechmaker' Presentation*		Date *31st March 2009*	
Present: *Anna A, Dong Z, David B, Lorna S, Jin W (Mary)*			
Action points from last meeting: *1. Anna to report back on initial research on Greek philosopher Aristotle as choice of speechmaker.* *2. David to report back on Winston Churchill.* *3. Mary to report back on Nelson Mandela.*			
Agenda for this meeting: <ul><li>to choose a particular speechmaker;</li><li>to draw up a project plan;</li><li>to allocate tasks between group members.</li></ul>			
Summary of discussion *After considerable discussion we decided that we would choose Nelson Mandela as our speechmaker: we thought Anna's research (Aristotle) was interesting but too ancient; Winston Churchill was very familiar to David and Lorna but not the rest of us and we weren't sure if we wanted to talk about wars! Nelson Mandela had the benefits of being a well-known and inspirational person who was still alive (!) and we could get lots of material on him and his life. We drafted out a rough plan—Lorna is going to circulate a tidied-up version to everyone—in which we decided to break our task up into 5 areas for Nelson Mandela as speechmaker: key biography; transcripts of 3 of his most famous speeches; background information on the history of apartheid in South Africa; photos, sound track, YouTube; etc. to add to our presentation; editing the various sections into our slides.*			
Action list			

ACTION	PERSON	BY
1. Tidy up plan, include dates and circulate e-version to team.	Lorna	2/4/09
2. Get key dates and facts on apartheid system.	Dong	5/4/09
3. Find transcripts of some of his speeches—circulate to team.	Mary	2/4/09
4. Carry out initial search for photos and YouTube.	David	3/4/09
5. Research on personal skills and qualities for speechmaking.	Anna	6/4/09

Date of next meeting: 7th April 2009, 2.00 pm, Library
Written by: *Mary (Jin)*

Fig 11.4 Example of meeting minutes

Step 4: Feedback

Here you decide as a team whether your ideas are worth pursuing. In rocket launch terms, it is the GO/NO GO decision point. You may have to go back and rethink your ideas and then go through some further research. In the example, the team chose Nelson Mandela as their speechmaker. They recorded this process in the meeting minutes, Figure 11.4.

Step 5: Draw up plan and Step 6: Allocate tasks

The team needs to decide on a plan of action. At the very least, this should list what is to be done and who is tasked to do it. You may wish to use an activity (Gantt) chart that shows the schedule of activities (refer to Chapter 3, Figure 3.4). Tasks need to be allocated at this stage—this is shown as 'responsibility chart' in Figure 11.2. Figure 11.5 shows how you might combine your project plan with a responsibility chart.

DATE / ACTIVITY	Week 1	Week 2	Week 3	Week 4	Week 5	Week 6	Week 7	RESPONSIBILITY
Tidy up plan and circulate to group	█							Lorna
Meeting secretary—writing weekly minutes	█	█	█	█	█	█		Mary (Jin)
RESEARCH								
1. Biographic details of Nelson Mandela								Lorna/David
2. Selected bio details to presentation content		█						Lorna/David
3. Transcripts of 3 Mandela speeches								Mary (Jin)
4. Selected quotes of speeches to presentation content		█						Mary (Jin)
5. Backround to apartheid system in South Africa								Dong
6. Selected points of apartheid system to presentation content		█						Dong
7. General qualities for what makes great speeches								Anna
8. Selected points of qualities to presentation content		█						Anna
PRESENTATION Content								
Initial draft			█					Anna/TEAM
Final draft				█				Anna/TEAM
SLIDE GRAPHICS—on to PowerPoint®					█			David
Photos/YouTube					█			David
PRESENTATION PROPS, HANDOUTS/FEEDBACK						█		Dong
SPEAKERS—Decide order in presentation						█		TEAM
REHEARSAL						█		TEAM
PRESENTATION EVENT							█	TEAM

Fig 11.5 Project plan combined with responsibility chart: example—'Great Speechmaker' presentation

Step 7: Work on tasks

The team in our example has yet to work on its various allocated tasks. Team members may go about this largely under their own direction, but it is usually good practice to keep in touch with other team members from time to time. In the example, they will do this informally between meetings by using MSN on Thursday evenings.

Step 8: Monitoring

Ongoing work will be monitored against the plan. If any corrective action needs to be taken, this should be picked up at regular meetings. Again, meetings will be minuted.

Step 9: Teamwork event/submission

Finally, the day of the team event—or in our case, the presentation—will arrive and the team will be judged on its performance.

Step 10: Review performance

It is important to keep going at this point—the full cycle is not complete until the team has reviewed its performance. For the 'Great Speechmaker' presentation, the team will receive feedback from the tutor and other students, as well as being able to conduct their own review. The review should be constructively critical with pointers for improvement. Finally, if you know you've worked hard on the project, why not acknowledge it in some way, even if it's only to yourself? Make a record in your personal learning log—it may come in handy for your CV.

Finally ...

Please note that you do not have to follow this approach exactly—the important thing is that you think about the benefits of adopting a similar approach and try it for yourself, noting what works best for you.

11.4 Developing social skills in teams

11.4.1 Tackling problem areas

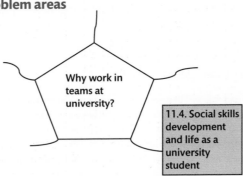

Why work in teams at university?

11.4. Social skills development and life as a university student

Team situations allow you to develop many social and inter-personal skills. You may have already identified some of these within your personal development plan. Some common problem areas are:

- shyness when talking to people you do not already know;
- making 'small talk';
- putting your own ideas forward.

Usually, if any of these apply to you, you will be aware of them. Less common, but equally problematical areas include:

- being too bossy;
- not listening to others' views;
- being (or appearing to be) aggressive;
- appearing to be 'too serious'.

You may or may not be aware of these behaviours—it may take a 'critical friend' to point these out during or after team discussions.

Overcoming shyness

It is quite normal to feel a little reticent when first meeting new people. Typical unhelpful *thoughts* might be:

- I'll say something stupid.
- People will wonder why I'm asking such a basic question.
- People will laugh at me.

Replace these thoughts with ones such as:

- It doesn't matter if I say something a bit strange—most people are just focused upon themselves and will probably not even notice or will soon forget.
- If I'm asking a question, it's quite likely that other people are thinking of asking the same thing.
- Does it matter if people laugh? What do I care?
- Go a stage further—think 'how could I make this meeting more enjoyable for others here?'

 Activity 11.2   Inter-personal skills

Identify an area of inter-personal skill that you wish to develop. You may already have listed this in your personal development plan. The next time you meet with your team, try to undertake a detached monitoring of your performance in this area. Do not worry if you do not always achieve this, but try to resume your monitoring throughout. Make notes afterwards in your learning journal. How do you think you might improve this particular inter-personal skill through your team activities?

Unhelpful *behaviours* might be:

- saying nothing!;
- looking away;
- looking bored!;
- not turning up for meetings;
- not telling people why you did not turn up.

Instead of these, make sure that you:

- *Always* say something—the sooner the better. It does not matter what you say to break the ice. Once you've entered the conversation things will flow.
- Look at people (no, not by staring!—just make eye contact from time to time). You may not find this easy to begin with, but persevere.
- Try to be more friendly—use people's names when you're talking to them.
- Smile more (yes, again this may feel strange if you're normally quite serious). Start by trying your smile when you meet someone. In time it will become natural.
- Go a stage further—try to encourage someone else to join the conversation.

As you practise more and more, you will become better. If this is one of your PDP goals, you can record your progress in your learning journal and discuss matters with your personal tutor.

And for those with language difficulties ...

Stammer or stutter? As a child I had a bad stammer, which always seemed to get worse when I had to speak in front of others. Persistence, help from a language 'coach' and graded experience gradually improved my speech. If this sounds like you, consider getting some one-to-one help from a speech therapist. You can include your team discussions and presentations as part of your improvement path. Often you will find others in your team who have experience of similar problems and will offer you their support.

English not your first language? You might feel embarrassed because you feel that you cannot express yourself adequately in English. Again, avoidance is not the answer. You have to tackle the issue, even if sometimes by sneaking around the side, rather than directly. Take advantage of any additional courses at university for improving your spoken and written English. Make friends with English speakers. Try to speak English as much as possible. Listen to English news reports and read English newspapers. Through practice you will improve, and so will your confidence. Make sure that you take your turn at speaking in meetings. Keep notes in your learning journal. Again, your team members may offer their support and advice.

11.4.2 **Learning as a 'community of practice'**

Jean Lave and Etienne Wenger advocate the social nature of learning and the concept of a 'community of practice', which they argue is where organizations need to be successful in today's knowledge society. The definition given below (Wenger, 2006) shows both the nature and structure of learning communities of practice:

> Communities of practice are groups of people who share a concern or a passion for something they do and learn how to do it better as they interact regularly.

(Wenger, 2006, p. 1)

Your team may therefore be thought of as a community of practice. In a wider sense, you might regard your university as a community of practice.

Communities of practice (CoP) are not new. However, research into them is. Through research it is possible to explore what encourages communities of practice to be effective and thus seek to improve our learning as participants. For instance, if we break down a community of practice into a 'domain of knowledge', a 'community' and 'practice', we can research its elements: we might observe that every CoP has a topic or area of knowledge upon which it is focused—its 'domain of knowledge'; we can consider the type and number of people who comprise the community; we can investigate the 'practice'—how the community goes about its business, its specific information and stories. By working as a team at university you are practising the skills required for the CoPs in which you will work (and perhaps establish) in your future work situation.

11.5 Developing self-concept through teams

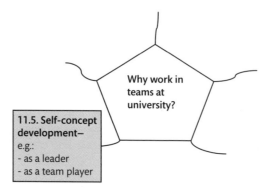

By working in a team at university you will be able to develop your identity as an individual in terms of the role you assume with other team members. For instance, are you the sort of person who likes to be in charge of others? Or would you want to be more like this sort of person? At university you have the opportunity to explore this and other group roles in a relatively supportive environment. You have time for reflection. You have advice on hand from your tutor and your colleagues. It is unlikely you will have all of these to help you in your future work situation unless you are fortunate enough to work somewhere that encourages such a trusting environment.

An influential model of group/team roles is that of Meredith Belbin. Originally devised during the late 1970s, the model has proved its worth and is often used on business and management courses to help students analyse themselves in terms of what Belbin calls 'team roles'. Originally a set of eight roles (Belbin, 1981), there are now nine roles (Belbin, 1996), which are used as the basis for identifying an individual's approach to working in a team. By completing a questionnaire, you can be scored against each of these roles and then given a role profile. These roles are shown in Figure 11.6.

BELBIN®

Team Role Summary Descriptions

Team role		Contribution	Allowable weaknesses
Plant		Creative, imaginative, free-thinking. Generates ideas and solves difficult problems.	Ignores incidentals. Too preoccupied to communicate effectively.
Resource investigator		Outgoing, enthusiastic, communicative. Explores opportunities and develops contacts.	Over-optimistic Loses interest once initial enthusiasm has passed.
Co-ordinator		Mature, confident, identifies talent. Clarifies goals. Delegates effectively.	Can be seen as manipulative. Offloads own share of the work.
Shaper		Challenging, dynamic, thrives on pressure. Has the drive and courage to overcome obstacles.	Prone to provocation. Offends people's feelings.
Monitor evaluator		Sober, strategic and discerning. Sees all options and judges accurately.	Lacks drive and ability to inspire others. Can be overly critical.
Teamworker		Co-operative, perceptive and diplomatic. Listens and averts friction.	Indecisive in crunch situations. Avoids confrontation.
Implementer		Practical, reliable, efficient. Turns ideas into actions and organizes work that needs to be done.	Somewhat flexible. Slow to respond to new possibilities.
Completer finisher		Painstaking, conscientious, anxious. Searches out errors. Polishes and perfects.	Inclined to worry unduly. Reluctant to delegate.
Specialist		Single-minded, self-starting, dedicated. Provides knowledge and skills in rare supply.	Contributes only on a narrow front. Dwells on technicalities.

Fig 11.6 Team role descriptions

Source: Reproduced with kind permission of Belbin Associates, http://www.belbin.com

Your questionnaire results may show you to be particularly strong in certain group roles. As with the learning styles questionnaire (Honey and Mumford, 2006) discussed in Chapter 2, you can use this knowledge in various ways:

- to appreciate your particular strengths and weaknesses within a group setting;

- as a baseline and guide for your group skills development (you could test yourself in the future).

In work situations, managers may test members of staff and, as Belbin states that the best groups have strengths in all of these roles, they may select team members on the basis that

 Student tips on skills and employability

Using awareness of team roles in the workplace

Steve is studying part-time for his business degree. He works in a large NHS hospital, where he is in charge of a team of technicians who have responsibility for the maintenance of sophisticated medical equipment (including MRI and X-Ray machinery). He has recently been promoted to this position from within the team. Here, he relates how he has used what he has learnt about teamwork in his degree, in relation to his own workteam:

> When I began my new role within management my biggest concern was delegating and getting people to accept me in my new position. I enrolled on a management degree to assist me. An area I found very useful was Belbin's team roles approach; this opened up a whole new concept in understanding people within their skill set rather than just their personalities. It helped me realize that not everyone is the same, and involving different characters and their approaches can help to create a healthy and efficient team. By understanding the needs of the individual one can often satisfy the person by allocating roles that not only suit their skill capacity but also their personality. This can motivate them, which in turn can help develop a successful team. For instance, one colleague was questioning everything, constantly asking why, what, how—which sometimes would frustrate and annoy other staff! I realized, however, that he was a useful team player, as we can often go along (as a team) never questioning anything—because we have always done things that way! I have since explained team role theory to staff within the department and now encourage him to be 'awkward' and question everything. Whilst in the past I may have tried to avoid such confrontation, I now actively encourage his approach and we now have very good dialogue within the team.

 Activity 11.3 Team roles

This activity may be used by you as an individual, or you may wish to extend it to include members of one of your teams. The aim is for you to think about the implications for you and your team members of your team roles—to act as a forum for discussion. It does not attempt to replace the actual Belbin test, which is available on a commercial basis (see Further reading). One way to complete the exercise is to use it as a subjective self-rating in which you compare yourself against each of the nine Belbin team roles; in the absence of the Belbin questionnaire you are asked to give your best self-estimate of each role on a scale of 1 (low) to 5 (high). If you wish you can vary this by also asking team members what they would rate you as—and you could do the same for them.
  Complete Figure 11.7

- Are there any surprises between how you rate yourself and how others rate you?

- In your team are there any clashes—for instance, too many shapers, an absence of completer finishers?

- What does this tell you?

Team role	Your score 1 (low)–5 (high)	Person 'A' score 1–5	Person 'B' score 1–5	Person 'C' etc. (extend as necessary) score 1–5
Plant				
Resource investigator				
Coordinator				
Shaper				
Monitor evaluator				
Teamworker				
Implementer				
Completer finisher				
Specialist				

Fig 11.7 Subjective team role self-rating exercise

all of the roles are adequately covered. Sometimes this approach is also taken by university tutors in selecting groups.

11.6 Developing coping skills through teams

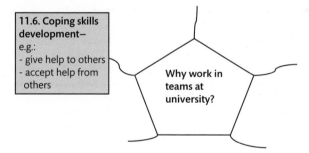

One of the benefits of teamwork lies in the ability of individuals to help each other to cope with any anxieties or problems. Viewed in the short term, teams can help you and your fellow students during the first year of your study as you adjust and 'orient' yourself to your new HE environment.

Your readiness to help each other (and to accept help) is something that is, in itself, a characteristic that will be needed when you join your future work team. As much of today's work environment is information-based, this help often depends upon the willingness of

---

Activity 11.4 Help?

- Which do you find easiest—to give, or to receive help?
- Why?
- Discuss with other team members.

Skills Example 11.2 An interview with members of the Great North Air Ambulance Service

This example considers teams at different levels: it consists of material from discussions with three members of the Great North Air Ambulance Service (GNAAS)—the operations director (Northumbria), the air desk controller and the helicopter doctor of the Durham Tees Valley base (http://www.greatnorthairambulance.co.uk/).

The air desk controller explained to me that the service operates three helicopters that cover the areas of Teesside, Cumbria and Northumberland, coordinated from Tees Valley Airport. Each helicopter has three crew on board: the pilot, a paramedic and a doctor. Teamwork occurs at different levels. One level involves the emergency services working together. It is a loose team in the sense that it is multi-disciplinary and people do not always meet face-to-face, although it does meet for major training exercises. When a serious accident happens, someone, often a member of the public, phones for an ambulance. The ambulance service may then decide to request an air ambulance, depending upon the situation. This request is made by phone to the air desk controller, who decides which of the three helicopters is best placed to help and the crew of that helicopter is then alerted. In the case of a road traffic collision, the police and the fire brigade will also be involved.

A direct level of teamwork is experienced on board the helicopter where the three members of the aircrew operate as a tight-knit unit. I asked the helicopter doctor, Dr Dave Bramley, what motivated him and the crew. His answer was immediate: the swift initial medical care and subsequent survival of someone in a medical emergency. Having to operate on occasion at the limits of their professional competence in often difficult physical environments was both challenging and rewarding. This was echoed by the photographs and newspaper clippings on the wall of the mess room showing helicopters, aircrew and grateful patients and their families. When I met the aircrew they had just returned from an emergency flight. What struck me most was their practised after-flight checks and preparation for the next flight; they went about their business in a methodical way, each member with their own work to do. The atmosphere was one of calm efficiency. Humour was used but in moderation, usually one-line comments between people who knew and trusted each other.

The operations director told me of a larger team structure to which the Great North Air Ambulance belonged—AAA (the Association of Air Ambulances: http://www.associationofairambulances.co.uk/). Like the Great North Air Ambulance Service, AAA is run on a charitable basis. It has been established as a representative body for the Air Ambulance Services in the UK.

individuals to share information. Beitler and Mitlacher (2007, p. 534), writing about business student attitudes to information-sharing, state plainly:

> ... the most successful companies will not be those whose individuals learn best but those whose employees are able and ready to share their acquired knowledge and information with their colleagues and subordinates.

(Beitler and Mitlacher, 2007, p. 534)

11.7 Conflict resolution

11.7.1 Why consider conflict?

Up until this point you have considered the central question of 'Why work in teams at university?'. You have seen how there is a process to team development, how you can learn in teams and how you can develop certain social skills by working with others. However, there is another crucial area to consider—one, in fact, that Stevens and Campion (1999) positioned first on their list of desirable team skills at work: conflict resolution. I did not give it the same priority for this chapter, as I did not want you to think that working in teams is always dominated by conflict. However, to pretend that it does not exist is to go to the other extreme and is equally unhelpful to you, for one thing is certain: at some stage, whether at university or in your future career, you are going to have to work in teams and you will face some form of conflict. The question is this: how do you handle it?

In this section you will explore different views and aspects of conflict, for not all conflict is necessarily 'bad'. You will examine techniques to tackle some of the more typical conflict situations that you may be presented with. You will identify a range of corresponding personal skills, some of which you may wish to develop further as part of your personal development.

11.7.2 What do we mean by 'conflict' in teams?

The word 'conflict' covers a whole spectrum of behaviour in teams, from mild disagreement or difference of opinion on some issue or other, through a range of work issues to, at the extreme, mutual loathing of team members! Typical sources of conflict are:

- differences between individuals or sub-groups in work direction or approach;
- the presence or formation of cliques;
- a desire to perform well as a team (!);
- confusion or resentment over allocated group roles;
- differences in perceived effort expended by individual members;
- personality clashes;
- cultural differences.

11.7.3 Is conflict always destructive?

Not all conflict is destructive. In fact, the reverse can be argued—that some conflict can actually be constructive. Also, to think that you can always avoid disagreement is unrealistic. Can you imagine a friendship where you never had an argument? In a team you will be working with people from different academic backgrounds, with different personalities and perhaps from different cultures: inevitably, you will not always agree as a team. The very differences that lead you to argue over your approach to team issues can be a rich source of idea generation, as they can open your minds to new possibilities.

They also allow you to refine your team's defence of its ideas against critical attack from others. For instance, in the 'Great Speechmaker' exercise in Skills Example 11.1, the discussion between the team members over who to choose (Churchill, Mandela or Aristotle) might have been quite heated. However, in going through this process the team would have fully explored the reasons for their choice. If questioned by their tutor at their presentation about why they chose Mandela, they would have a good, ready response.

One piece of advice on team conflict that you will hear (and that is recommended here) is not to let disputes become personal. Personal insults should not be tolerated by the team. Fight passionately for your point of view, by all means, but stick to the issues. However, it's not always that simple—even without personal insults you will find that you may identify so strongly with 'your' argument that you feel personally offended if the 'other' argument wins the team's vote. This feeling is something you will have to learn to cope with. Record it in your learning log when the hurt has receded a little!

11.7.4 Conflict resolution styles: win–win, compromise and win–lose

When the various inputs, opinions and ideas from your team members take on a life of their own and gel into a really great outcome, far better than any one of your individual ideas, or even all your best individual ideas put one on top of the other, you have true collaboration. It is what is called 'synergy'. It is represented by the mathematically incorrect 'equation' $2 + 2 = 5$. This is also highly desirable from individuals' points of view, as it means that their ideas have all fed in to this process. Everyone has 'won'—it is what is known as a 'win–win' situation.

True collaboration and win–win represents the pinnacle of teamwork. At other times you will have to settle for less—compromise. Compromise may still give reasonable results; it means that you will not get all that you want, but hopefully you will get something worthwhile. How much you get in your favour will depend upon your bargaining position and your ability to negotiate with the other side. In a good negotiation both sides must feel that they have got a reasonable deal.

Win–lose represents an aggressive, winner-takes-all approach. Of course, it can feel good to win. Some people will admire you for your superior strength or ability. However, use this strategy with caution—you may end up by winning the argument but by ultimately losing support; your feeling of 'victory' may be matched in intensity by your opponent's desire to even the scores at some future point. Even in a democratic process, when the team votes on one initiative versus another, there may be an element of win–lose between sides. In such cases, both sides should try to depersonalize the decision as much as possible and get on normally with their work as soon as the decision has been made.

11.7.5 Other strategies—agreeing to disagree, giving ground, arbitration

Agreeing to disagree is one way of attempting to avoid conflict. In a team, for instance, there might be a matter of principle on which one particular team member cannot agree with the other members. In such cases, the individual might agree to proceed on the basis that his objection is noted in the team minutes. If it is a question of judgement, which subsequently is shown to be in his favour, he at least has the satisfaction of saying, 'I told you so!'. At other times disagreement might be more widespread—for instance, on the basic direction that the team should take. It is best if the team can thrash out a way forward that everyone can agree on, but if this proves impossible within the time available, then a vote may be necessary and a pragmatic 'agree to disagree' approach taken. The team can then proceed. It is vital that if this approach is taken, the 'losing' side puts its differences aside after the decision and puts their full effort into supporting the (overall) team decision.

Winning every argument is not always a good idea. It will drain your reserves and take time. Sometimes you might not really value the outcome very highly. This could be the basis for some negotiation; if the other party values an outcome in their favour, then you could attempt to trade this for something that you want. People—in this case, your team members—often prefer others that they can negotiate with, rather than those who adopt a 'take it or leave it' approach.

One other method you may wish to consider is called 'arbitration'. Arbitration is commonly used to solve industrial disputes between unions and management when they cannot agree. The process depends upon having someone who is neutral acting as the 'arbitrator'. Both sides must respect and trust this person. In arbitration, both sides put their case to the arbitrator, who then makes the decision. Both sides must abide by what the arbitrator says. Sometimes at university a tutor may agree to take on the arbitrator role—but it does not have to be an authority figure, as long as both sides agree in advance to respect the decision.

11.7.6 Individual conflict competences to develop in teams

Teams give you an ideal opportunity to develop the following competences for your personal development plan:

- diplomacy;
- negotiation;
- creativity;
- communication;
- empathizing;
- listening.

You will already have covered these as skills areas in previous chapters, with the exception of creativity, which follows in Chapter 12.

 Activity 11.5 Conflict

Discuss the following statements with your team members. Then read the following section on team behaviours and update your discussion as necessary.

1. I prefer to speak only to friends in my team.
2. I do not like speaking to people in my team that I do not get along with.
3. It is necessary to speak to everyone within the team.
4. Mistakes are acceptable.
5. We learn from our mistakes.
6. Mistakes should be hidden.
7. Conflict can be beneficial in certain situations.
8. After a group decision we should all accept what has been agreed.
9. We should support group decisions even if we personally preferred an alternative course of action.
10. If we do something good as a group we should be quiet about it.
11. If we do something good as a group we should boast about it.
12. If we do something good as a group we should celebrate in some way.
13. I like helping other people in my group.
14. Other people in my group may need my help.
15. I expect help from other people in my group.
16. I may need help from other people in my group.

11.7.7 Team behaviours to adopt

The following team behaviours are recommended ideals to strive for:

- **C**ommunicate with everyone in the team—don't go into cliques.
- **O**penness—adopt a 'no blame culture'.
- **A**gree and move on—and support.
- **C**elebrate success—you deserve it.
- **H**elp each other.

Most of these follow on from the previous discussion and Activity 11.5. Cliques and the no-blame culture deserve a little more explanation.

Cliques

In a 'clique', a number of individuals from the team will tend to talk to each other, to the extent of inadvertently or deliberately excluding other members of the team. When taken to extremes, this can have an adverse effect upon the team: essentially the team is in danger of splitting into two or more sub-groups. The problem is that your team will be assessed on its overall team performance, and this is very likely to suffer. So, whilst it is quite natural to be more friendly with some members than others, you need to think about the overall task the team, as a whole, has to perform: you need to communicate with all team members when you are working on the task.

'No-blame culture'

In a 'no-blame culture', you accept that what you might regard as 'mistakes' will—in fact, *must*—occur at some point. The only way never to make a mistake is to do nothing. But, of course, that is unacceptable. However, one thing a no-blame culture does not equate to is a 'don't care' culture—quite the reverse. What you want to cultivate in your team is an environment where people are open and honest about their work. When things do not go according to plan, the 'mistake' needs to be investigated quite dispassionately; the aim should be to learn as much as possible from what has happened so that you can *improve*. What you are developing is a culture of *continuous improvement*—a quality concept you will come across in management thinking in your programme, as well as in industry.

11.8 Cultural issues

11.8.1 Working with others

Your fellow students may come from countries all over the world, so it is quite likely that you will work in multicultural teams. Also, it is quite likely that in your future career you will spend some of your time in multinational teams or that you will be doing business with people from different countries. You will experience cultural differences between the various people you work with; some of these you will easily accommodate, but others you are likely to find

Activity 11.6   Great Speechmaker: continuation

Please note that to make this example more meaningful, a mix of real-life situations has been used. To some extent these are stereotypical of different cultural behaviours. You should bear in mind that, in any given situation, people will not necessarily fit these stereotypes. Having said this, however, researchers do attempt to draw general conclusions about national cultural characteristics (see Further reading at the end of this chapter). For this activity, read the continuation case study below and make your own notes. You should then try to make connections between your notes and the rest of this section on cultural issues.

Case Study: A Great Speechmaker: continuation

You will recall Skills Example 11.1: A Great Speechmaker—and the team of Anna, Dong, David, Lorna and Jin (Mary). The team started their task well enough, drawing up an agreement as to how they should work together (Figure 11.3) and deciding to choose Nelson Mandela as their great speechmaker (Figure 11.4). However, the team has been experiencing several operational difficulties lately. One of these is that David has started to take more of a leading role as he felt that 'things weren't happening quickly enough around here'. Lorna is fine with this, but Anna feels that he should be more relaxed, as she explained that 'there was plenty of time left' to complete the task. Dong and Jin (Mary) do not say much to the others, but privately they have expressed disquiet to each other at David's approach, which they regard as not very polite and certainly not very team-centred. Another issue is the reluctance of some of the group to ask their tutor in class about any aspects of their task that they do not understand; instead, they have started to ask Lorna these questions after class. At first Lorna was pleased to help her fellow team members, but has recently said to Anna that she does not see it as her job to act as their 'coach'.

difficult to deal with, especially when you first encounter them. As with a lot of things, if you are aware of what to expect you are likely to adapt more easily to the situation—hence this section's advice and suggestions.

11.8.2 **The teacher is always right?**

In some schools and colleges the teaching system can be quite rigid and authoritarian. There may be a much greater emphasis upon recalling facts. There may be the underlying assumption that the teacher has all of the answers and that learning is a matter of transferring these 'right answers' to the minds of students. In such cases, it may be considered rude to ask the teacher questions on the basis that (a) it might suggest that the teacher has not given you sufficient information—that you *should* understand; (b) it is not appropriate, as it might suggest that you are questioning the credibility of what the teacher is saying. If you recognize this approach as characteristic of your own education, please be encouraged to know that tutors will be aware of these differences and will generally support you—but it will still be necessary for you to take some bold steps if your university has a style where it is in fact OK, indeed *desirable*, for you to:

1. ask questions in class if you do not understand—you will not be thought of as disrespectful by your tutor;

2. put forward your own thoughts—for example, in workshops;

3. test theories and ideas openly with other students and with your tutor—in other words to be critical.

11.8.3 Attitude towards time

There are sometimes perfectly natural differences in how people from different back-grounds and cultures regard the passage of time. These differences overlay their natural personalities, so what we are talking about here are general characteristics (see Further reading at the end of the chapter). If you are not aware of these differences, you might think that the other person is either being lazy if they continually arrive late for meetings or, on the other hand, too serious about timekeeping if they accept no deviation what-soever from a schedule. If you feel that your team's assessment grading—and hence your own mark—will be adversely affected by others' time-keeping, this issue can easily become problematic.

There is an old saying: 'When in Rome, do as the Romans do.' As a student you should ac-quaint yourself with the attitude of your university tutors to keeping to deadlines. Of course, your tutor will not mind if you are super-efficient at handing work in on time, but you may have to be careful with other students in your team if you do not want to appear to be too task-driven. However, if you sense that your attitude to work is a lot more relaxed than ei-ther your tutor or your fellow students, then you may need to pay more attention to your time management if you are not to have arguments over time-keeping. This is an area that should be discussed and agreed upon soon after the team has formed (see Figure 11.3, Team agreement).

11.8.4 Group versus individual

The importance of working in teams has already been covered at some length in this chapter. However, you should be aware that studies (Hofstede, 1980) have shown that attitudes towards group work versus working as individuals vary from country to country. This means that some of your team members may be used to working in a group environment, whilst others may not. Moreover, those who view the individual as the central focus may find it hard to adjust their thinking.

11.8.5 Level of risk-taking

Again, this is an area that overlaps a person's personality. We all have different attitudes to-wards the amount of risk we are prepared to tolerate. However, studies (Hofstede, 1980) have shown that there are marked differences between national norms. Perhaps where this becomes most apparent in your university teams is in the goals that you will set yourselves; for instance, do you go for the 'safe option' where you feel that you will obtain an average grade, having done a reasonable amount of work, or do you go for something more ambitious ('too ambitious', the other members of your team might say).

Chapter summary

This chapter has covered a range of practical and psychological aspects of working in teams. To be an effective team member you need skills in both of these areas. In practical terms, you have explored methods for helping your team engage in project work. These have included team agreements, team minutes and project plans. After a while, the mechanics of these will become second nature. The chapter then emphasized the human dynamics—both complex and variable—within any team. You have seen, for instance, the need to incorporate different team roles within your teamwork. You now have a range of strategies to handle difficult situations that may occur within your own teams. Further, you have learnt a common language to use when reflecting, with others, upon your team's performance.

 ## End of chapter exercises

Exercise 1

What factors do you think influence how much time a group spends on the stages of forming, storming and norming? Illustrate your answer with examples.

Exercise 2

Your team has been asked by your tutor to work together on a presentation. After the presentation you will each have to write an individual report, which has two sections: the first section discusses the subject matter of your group presentation, although it allows you to add your own research if you wish; the second section asks you to give an analytical report of how your team worked on the presentation. Your tutor is only going to award marks for your individual report—no marks will be awarded for the presentation itself, although you will receive written feedback. How much do you think it matters if your group performs poorly on the presentation? Discuss.

Exercise 3

Think of a conflict situation that you have experienced within a team (at work or at your university). How was the situation approached by the various team members? How successful was the outcome? Have you learnt anything from this event?

 ## Further reading

For an in-depth discussion of groups and teams read:

Buchanan, D. and Huczynski, A. (2006) *Organizational behaviour: An introductory text.* 6th edn. London: Prentice Hall.

To find out more about Belbin's team roles (note this is a commercial site) go to: http://www.belbin.com (accessed: 24 September 2012).

To read more about communities of practice, you can view Etienne Wenger's website or consult the article by Akkerman, Petter and de Laat. http://www.ewenger.com (accessed: 24 September 2012).

Akkerman, S., Petter, C. and de Laat, M. (2008) 'Organizing communities-of-practice: Facilitating emergence', *Journal of Workplace Learning,* 20(6) 383–399.

To read about the effects of national culture within business, read books by Geert Hofstede, whose original work involved a large-scale study of managers within different countries who worked for IBM. One of his latest books is listed below, or you can access his website.

Hofstede, G. and Hofstede, G.J. (2005) *Cultures and organizations: Software of the mind.* New York: McGraw Hill. http://www.geert-hofstede.com (accessed: 24 September 2012).

Another book to read on national culture is:

Trompenaars, F. and Hampden Turner, C. (1997) *Riding the waves of culture: Understanding cultural diversity in business.* London: Nicholas Brealey Publishing.

For a good mix of theory and practical advice on operating within the work situation in a team:

Verma, V.K. (1997) *Managing the project team: The human aspects of project management: Volume 3.* PA 19073. London: Project Management Institute.

 For further information, please visit the Online Resource Centre at **http://www.oxfordtextbooks.co.uk/orc/gallagher2e/**

12 Creativity and Innovation Skills

◉ Chapter guide

Student viewpoint

You may find that some of your most satisfying and enjoyable moments happen when you are being creative. Some jobs specify creativity skills and allow you to use these abilities fully, whilst there is often an element of creativity required in business or management activities. This chapter supports the view that you can improve your creativity skills through the application of thoughtful processes to problem-solving. One of the creativity techniques you will use in this chapter is mind mapping. Here are some thoughts about mind maps from full-time MSc Management students Elaine, Judith, Jeremy and Ian:

'I used to use them at work (e.g. for managing change in a retail environment) but now that I'm at university I use them constantly for assignments—the visual aspect brings the relationships between issues to life.'

Elaine

'Yes, I used to use them too at work (pharmaceutical industry), for instance in product launches when I had to organize activities around the launch.'

Judith

'I'm more of a lists person myself but I do see the potential benefits to the technique and having listened to Elaine and Judith I think I will try using them as well.'

Jeremy

'It's good to hear how useful they can be in the workplace. I find them good in university for when I've got to pre-read several chapters before a seminar—what I do is to draw a sort of mind map whilst and after I'm doing my reading to summarize the links and content of what I've read.'

Ian

By the end of this chapter you should be able to:

- Explain what is meant by being academically creative
- Show how entrepreneurship is linked to creativity
- Recognize that technological and social contexts are important factors in creativity
- Apply four creative techniques—brainstorming, mind mapping, use of metaphors and attribute listing—to creative problems
- Outline the four stages of creation of a piece of work

Introduction

Good ideas are the starting point for new product development in business—and without new products, organizations would eventually wither and die. Good ideas are what people seek in crises, whatever the context, personal or business. You may well pride yourself upon your good ideas, for your ability to solve your own problems. However, arriving at good ideas isn't easy—you may have heard the saying that 'good ideas are the result of 99% perspiration and 1% inspiration'—usually from someone who has finally created an innovative product after years of toil. Like all good sayings, it has a substantial element of truth and wisdom.

Good ideas are the result of the somewhat elusive 'creativity' process, which requires 'creativity skills'. Business is concerned with 'innovation' skills too. Many business degrees are written with the intention of fostering the development of both creativity and innovation skills. This chapter will lead you through the concepts of creativity and innovation. It will look at these through the eyes of a student seeking personal growth, a university lecturer and an employer.

Chapter outline

There are three areas covered in the chapter. Section 12.1 explores creativity from student, university and employer viewpoints, considering broad understanding and relevance. Section12.2 outlines the influence of various contextual factors—such as technology and the social environment—upon creativity. These opening sections lead into the very practical Section 12.3. This shows you how you might improve your own creative skills by experimenting with a number of creative techniques, including that of mind mapping mentioned in the Student Viewpoint at the beginning of the chapter.

12.1 Student, university and employer viewpoints on creativity

12.1.1 How can developing creativity skills benefit you as a student?

You will notice that up until now there has been no attempt to define 'creativity'. In fact, this is not easy to do! You will spend some time later in this chapter on this very point,

Activity 12.1 Creativity benefits

Write a list of bullet points of the benefits you think you would derive from developing your creative ability further. Include your home and social life, your life at university and your (possible) career.

Commentary on activity

Your list may have included comments such as 'to help me to arrive at better ways of juggling my life/ work balance, to have a sharper or more agile mind, to help me solve problems better', etc. You may have identified it as one of the differentiating factors that marks you out as 'a cut above the rest' when it comes to the job market. You may have found from the above exercise that at times the benefits you listed overlap personal, academic and career needs and aspirations.

What follows next is a discussion of creativity skills from the perspective of a university lecturer and an employer, including a look at entrepreneurs and intrapreneurs. The purpose of these sections is to help you to improve your awareness of how they see creativity and innovation skills so that you can perform better at university and, ultimately, in the work situation.

but for now let us simply define being creative as 'having the ability to come up with a good idea'.

12.1.2 University lecturers' perspectives on creativity

The answer to this will differ from one business school to another, depending upon its bias of academic rigour to commercialism, but in general we might say university lecturers are interested in your ability to:

1. gather and synthesize (i.e. put together various ideas into one) information from a variety of sources;
2. analyse that information;
3. reach conclusions consistent with that information;
4. suggest recommendations for further action;
5. transfer and apply methods of learning process and knowledge from one situation to another;
6. reach novel solutions;
7. reach solutions using both linear (like a flow chart process) and non-linear thinking (for instance, an intuitive thought);
8. reach aesthetically pleasing solutions (these do not have to be complex—indeed, the beauty of some solutions is their simplicity);
9. use unconventional thinking or methods;
10. use creative techniques to assist idea generation and subsequent processing.

The advice here is to picture yourself as the would-be lecturer. What would you want students to present you with in terms of the creativity criteria for the assignment if you were the lecturer? Well, at the very least, that they had complied with items 1–4, above. Then you would be looking for evidence that they had at least gone through the process of using the creative techniques (item 10) you had taught them in class or asked them to look at in their reading. Then you would start looking for items 5–9; not all of them, of course—just one of them might be sufficient. What you would be looking for is something that would make you say (and it's usually out loud!) 'Aha! An excellent idea/method/product!' The more 'Aha!' exclamations the better! There is just one rider to all of this, but it is an important one: in the area of fine art, the beauty of the final product may be all; in business the beautiful idea is one that can be used.

12.1.3 Employers' perspectives, entrepreneurs and intrapreneurs

It is clear from various reports compiled by both employers' associations and via academic fact-finding investigations with employers, that one of the desirable attributes employers say they want from graduates entering their organizations is the capacity to have a 'can-do' attitude. Instinctively, employers talk of the need for graduates to be 'innovative' and 'creative', to be the 'new blood' of the organization with fresh new ideas. They expect enthusiasm and energy, to update the organization with the application of state-of-the-art techniques and perhaps even to propose and implement novel ideas.

 Student tips on skills and employability

A little bit of innovation goes a long way

Jen had taken a summer vacation job working in a tented holiday village on the French Riviera. The village belonged to a large company and was one of a number providing outdoor pursuits to children and families. Jen was put in charge of the village shop and left to make her own decisions. Here, she describes how she transformed *her* shop into the most profitable of the company's shops in France:

Soon after I arrived I made a number of changes—some of them were obvious, others less so. For instance, I noticed that the layout of the merchandise was poor—insufficient goods on show, lack of visible pricing and rather boring presentation. I organized products into categories (e.g. all chocolates together) and revamped their presentation so they were easy to see. Another thing which immediately struck me was that the shop looked more like a shed, as it was plain wood; so, I managed to find some surplus paint and, with the help of a few friends (also staff) I painted it a much more bright and cheerful colour.

After a while I started to notice that the shop was becoming a meeting place for both children and families. I took advantage of this, promoting it as a place to meet by providing some tables and chairs, which I obtained from elsewhere on the site. I soon found that sales started to improve as people drifted in. I experimented with providing some music. I found that I could connect my ipod to the existing speakers. The kids really liked this and were soon requesting their favourite songs. I guess all of these small improvements added up and certainly made the running of the shop an enjoyable experience for me, rather than just a job.

Closely linked to the concepts of creativity and innovation are what we may term 'entrepreneurial' concepts. Consider the following definition for entrepreneurship:

> Entrepreneurship is the ability to create and build something from practically nothing. It is initiating, doing, achieving, and building an enterprise or organisation, rather than just watching, analysing, or describing one. It is the knack for sensing an opportunity where others see chaos, contradiction, and confusion.
>
> (Timmons 1989, p. 1)

Athayde (2009, p. 484) states that in young people attitude is very important and that entrepreneurial potential is indicated by the following:

- Creativity—being imaginative, enjoying different ways of doing things, being good at doing things differently
- Personal Control—the extent to which you believe you have control over events in your life
- Achievement—setting goals, having drive and energy
- Intuition—feeling it is right to go on when dealing with ambiguity and uncertainty
- Leadership—the ability to persuade others to follow.

Thus, although innovation and creativity are essential requirements of entrepreneurship, entrepreneurship is a much broader concept than these alone. O'Connor and Ramos (2006, p. 213) add to the discussion when they propose that would-be entrepreneurs need 'empowering' in the following abilities:

- Differentiating ideas from opportunities
- Understanding that which creates value
- Operating within a team
- Packaging concepts and presenting opportunities
- Integrating fundamentals of marketing, finance and legal requirements for a start-up business.

From a business point of view, entrepreneurs play a vital role in starting new business ventures. They are visible; often regarded as almost heroic figures (think of Richard Branson and Alan Sugar). Businesses need entrepreneurs. In line with this, some business courses now incorporate enterprise and entrepreneurship within their curricula.

The extent to which entrepreneurs can be 'trained' on business courses is a subject of fierce academic debate, with adherents on either side. Athayde (2009, p. 481) cites the work of Gibb, as saying, 'enterprise skills are not fixed personality traits but can be learned and developed through experience'. Wilson, Kickul and Marlino (2007) propose that entrepreneurs need to have self-belief that they can achieve their business goals—that they need to have what Bandura (1997); Bandura and Schunk (1981) called 'self efficacy' (refer back to Chapter 2, Section 2.6 for further discussion). They quote examples of the 'mastery' skills required for the domain of entrepreneurship, allowing students the opportunities to use enterprise skills such as 'feasibility studies, develop business plans and participate in running simulated or real businesses' (Wilson, Kickul and Marlino, 2007, p. 392).

Activity 12.2 Self-efficacy and entrepreneurship

In Chapter 2, Section 2.6, four sources of developing self-efficacy were outlined. (Please refer back to this chapter if you need to refresh your understanding.) These sources are:

1. mastery experiences;
2. vicarious experiences (observing others);
3. social persuasion;
4. physiological/emotional states.

For this in-depth activity you should choose a famous entrepreneur and research their path to success (you may wish to use Internet articles, websites and biographies). You should seek out specific examples of the four sources of self-efficacy development, as listed above, and any other characteristics or abilities, such as those previously mentioned in this section. Ideally, you should share your findings with others and compare notes on what you have learnt.

Intrapreneurs

The concept of *intra*preneurship shares certain traits with *entre*preneurship. A definition is given below:

> Internal entrepreneurs (Intrapreneurs) can ... be understood as co-operating organization members, which innovate, identify and create business opportunities, assemble and co-ordinate new combinations or arrangements of resources so as to yield or enhance value. They initiate actions to fill currently unsatisfied needs and claims or to do more efficiently what is already being done.
>
> (Wunderer, 2001, p. 194)

Entrepreneurs vs intrapreneurs

It is probably true to say that successful entrepreneurs are a fairly select elite, whilst the scope for being a successful intrapreneur is much greater: an organization may perhaps have only one

 Skills Example 12.1 Keith Gill—entrepreneur

Keith Gill is an entrepreneur—a man with drive, determination, a keen sense of where the market is and a willingness to take financial risks. He has already been hugely successful with a previous product range (the Phileas Fogg range of savoury snacks) in the quality snack market, where he successfully competed with the giants in the snack market industry. More recently, he was the co-founder of the Tanfield Food Company, which manufactures and sells top-of-the-range gourmet sealed-in-the-bag meals (such as prime Aberdeen Angus beef, venison, etc.).

At the heart of his creative philosophy are two simple statements:

'Break rules!'
'Challenge convention!'

Mr Gill is clearly not someone who could be accused of being impractical: indeed, his success is down to knowing precisely what the market will deem as desirable and then thinking creatively of how to satisfy that desire—and then having the drive and courage to make that vision a reality. Like many successful entrepreneurs, he loves what he does. For him, making money is a by-product of his success. His motivation stems from challenge and achievement.

Activity 12.3 Challenging conventions

- Consider Keith Gill's two statements about breaking rules and challenging conventions, outlined above.
- For each statement draw up a list of 'fors' and 'againsts'.

entrepreneur, but there is sometimes ample opportunity for internal intrapreneurs. You should note for the purpose of this chapter that both entrepreneurs and intrapreneurs possess a mix of personal, innate qualities and skills, which can be developed over time: a university degree can encourage the former and assist the latter by providing a mix of structured and unstructured opportunities for would-be entrepreneurs and intrapreneurs. As mentioned previously, the focus of this chapter addresses two of the above ingredients: innovation and creativity.

12.2 Creativity: a more detailed understanding

So far, the discussion has considered 'creativity' as though it is something that everyone understands, and moreover something to which we all attribute a similar meaning. However, this is not the case, for as we shall see, 'creativity' may have various meanings.

12.2.1 Personality, product, process, usefulness

First you may note that creativity may be generally linked to three areas: the creative personality, the creative product and the creative process. Thus you might say that Charles Dickens had a creative *personality*, that his novels were the creative *products* of his thinking and writing (the creative *processes*). Put in this way there are obvious links between the three areas, although some would argue that Dickens would still have had a creative personality even in the absence of writing his books—we would simply not have known about it! It's probably true to say that all three aspects are relevant. Some people would add to this the idea of *usefulness* (Sternberg and Lubart, 1999)—for instance, Sir Clive Sinclair's three-wheeled C5 car was certainly innovative, but was of limited use.

12.2.2 The influence of context

Technology

One area that has not yet been considered is the idea that creativity is dependent upon the context. Leonardo Da Vinci's (1452–1519) design for a helicopter, for instance, was of limited application because the *technology* to construct it had yet to be developed (this had to wait until 1842, when the first engine (steam) powered model was built by W. H. Philips, although this was still not full size nor a commercial proposition).

Social environment

Likewise, the *social context* is a key variable. Thus the astronomer Galileo's (1564–1642) assertion that the Earth orbited the Sun (as opposed to the notion that the Sun orbited a stationary

Earth) was refuted for many years by the powerful Church leaders of the Inquisition, to the extent that Cardinal Bellarmine ordered him not to 'hold or defend' this scientific fact (see Further reading for notes).

12.2.3 A more precise definition of creativity

The definition of creativity given below incorporates aspects of personality, product, process, usefulness and context:

> Creativity is the interaction among aptitude, process, and environment by which an individual or group produces a perceptible product that is both novel and useful as defined within a social context.

(Plucker, Beghetto and Dow, 2004, p. 90)

The above statement will be taken as a workable definition for this chapter.

12.3 Improving your personal creativity

12.3.1 Four techniques

Four useful creative techniques are listed below:

1. brainstorming;
2. mind mapping;
3. metaphors;
4. attribute listing.

Brainstorming is a technique that you have probably used before, but it is included here because it is such a useful method. The second of these techniques, mind mapping, has been popularized by Tony Buzan (1996), and you may already have read one of his many books on the technique. You may also have come across similar-looking versions under the headings of 'spider diagrams' and 'rich pictures', which additionally uses small drawings and symbols (e.g. crossed swords might represent conflict). The third technique—metaphors—is a means through which we might view the familiar in an unfamiliar way, and thus helps us break free of our present thought patterns and assumptions. The fourth technique—attribute listing—is a way of charting a product or service in terms of key characteristics—'attributes'—and analysing them individually or in combination. Each of these techniques is discussed in turn.

12.3.2 Brainstorming

Sometimes now referred to as 'thought showers', the practice of brainstorming is simple but effective and generates a high volume of ideas: participants are encouraged (sometimes by a facilitator) to make the group aware of any and every thought they may have on a particular problem/task—these are then immediately transferred, usually in written form, to a communal flip chart, sheet of paper or white board. At this stage, no ideas or comments are barred—no matter how bizarre. Often, comments that would have been laughed off and disregarded take on a new meaning or allow different thinking along the lines of 'what-if?' Of course, the essential pre-requisite for this technique to work is that the group feels that they can, essentially, make fools of themselves! Some people may feel unable to do this. One technique to encourage people to open up is to use so-called 'ice-breakers', whereby participants are encouraged to open up to each other and relax in each other's company.

There are many such techniques for ice-breaking, from the simple idea of asking people to introduce themselves to their 'neighbour', to particular 'fun activity' games. You are left to investigate these. However, one factor that both relaxes and opens the mind to different ways of thinking is the use of humour. The psychology of humour is beyond the scope of this book, but as a rule in creativity, try to encourage its use: a few of us are naturally entertaining (what a wonderful gift!); however if, like me and the majority of people, you could not tell a joke to save yourself, do not despair! What is required is the willingness to play with ideas and to be able to laugh at yourself—only then will you be able to completely let go of the rules and conventions that bind your thinking.

To complete the technique, after gathering together all the ideas and associations (many of which trigger further ideas in others' minds, allowing for a building of concepts), the group must then attempt to make some sort of sense of the mass of notes and scribblings—it is only at this point that rejection occurs and conclusions are reached for the group to subsequently action.

12.3.3 Mind mapping

Drawing on paper is remarkably creative in itself. The apparently simple act of picking up a pencil and beginning to 'free-draw' is one which allows the 'artist' to express ideas, thoughts, feelings. It is something that appears to come naturally to many people, an extension of themselves. Sometimes the artist has a very definite idea in his mind's eye, sometimes only a faintly conscious notion of what will appear. Indeed, some artists will reflect 'in action' and develop their drawing in an organic fashion. The finished drawing remains as the final product of the creative exercise.

Mind maps possess many of the properties of such free-drawing; they help to generate an overall picture that is a visual depiction of ideas and thoughts. The finished drawing remains as a plan and record of those thoughts. Mind maps are typically used to help generate ideas and show the linkage between those ideas.

I use mind maps all the time. I find their use second nature now. This book owes its origins and development, at least in part, to the technique. A typical hand-drawn mind map, tidied up only to the extent that it is now legible, is shown in Figure 12.1. You can buy software to draw mind maps, but one of their benefits is that you can draw them anywhere using just a sheet of paper and a pencil. Mind maps are, first of all, working diagrams; presentability is really only an issue if you wish to use them more formally to show other people your logic.

Figure 12.1 shows a project that concerns the design and implementation of a training course to improve group communication. The group is an organizational one and comprises an office manager, an accountant, a sales manager and an operations team (which itself consists of an area manager, supervisors and operatives).

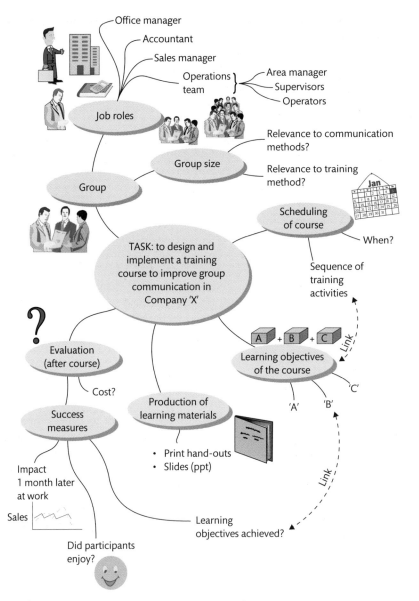

Fig 12.1 Mind map

1. To draw the mind map it is usually best to start at the centre of a blank piece of paper with the overall aim or statement of what you are investigating. Expect your first attempt (at least) to need redrawing, as at this stage you will not know what will emerge.

2. Draw links (usually lines—these may be straight, although curved lines do give the diagram a more organic feel) to associated items, drawing out from the central hub. You will see that I have included links to the group itself, the learning objectives of the course, scheduling of the course, production of materials for the course and evaluation of the course. You may prefer to label along the lines themselves—Tony Buzan does this.

3. From each of these I have then made links to items associated with them, radiating outwards again. I have then noted that there are logical links between learning objectives (which appear both in evaluation and in learning objectives and which may be linked to the sequence in which activities are scheduled to take place), which I have indicated using the dashed two-way arrows. This is something I intuitively do, as I find it helps me, but you will see mind maps in texts that do not do this.

4. Remember: the idea of the mind map is to represent your thoughts and logic on paper, and to extend both of these—do not be afraid to experiment by adding whatever you think is appropriate to the diagram (in this case, additional logic arrows). Add colour, highlight obvious connections, add signs/symbols/cartoon drawings, order of priority— whatever you feel helps you: it's your mind map and if it helps, then it's right!

5. This advice may be all you ever need on mind mapping. However, if you want to go further, then read one of Tony Buzan's various books on mind mapping (Buzan is perhaps currently the most prolific author of mind mapping guides: two of his books are listed in the Bibliography section at the end of the book to get you started on your search for other things he has written.)

12.3.4 Use of metaphors

So, what exactly is a metaphor? Here is a definition:

> The essence of metaphor is understanding and experiencing one kind of thing in terms of another.
>
> (Lakoff and Johnson, 1980, p. 5)

To say that Sir Edmund Hillary and Sherpa Norgay Tenzing were the first to conquer Everest in 1953 is using the image of an epic struggle fought against some powerful foe, of a military victory. In reality, the mountain is an inanimate object, oblivious to the presence of man's intention to climb it. And, yet, the use of such language allows us a 'glimpse of reality' (Koro-Ljungberg, 2001, p. 367): you are very unlikely to breathe the thin air of the Earth's highest point, but through this description you can gain some understanding of the human reward and sacrifice of such an achievement.

Extending this approach, the use of metaphors can help you to understand yourself better and to make more sense of your life experience (Mahlios and Maxson, 1998). Exercise 1 in Chapter 2, 'Looking ahead', on personal development, which asked you to represent how you viewed your life in terms of your own drawings and images, is a good example of metaphors used in this way.

 Activity 12.4 Metaphors

This is a metaphor exercise, sometimes used to 'break the ice' in personal development sessions, and it follows the above theme: 'If you were to choose to be an animal, what sort of animal would you be? Why do you say this?'

A typical metaphor that you might use in everyday life could be:

Are you a Man or a Mouse?

In a similar vein, a saying (in fact, wise sayings and proverbs are full of metaphors) is:

It is foolish to pull the tail of the sleeping tiger.

Thus, metaphors are excellent devices to help you understand and articulate your feelings, as well as to provide insight.

You can also use metaphors with your mind maps. Perhaps the simplest way to do this is to add drawings or other images to the mind map (another technique—rich pictures—depends upon this). For instance, you could represent studying by drawing a pile of books, an unknown by a '?' symbol, a financial consideration by a '£' or a '$' sign, conflict by the use of crossed swords, being happy with a pictogram smiley face, etc. or make up your own drawing. This really energizes your mind maps, and is particularly useful if you want to share your ideas with others.

Finally, do not start thinking that metaphors only apply on the personal front. In the world of business they are everywhere: remember, 'Out there it's a jungle!'. Military metaphors abound (not surprising then that we talk of 'strategy' and 'tactics', and books such as *The Art of War* by Sun Tzu, a Chinese general who lived and fought in antiquity, are still top-sellers in the business books section of many airport bookshops). On a more contemporary note, the ways through which you think of your own organization—for instance, you may feel like you are just part of a huge 'machine', or you may think of the organization as a living organism—have been thrust into the realm of academic debate by the highly influential book *Images of Organization* by Gareth Morgan (1986).

12.3.5 Attribute listing

Attribute listing is a creative technique that has been used extensively in the design of new products and services. At the most basic level, you would start by making a list of what you regarded as a product/service's attributes. These attributes may be broadly categorized as:

- physical;
- mental;
- emotional;
- social.

 Activity 12.5 Machine metaphor

Research some of the classic footage or commentaries of Charlie Chaplin in the silent movie *Modern Times*, as he works on the assembly line—many clips/articles are available online. In what ways is the organization operating as a machine? Is Charlie part of the mechanism of this machine? What message do you think your chosen film clip(s) is trying to give?

Skills Example 12.2   Attributes

Assume, for example, that you are reviewing the operation of a customer services department, which has been set up to handle enquiries and complaints about your company's products—waterproof jackets for walkers and climbers. You have been asked to raise some fundamental questions about the department, what it does and how it might operate in the future. A typical physical attribute is size: in this case, how many people could be employed in the department? A mental attribute might be level of advice given to customers—for instance, basic, intermediate, advanced. An emotional attribute might be level of friendliness versus strictness that you want to convey to customers over complaints. A social attribute might be whether or not you wanted customers' opinions to feed into your new product design, and for them to be registered to receive updates on new products as part of the customer community.

The identification of attributes is a very useful process as it allows you to explore the product or service in new ways. It is easy to use this process in a group brainstorming session. Once you have identified attributes, you can do further things with them. One of these is to go through the following checklist:

- Adapt?
- Modify?
- Magnify?
- Reduce?
- Substitute?
- Rearrange?
- Reverse?
- Combine?

If you apply this to the customer services department in Skills Example 12.2, introducing changes would certainly serve to *modify* or *rearrange* the service in some way. Perhaps the service could be *adapted* to promote sales of new products? Could some attribute of the

 Activity 12.6:   Attributes—design of refurbished doctor's surgery waiting room

Imagine that you are part of a patient focus group due to give recommendations to the architect redesigning your local GP's (doctor's) surgery waiting room. At present, the group has noted that the waiting room is rather bleak, with drab surroundings, fixtures and fittings. There is little to do, other than wait, and children in particular can become noisy and troublesome. Lighting is poor (there is no natural light). There is only one toilet, which has a door within full view of those within the room. The reception area is at one side of the waiting room, again within view and earshot of waiting patients. Sealed specimen samples for testing (e.g. blood, urine, etc.) are also handed in by patients to reception.

   Give suggestions for improvements to the design of the waiting room. Your answer should recognize physical, mental, emotional and social attributes.

service be *magnified* (e.g. number of staff) or *reduced*? Does the company actually need to provide customer advice on its products over the telephone—might it not *substitute* this part of its service by putting detailed information on a website? Why not *reverse* the idea of customer complaints to product improvement and reward customers for good ideas? The last item on the above list—combine—deserves additional discussion.

Morphological analysis

An area that has seen wide-ranging use considers how attributes may be combined in different ways. Originally pioneered by Swiss-American aerospace scientist Fritz Zwicky (Richey, 1998) and extended to computer analysis, it is a powerful technique. However, you can use its main principle—that of investigating different combinations of attributes from a basic matrix. The example shown in Figure 12.2 is for a digital camera. The shaded cells show one possible combination amongst many.

You will note that there is a very large number of possible combinations for even this basic example, and that is why the method has been used with computer programs. However, you may use it more simply as a diagram to look at specific combinations that you would like to investigate further.

Attributes →

Attribute A, e.g. size	Attribute B, e.g. colour	Attribute C, e.g. shape	Attribute D, e.g. operating difficulty level	Attribute E, e.g. level of help	Attribute F, e.g. user
Mini	Silver	Flat/lozenge	Point-and-shoot	Instructions booklet	Beginner
Small	Black	Spherical	Semi-automatic	On-screen	Intermediate
Medium	Red	Box	Basic manual		Advanced
Large	Green	Cylindrical	Basic menu		Professional
	Blue		Advanced menu		

Fig 12.2 Attributes chart (morphological analysis) for a digital camera

12.3.6 **General ways to improve your creativity**

The techniques of brainstorming, mind mapping and metaphors should be helping you to focus and develop your thinking—but there are other, more general ways, which you can use in conjunction with these. This section considers how you use both the left and right sides of your brain and then the concept that the creativity process consists of different stages. By being aware of these stages, you are able to take advantage of the natural way in which your brain works in terms of creativity.

Left versus right brain

One of the popular viewpoints on creative thinking is that the human brain's left and right hemispheres are reserved for different types of thinking: the left hemisphere for logic, reasoning, words and numbers; the right hemisphere for images, imagination, rhythm, colour and intuition. The inference is that 'right-brained' people are more creative; the observation has been made that business schools focus on the left, logical hemisphere. This viewpoint has its origins in the work of a Nobel prize winner, Robert Sperry (1968), who studied the physiology of the brains of hospital patients who had suffered head trauma, with the result that the left hemisphere of their brain could not communicate with the right hemisphere.

However, more recent work has shown that applying Sperry's findings without further refinement to the creativity of 'normal' people is too simplistic, and the view now becoming prevalent is that we use both sides of our brains when we are creative, so that the term 'whole' brain thinking (Buzan, 1989; Mento, Martinelli and Jones, 1999) is perhaps now more appropriate. For instance, an article by Professor John Stein (2007) in the *Independent* states that there are 'four stages in [the] creation of a piece of work':

1. preparation—this equates to initial idea generation, e.g. initial thoughts, gathering information;
2. incubation—this stage is when you take time to mull over your ideas and available information; this may be conscious or sub-conscious;
3. illumination—the stage at which things fit together and make sense;
4. verification or execution—actually putting your idea(s) into action.

At the preparation stage, the mind must be allowed to roam free (favouring the right hemisphere), whilst in the last stage of verification (for instance, committing your ideas to a plan and schedules), it must be ordered and disciplined, thus favouring the left, more logical hemisphere. Incubation and illumination are curious phases—largely they occur without our conscious attention: incubation is the process through which we mull thoughts over subconsciously—'sleeping on an idea' is a prime example of this. Finally, remember to make use of all of your intelligences (refer back to the concept of multiple intelligences in Section 1.5); this is not only to appeal to the intelligence preferences of others, but also to enrich your own creative thinking.

Chapter summary

This has been a wide-ranging chapter. You have been on a journey that has raised your awareness of the importance of creativity and innovation to academics, industrialists and students alike. You have worked through four specific creativity techniques, as well as some more general methods. Hopefully, you appreciate a little more how your own mind works and are more ready to explore and be 'playful' in your thinking—and more ready to trust your intuition or even to do nothing (!) while your mind works subconsciously. You have seen how the context in which you work is interrelated with yourself or your team; you may be able to use this knowledge to promote your own creative development or the creativity of your team.

 ## End of chapter exercises

Exercise 1

Discussion question: 'In what sense can you relate creativity to the following:

a. designing a logo or sign;

b. a sales campaign to sell baby powder to women;

c. a road-side-assistance mechanic fixing a car;

d. a Picasso painting?'

Exercise 2

Draw a mind map showing your thoughts on the next stages of your personal/career development. Extend some of the branches to the next level(s).

Exercise 3

Refer back to Skills Example 12.2, the customer services department for the company selling waterproof jackets to walkers and climbers. Refer also to Figure 12.2 and draw up an attributes chart for the customer services department, showing the various attributes of its service.

 ## Further reading

The following books are recommended for practical advice on creativity techniques:

Buzan, T. (1989) *Use both sides of your brain*. 3rd edn. New York: Plenum.

Buzan, T. (1996) *The mind map book: How to use radiant thinking to maximise your brain's untapped potential*. New York: Plume.

De Bono, E. (1990) *Lateral thinking: Creativity step by step*. New York: Harper Collins.

The article below considers different types of creativity. It is referred to in the Online Resource Centre:

Bleakley, A. (2004) 'Your creativity or mine?: A typology of creativities in higher education and the value of a pluralistic approach', *Teaching in Higher Education*, 9 (4), pp. 463–475.

You will find many websites on creativity. Some of them are little more than advertising sites for training courses and books, although you may still find some useful information. Here are two of the more useful sites:

Official site of Edward de Bono, one of the most well-known experts on creativity, can be found at: http://www.edwdebono.com (accessed: 4 August 2012).

According to it's own strapline, 'Innovation Tools is the world's largest website focused on business innovation, creativity and brainstorming.' This can be found at: http://www.innovationtools.com (accessed: 4 August 2012).

If you are interested in further information on Leonardo da Vinci, please refer to: http://www.bbc.co.uk/history/historic_figures/da_vinci_leonardo.shtml (accessed: 4 August 2012).

For information on early helicopter history please refer to: http://www.aerospaceweb.org/design/helicopter/history.shtml (accessed: 4 August 2012).

For information on Galileo and the controversy of Earth/Sun orbiting please refer to:

Machamer, P. (2009) 'Galileo Galilei', *The Stanford encyclopedia of philosophy* (Summer edition).

Zalta, E.N. (ed.) (2009) [online] Available at: http://plato.stanford.edu/archives/sum2009/entries/ galileo (accessed: 4 August 2012).

 For further information, please visit the Online Resource Centre at **http://www.oxfordtextbooks.co.uk/orc/gallagher2e/**

13 Carrying Your Skills Forward

◉ Chapter guide

Student viewpoint

I asked various first, second and third year part-time management students the question:

How important is it for you to keep on developing skills/knowledge after you complete your degree?

Here are some of their replies:

'Perhaps the main focus is to incorporate skills and knowledge in such a way that they will improve my workplace performance.'

William

'I feel that is important … as it will help me to adapt to constantly changing working environments … it leads to a broadened future, allowing greater change in life.'

Philip

'Extremely important [for me] to continue developing IT skills, project management skills … possibly leading to a Master's degree and doctorate.'

Linda

'Very important. I am considering joining the NHS graduate programme. … I have not ruled out going on to a postgraduate degree.'

Karin

'Assertiveness and organizational skills are very important to me. I'd like to continue improving them.'

Maureen

➔ By the end of this chapter you should be able to:

- Outline typical training/work activities that further develop the skills you have learned at university, as described in this book
- Focus on the importance of communication skills in the world of work

Introduction

As we have already discussed, there are two main reasons for learning skills at university: one of these is to provide you with study and personal skills, which you will use throughout your course; the other is to provide you with the basis for skills development in your future career. The purpose of this concluding chapter is to encourage you to think more deeply now about your personal development whilst at university, and how you might tailor your present development goals to your future career. You will be shown typical examples of the activities and skills you may be engaged in at work, within a business or management environment.

Chapter outline

The focus for the chapter is in carrying forward the skills you will develop during your programme of study into your first job after university. It thus revisits each of the chapters covered in the book and shows examples of how each set of skills could be used in the work situation.

13.1 Developing skills in your first job after university

Your graduation is likely to be a significant personal milestone. At this point you will possess the qualification to allow you entry to higher-level career opportunities. You will have gained considerable knowledge and skills during your course. However, it is worth noting that employers are likely to recruit you for your future potential as much as for your current abilities. You still have a lot to learn in their eyes. In fact, many employers welcome this, because they want you to learn how they do things in their organization—their culture. In terms of management development, Pedler, Burgoyne and Boydell (2007, p. 22) suggest there are 11 essential qualities, which can be grouped into three major categories: first, 'basic knowledge and information', which concern the profession and the organization; secondly, 'skills and attributes', which include social skills and problem-solving skills; and finally, thinking ('meta') skills, which include creativity and the ability to realize when to learn a skill and when to use other people's abilities.

You will appreciate that the first of these categories—basic knowledge and information—is one where you are likely to need substantial development. You may have basic facts concerned with business theory, obtained during your degree studies, but you are unlikely to know much about the organization you have just joined, or have detailed know ledge of its particular industrial/commercial sector. The other two categories for managerial development—'skills and attributes' and 'meta skills'—share much in common with the skills you have been developing already within this book. However, the point is that you will go on developing them in your new workplace. Of particular attention are social skills and carrying forward your own learning skills.

The rest of this chapter will consider typical areas of development, which you might be involved with during your first year in your new organization. Some of these experiences will be planned, others will occur in an unplanned way during the natural course of your work activities. We will refer back to previous chapters in the book by considering 'carrying forward' all the skills covered. Throughout this section we will use the (fictional) learning journal of Sam Blixen, who you may recall from Chapter 4 on communications was the graduate recruited to the role of Business Development Manager for Green Vale 'n' Dale Recycling. The journal will follow his learning journey during his first six months at Green Vale 'n' Dale. The format of the journal is according to Figure 13.2.

13.2 Carrying personal development skills forward

13.2.1 Induction training

When you join an organization you will probably go through a series of processes designed to familiarize you with your new workplace and to give you sufficient skills and knowledge to enable you to begin your work. Sometimes these processes will have a different primary motive—for instance, your job interview(s) will be biased towards the selection process, but you will probably have the opportunity to ask questions about the organization and you may be given a tour of the operations. At other times—for instance, your 'induction'—you will attend a company briefing session, which is designed solely for the purpose of giving you relevant information on the company and its procedures.

You may be fortunate enough to be employed by an organization that makes a serious commitment to your development. In such cases, you can expect your first weeks or months to be devoted to a particular training programme. Some companies may refer to this as 'induction training', although you should be aware that other companies only use this term for familiarization with procedures and staff during the first day or days of your employment. In general, the more senior your new job, the more likely it is that you will undergo a prolonged 'induction' training. This might consist of sitting alongside experienced staff and picking up skills directly from them; it might involve attendance at specific training events (for instance, in sales techniques or product information); it may consist of working in various parts of the company to gain familiarization with how the 'parts' of the business (for instance, marketing, sales, operations) work together. If you are on an industrial placement you may be involved in a similar process.

Finally, if you are fortunate, you will be allocated an effective personal mentor. This person(s) will help you to adapt to your new environment and will be there to offer practical and perhaps emotional support when you need it. Figure 13.1 shows a schedule of initial training (induction) for Sam Blixen. This has been designed to familiarize him with the major aspects of the company. The training schedule is not shown here as a model plan; however, it does show some of the ways through which new starters may gather experience within an organization. The training has not been specifically tailored to him at this point, although the HR director has talked to the managing director about the role of business development manager. Together they have designed a series of experiences over the first six months that they feel are likely to be beneficial to a new starter in this post. The reviews in the process are intended to feedback Sam's progress and allow for possible changes to his induction training.

Sam's first entry in his learning log (Figure 13.2) follows the meeting with Green Vale 'n' Dale's HR manager to discuss his training and development during his first six months with the company.

13.2.2 Planned development versus self-directed learning in the workplace

As you can see from the example, Sam Blixen is about to embark upon a six-month induction training programme. The design of such training programmes need not concern us, as

Weeks →																				
ACTIVITY	1	2	3	4	5	6	7	8	9	10	11	12	13	14	15	16	17	18	19	20
Meeting with HR director to discuss induction training	▨																			
General overview of the company, inc. Health and Safety	▨																			
Operations department—work experience		▨	▨	▨																
Sales department—work experience						▨	▨	▨												
Finance department—work experience									▨											
Progress review points					x			x	x							x				
Working at Head Office on various projects (*agreed with MD)												▨	▨		▨	▨	▨	▨	▨	▨
National recycling exhibition—NEC, Birmingham						2 days														
Company executive training programme—London														week						

Fig 13.1 Induction training schedule: Sam Blixen (Business Development Manager, Green Vale 'n' Dale)

they will be left to the HR manager. Hopefully these planned events will help you develop the necessary competences in the workplace; however, this should not stop you from setting your own, additional objectives and being on the look-out to pick up any useful knowledge or skills on an everyday, informal basis. Sometimes your most important learning comes

LEARNING JOURNAL Sam Blixen	
Date: 5th January 2013	
What was critical incident concerned with?	Meeting with HR manager to discuss my first 6 months' training and development plan
Details of what happened	I was told that I would go to Cardiff operations site, working alongside site manager. Then I would work in Sales and Finance departments. I would then stay at Head Office for remainder of time, working on specific projects. I would also attend specific training events (finance course and exhibition). I was asked for my ideas. Told to start a learning journal. This is my first entry.
My initial thoughts	Training seems appropriate. Should help me.
My initial feelings	Good to feel valued like this.
What skills/behaviours did I use?	Listening. Showed interest. Thought of additional ideas for my training—however, managed to persuade HR manager of only one of these.

Fig 13.2 Learning journal: Sam Blixen, 5 January 2013

Performance rating of my skills/behaviours (1 poor–5 excellent)	Listened quite well–3 (still confused a little with some new terminology) Persuasion–2
Confidence rating of my skills/behaviours (1–5)	Listening–quite confident that I will be able to follow conversations with these people–3 Persuasion–fairly confident–I think my performance will improve–3
What have I learnt?	This company likes a planned approach to training. It takes it seriously. They will allow me to contribute but will not always agree with me. I must be patient.
What will I do differently next time?	Reasonably happy with my approach but perhaps I will try to think of likely questions in advance of the next training/review meeting.

Fig 13.2 Continued

from events that no one could predict. An example of this is shown in Figure 13.3–Sam's learning journal extract on the day he was working alongside Simon, one of the lorry drivers.

13.2.3 Ongoing appraisals and personal development

Induction training is designed to give you familiarity with your new job. After this you will receive regular appraisals, usually by your line manager. This may continue throughout your working life! Part of this process is to review your recent performance; another part is to consider your personal development and training needs. In terms of your personal development, you may have a personal development plan—much like the ones you will use in your

 Activity 13.1   Sam Blixen

You will recall that at the beginning of the chapter you read about the skills and attributes that employers are looking for in their graduate recruits. Can you detect any of these in Sam Blixen, based upon his two learning journal accounts, Figure 13.2 and Figure 13.3?

LEARNING JOURNAL: Sam Blixen	
Date: 20th January 2013	
What was critical incident concerned with?	Accompanying Simon today (one of the lorry drivers). We had to collect a load of wastepaper from a printing company in Bristol. Argument with car driver.
Details of what happened	Printing company located in narrow, busy street. We were just about to park the lorry when a car sped past us and parked in the space we were aiming for. Simon politely asked him to move as we had to collect material and we would otherwise block the road to traffic. An argument ensued between the car driver and Simon. Simon was getting angry. I tried to calm both of them down but was not very successful. Eventually the car driver left but was very unhappy and threatened to phone our Head Office.

Fig 13.3 Learning journal: Sam Blixen, 20 January 2013

My initial thoughts	People can be so petty! It would be easy to give the company a bad name by getting into such arguments with the general public. Why doesn't the printing company have a dedicated loading area? Driving a lorry isn't an easy job when this happens!
My initial feelings	Angry when the driver zoomed in front of us. A bit nervous at one point when it looked like there might be a fight. Felt that we were right and the driver was wrong.
What skills/behaviours did I use?	Communication and persuasion—tried to calm both Simon and car driver.
Performance rating of my skills (1 poor–5 good)	Not very good—2.
Confidence rating of my skills (1–5)	I need more practice. I'd rate myself a 2 at calming people down.
What have I learnt?	- People sometimes don't think about the practicalities of getting rid of their wastepaper—it might be our business but it's not theirs. - Lorry drivers are company ambassadors—our contact with the general public. - The situation can force us into a corner. - People (including myself) can't always control our emotions.
What will I do differently next time?	Might not do anything differently in a similar situation but will have a talk with the Operations manager about this and other similar cases. May table this as a general issue for discussion at area managers' meeting. Possible vetting procedure when we take on a new contract with customer. Also possible implications for customer service training for drivers.

Fig 13.3 Continued

studies. This plan may have been agreed with someone from Human Resources or it may have been the result of a discussion with your line manager. In either case, the intention will be to set out a planned development for you, perhaps over the next six months or year. You will be monitored against development targets. You may be asked to keep a learning journal. Again, you will see that this approach is not so very different from what you are being asked to do in your studies.

13.3 Carrying communication skills forward

Good communication is the lifeblood of any organization. Any new employee must learn how communication works within the organization and also how the organization communicates externally to its customers and others. Although it will be an advantage to the newcomer to have worked in the same industry in their previous job role, each organization has a unique history and work culture—its own way of doing things. Just as importantly, each workplace is unique because the people working within it are unique; it takes time to get to know who the key 'players' are and how both formal and informal groups communicate. Induction training, mentioned previously, is designed to give you some familiarity with your new job and the people you will be working with. You may then wish to make a conscious effort to extend your communication contacts within the organization, external parties linked to your job, and to your professional and personal contacts; this process is referred to as 'networking' and is discussed further in Section 13.3. Following on from this, attention is given to email, one of the most common forms of communication for both internal and external organizational communication.

13.3.1 **Networking**

Making contacts with people for the purpose of sharing information is sometimes called 'networking'. It is something that you do naturally—for instance, your circle of friends may be described as your 'social network'. In the organization it is very useful to be able to contact a wide number of people; you might want to ask them for their advice; they might wish to ask for your help. Good networking skills allow you to be aware of what is going on. And, as they say, knowledge is power—so being a good networker gives you access to information that you may find extremely useful, allowing you to perform your role more effectively. You might also have the ear of people who can make decisions—as the saying goes, 'It's not what you know, it's who you know'. Some people frown on using personal contacts in this way. However, if there are two equally competent candidates applying for the same promotion, the candidate with the higher profile and better contacts often has the edge. In terms of the workplace, there is a range of networking possibilities that you may wish to develop. You might wish to consider these as either internal or external networks.

Internal networking

Consider the example of Sam Blixen. By spending time (Figure 13.1) in the operations, sales, finance and head office of Green Vale 'n' Dale, he will have the opportunity of building up his own circle of contacts within the company. Other likely networking opportunities are scheduled meetings with others, including line managers and senior managers. Informal networking also happens frequently; venues at work include the company cafeteria, coffee shop, gym and around the drinks machines.

 Skills Example **13.1**   Networking

You will see that Sam Blixen has been scheduled to attend a recycling exhibition at the National Exhibition Centre in Birmingham—this will give him the chance to talk to others who work in his industry. He has also been booked on a course for 'executive managers'. He will not know who else will be attending this (although he should be able to obtain a list of delegates while he is there), but if he is a good networker he will be ready to add names to his personal list of contacts.

 Activity **13.2**   Career mind map

Draw a mind map of possible career contacts, with yourself at the centre.

External networking

Depending upon your job, you will be expected to build up a circle of business contacts. Opportunities for this may include the following:

- visits to customers or clients;
- trade exhibitions;
- professional bodies events (e.g. chartered institutes);
- sales promotions;
- training events;
- site visits;
- invitations to product launches;
- company hospitality events (sports, dinners);
- awards ceremonies.

13.3.2 **Email skills**

Let us consider one type of electronic communication: email. In doing so, we will raise issues relevant to other types of e-information, which time and space do not allow us to consider in this book. This is appropriate for, as Byron (2008, p. 324) tells us:

> Email ... is presently the dominant form of electronic communication in the workplace, and many of the theoretical arguments presented may be applied to other electronic media used at work, such as instant messaging or collaborative electronic technologies.

Email has certain characteristics that separate it from face-to-face communication. The most obvious of these, as mentioned, is the lack of visual and audio cues (facial gestures, tone of voice). This may not be important for factual information or non-contentious issues, but it is a key component of messages with personal and emotional overtones. (The use of emotions—such as smiley/sad faces—hardly replaces the complexity required to adequately convey emotion, and their use may be seen as childish or unprofessional.) Secondly, it tends to be used as an ongoing series of sent and received messages spread out over time; the term 'asynchronous' (Friedman and Currall, 2003, p. 1327) is used to describe this. The sender or receiver can decide when to send or open their message. This has several implications: structurally it is not possible to interrupt the message (as in conversation) or ask for feedback as the message progresses; because it is technically possible to send a message very quickly there is the (often unrealistic) expectation that a reply should be equally fast.

From a more psychological viewpoint, there is the opportunity for the reader to dwell on the received message and to let imagination take over. Friedman and Currall (2003, p. 1339) use the term 'ruminate' to describe a mentally unhealthy tendency to do this to excess. If this 'rumination' is combined with an individual's tendency to always think the worst of any possible outcome (the term 'catastrophize' describes this well!), then the door is open to fear. And fear, as we have already warned, is a very potent barrier to communication: it locks the individual into instinctive defence mechanisms, blocking reasoned response (Goleman, 1996).

In fact, the potential problems with email may go even deeper than the associated barriers to communication just mentioned: Friedman and Currall (2003, p. 1326) raise the spectre of 'email communications that had spun out of control' and which can actually lead to an *escalation* of conflict. They point to the exaggeration of communication barriers such as message ambiguity and dislike. Further, they suggest that people are less restrained by social niceties and can become increasingly aggressive, even threatening, in an ongoing tit-for-tat escalation of exchanges. They say that in face-to-face conversation we have the ability to defuse potential conflict by interrupting the other person in mid-message. In emails, we can simply continue. In fact, we can build up a 'case', which catalogues many points.

 Activity 13.3 Netiquette

One of the problems with email is that there is no formally recognized format for sending messages in terms of their politeness or etiquette ('netiquette'). Beginnings and endings of emails are particularly troublesome. There are some tricky questions:

- What words do you use to start or end an email?
- How will it sound to the other person?
- Do I just copy their style?

There are no definitive answers to these questions; much will depend upon who you are writing to, in what context and how well you know them. For the sake of this exercise, assume that you are writing to someone who is a colleague (rather than a close friend) in your university or organization about a work-related matter.

a. Comment on the appropriateness of the following email introduction wordings and what they 'say' to you:

> *Hi*
>
> *Hello*
>
> *Dear (first name)*
>
> *Dear Mr/Mrs/Miss/Ms (family name)*
>
> *Dear colleague*
>
> *Nothing—straight to the message*
>
> *First name.*

b. Comment on the appropriateness of the following email exit/end wordings and what they 'say' to you:

> *Regards, (first name)*
>
> *Kind regards, (first name)*
>
> *Cheers, (first name)*
>
> *Yours, (first name)*
>
> *Yours truly, (first name)*
>
> *Yours faithfully, (full name)*
>
> *Nothing*
>
> *First name*
>
> *Full name*
>
> *Initial of first name, e.g. J.*

Byron (2008) talks of the 'miscommunication characteristics' of email and says that receivers often interpret neutral or negative messages as more negative than they actually are and interpret positive messages as less positive. Further, he points out that these misinterpretations are unlikely to be corrected.

Drowning in email? (Or 'But I sent you an email! ...')

As Byron (2008, p. 313) points out 'employees receive a large volume of emails and consequently read them quickly', and can easily miss important parts of the message. This might be the least of it: a manager who takes a week's holiday (or is absent due to illness) can easily be confronted with a hundred or more emails upon his return. Under such circumstances, the issue is not one of how quickly to read but *whether* or not to read. The danger is that you will miss a vital email if you use this strategy. Also, emails put to one side can easily be forgotten.

Implications for the use of email

The following is tentatively suggested as guidelines from the above:

1. Accept that email is essential for organizational life and can be very useful but ...
2. Use email predominantly for factual information.
3. Keep messages focused.
4. Try to reply to emails promptly once opened.
5. Do not rely on an email as being the only instance of conveying a vital message.
6. Try not to use emails for tricky personal or emotional messages.
7. If you do use emails (especially with those who you do not know very well, or those who you do not particularly like) be aware of their negative characteristics.

13.4 Carrying critical research skills forward

No one tells you in the 'real world' why your business is doing well or why it is experiencing problems. It is not like your studies, when you've been given an example of a poor set of accounts in a finance module—in such a case, it is more than likely that the problem has a financial cause. The reality is that many problems in business are not easy to diagnose; some may have multiple causes. The real skill is thus in asking the right questions, rather than immediately looking for solutions. You will recall that this questioning lies at the heart of the critical approach.

One of the areas that management is constantly striving to improve is quality. This applies not just to products but to customer service. Customer complaints are often rooted in quality problems. Quality improvement groups are now quite common in large companies. They seek to ask the right questions in the first place and try to relate cause to effect.

Student tips on skills and employability

Using newly acquired university skills in the workplace

Steve is studying part-time for his business degree. He works in a large NHS hospital, where he is in charge of a team of technicians who have responsibility for the maintenance of sophisticated medical equipment (including MRI and X-Ray machinery). He has recently been promoted to this position, from within the team. Here, he relates how he has used what he has learnt about SWOT analysis from his degree studies (used in Exercise 3 in Chapter 8; also see Further reading at the end of this chapter) to his own work situation.

> When I began my degree we looked at different management tools that can be used within the workplace. Whilst we went through the process and completed assignments I was sceptical that anyone in the 'real world' would actually use such tools. However, recently at work I was invited to join a Research and Development group which was to produce an overall vision for my work department. Those invited included senior managers, directorate managers and consultants and we were all put into mixed groups. Lo and behold, the tool we initially used was SWOT analysis! Knowing how this and other tools worked allowed me to be greatly involved within the development group and key suggestions put forward were used within their vision statement. Without this knowledge gained at university I would have been like a fish out of water and a peripheral player. Knowing what I was talking about also gave me the confidence to put forward suggestions and debate them, something I would not have felt able to do in the past.

13.5 Carrying reading skills forward

In his new job, Sam Blixen will be glad that he spent time in his studies improving his reading skills. He will be confronted with a mass of information. He will need to use his SQ3R techniques: survey, question, read, recall (note-take, etc.) and review. Here are some examples of the types of information that he will read:

- company brochures/sales literature;
- quality manual;
- health and safety information;
- product/operations information;
- company financial reports;
- industrial journals;
- financial newspapers;
- industry/market reports concerning facts and statistics;
- minutes of meetings;
- internal reports.

 Activity 13.4 Job sector research

Carry out the SQ3R technique on a job sector you are interested in. Include some of the above sources of information.

13.6 Carrying writing skills forward

Perhaps the most common form of writing you will have to do at work concerns reports. These may vary in length. Often you will be required to write rather brief, succinct reports, as busy managers do not have much time to read lengthy documents. This is a case of thinking carefully about who your reader is and writing accordingly. Many (necessarily) long reports are accompanied by an 'executive summary', which gives a condensed account with the main points highlighted. Here are a few examples of different types of reports:

- manager's operations report;
- area manager's monthly report of sales figures;
- financial manager's report on annual profit/loss for the company;
- feasibility study of new proposal;
- customer feedback report.

Writing letters is yet another writing activity. Examples might include letters to:

- customers/clients;
- staff;
- contractors;
- utilities companies (electricity/telephone/water/gas).

A brief guide to typical letter layout is shown in Figure 13.4.

Another area of writing involves company documentation, for instance:

- instruction manuals;
- quality procedures;

Your address
Date

Title and name of person you're writing to
Their address

Dear Ms/Mr/Mrs (insert family name)
Topic of your letter in bold
Main body of your letter

Yours sincerely
Signature
Your name

Fig 13.4 Typical letter layout

> **Personal details**
> Name
> Address (home and college address if different)
> Telephone number (home/mobile/college if applicable)
> Email address
> Personal profile—a brief summary of who you are and skill competences
> **Education and qualifications**—start with most current first, including if you are currently studying and when you are due to finish
> **Employment history**—starting with most recent first and a brief summary of each job
> **Any other skills, achievements or training**
> **Interests or pastimes**
> **Referees**

Fig 13.5 CV structure

Source: Reproduced by permission of Oxford University Press

 Activity 13.5 Your CV

Is your CV up to date? Revise it in line with either the framework given above or another credible model.

- company brochures;
- company magazines.

One document that you will need to update is your CV. Figure 13.5 shows the structure given by the *Compact Oxford English Dictionary for Students* (2006, pp. 66–7) in the section 'Effective writing for college and career'.

13.7 Carrying presentational skills forward

Giving presentations at work is quite common, especially for supervisors and managers. Of course, they are not always called *presentations*, but that is what they are. Perhaps the most usual type of presentation is the briefings that supervisors give to staff. These might be given each day, or be reserved for weekly/monthly events. Briefings may be quite to the point and limited to giving information and instructions, or they may give scope for staff to feedback. Other types of presentation include giving a sales or technical talk to customers and training members of staff. You will probably have to give a presentation if you apply for a job or a promotion in your organization.

13.8 Carrying quantitative skills forward

When you take on managerial responsibilities you are expected to be able to handle data of various sorts. Even if your responsibility only extends to running a small team, you may be expected to work within a budget. Budgets may relate to staffing time or to materials or other resources. You will be expected to understand monthly profit/loss reports. You might be given further training and development, for instance attending courses with titles such as 'Finance for non-financial managers'. If you work in sales or marketing you will need to monitor the sales and projected sales of various products. You may be asked to justify proposed expenditure on new equipment. Some of these skills you will learn at work, dependent upon need. Sam Blixen has been given several projects to work on at Head Office during his first six months in the job. Two examples of these are given below:

 Skills Example 13.2 Top 10

Top 10 exercise

The managing director has asked Sam to prepare a report for him, which identifies the top 10 customer accounts in terms of annual sales value, and then in terms of profitability (not necessarily the same thing!). This exercise has a dual benefit: it provides the managing director with up-to-date figures, and just as importantly it provides Sam with an initial idea of who the company's key customers are. Sam will need to use his research, report writing and data presentation skills.

 Skills Example 13.3 Investment appraisal

Investment appraisal for new paper cutting machine

The company is currently collecting remnant paper, which is wound tightly around cardboard tubes. At present the valuable paper is separated from the poor quality cardboard by hand-cutting; this is very time-consuming. A new Swedish machine, a type of circular saw, is now available, which promises to dramatically reduce the time requirements for this operation. Sam has been asked to assess the case for buying one of these machines in terms of finance and production. This 'investment appraisal' will then form the basis for the decision as to whether or not to purchase. Sam will need to use his quantitative skills to evaluate the cost/benefit of the new machine. He will also need to use his data presentation skills.

13.9 Carrying team skills forward

In the work situation you will often be required to work in teams—either as a team member or as a team leader. Such arrangements may reflect how you work on an everyday basis or they may be temporary; for instance, when you are part of a project team. You may also work as part of a team that does not communicate face-to-face, that may be geographically widespread—a so-called 'virtual team'.

Organizations are keen to promote teamworking skills; some have specific training events to encourage it. An element of competition between teams is sometimes injected into work. Team performance may attract special team bonuses and a mention in the company

Skills Example 13.4   Quality

Sam has been asked to take a lead role in implementing a quality system (an international standard called ISO 9001: 2008) across Green Vale 'n' Dale. The system is to be implemented in its various regional depots. Sam's job is to work with the managers at each of the depots and liaise with the quality consultant who has been brought in to assist with the project. Sam wants to establish a series of meetings with the managers and encourage them to be effective team players in this quality project. He will need to use his communication and teamworking skills. Also, he will have to be ready to listen to the concerns and feelings of the managers: the most difficult aspect of this task is likely to be persuading the managers to 'buy in' to the new system.

Skills Example 13.5   Team event

Every year a charity run is organized by one of Green Vale 'n' Dale's major clients. For the past five years, Green Vale 'n' Dale has contributed to the sponsorship of this event and has entered teams of runners from its various locations. This year Sam has decided that he will organize a team from Head Office. It turns out to be a fun occasion. It's also a chance to meet staff from other parts of the country. A staff barbecue is held afterwards, hosted by the managing director, who at one stage dons a chef's hat and is photographed smiling broadly with barbecue fork in hand. This is good internal public relations for the company—the photograph will appear in the company magazine; it will demonstrate that senior managers are not purely money-orientated and that they have an interest in the wider community. These senior managers may note that it was Sam who organized the event; this would demonstrate to them his ability to be proactive and to network—transferable skills. This can only be to Sam's career advantage. Sam will also benefit directly by learning organizational skills from the event.

magazine. Charitable events often attract company interest, a by-product being teams of people within the organization working together.

13.10 Carrying creativity skills forward

Certain job sectors thrive on innovation: for instance, fast-moving technological companies (e.g. IT hardware and software); and the fashion industry (clothing, sportswear, shoes). If you work in these sectors and are involved in design, manufacturing or marketing you will constantly be using your creative skills. However, you can use your creativity skills in any organization by using the techniques discussed earlier in this book, such as brainstorming and mind maps, to help you problem-solve and explore new ideas.

'Necessity is the mother of invention'

You can't always be creative on demand. And creativity isn't always something that you seek out—sometimes it finds you. In other words, if you're faced with an unforeseen problem, you may be encouraged to come up with a creative idea. Here is one instance that Sam Blixen experienced:

Skills Example 13.6 Company brochure

Sam Blixen had been given the job of producing a company brochure. He went about the task enthusiastically. Photographs were taken, design agreed and content written. The first batch of 6,000 copies arrived. It was then that someone noticed something was not quite right on the first page, as shown in Figure 13.6—spot the obvious mistake:

Yes, the company name—correct in the logo, incorrect in the headline! At times like this, people blame one another. But it doesn't solve the problem. However, eventually an ingenious compromise was reached which, although not the perfect answer, as it meant additional cost, allowed the brochures to be used. You can see creativity in action below—it's in the idea to add a sticker at the crucial point as though it was a deliberate marketing device, as an update to the brochure (Figure 13.7).

Fig 13.6 Company brochure—with mistake

Fig 13.7 Company brochure—fixed!

Chapter summary

In this chapter you have seen how all the skills that you have been developing at university may be used in your future work situation. You have seen how employers want graduates who have a pro-active, thinking, enthusiastic attitude to work; that they are looking for people who can keep adapting and learning—because that is what it takes these days to survive in business.

This chapter has given you the opportunity to relate the skills that you are currently developing within your programme of study, to those that you will need in the work environment. You may have noted that some of the most important managerial requirements are for the so-called 'soft skills' such as social, team and communication skills—skills that you may find readily transferable from one context to another.

You will have noted that, in all probability, you will continue to develop various skills as part of your continuing professional development.

 ## Further reading

Jobs and careers:

An excellent website to visit for details on student and graduate jobs is TheBigChoice.com, which can be found at: http://www.thebigchoice.com (accessed: 14 August 2012).

Areas covered include advice on part-time work, as well as finding work placements and internships.

Another website, already mentioned earlier in the book, is Prospects, which can be found at:
http://www.prospects.ac.uk (accessed: 14 August 2012).

SWOT analysis:

This was covered briefly in Exercise 3 at the end of Chapter 8. However, this is one technique which you may encounter again, for instance in the Marketing subject area of your degree, as well as in Strategic Management. SWOT is an abbreviation for Strengths, Weaknesses, Opportunities and Threats. Often used as a management tool to consider the strategic viability of an organization/ body with regard to its future plans, it may also be used at other levels (e.g. at a higher level such as government or, conversely, at a personal level). Basic coverage of both types of SWOT are available online at MindTools, at http://www.mindtools.com (accessed: 13 August 2012).

For an in-depth discussion—appropriate to years 2 and 3 of your degree—the following article gives both the historical development of SWOT as a strategic tool and critically appraises its use:

Chermack, T.J. and Kasshanna, B.K. (2007, December) 'The use and misuse of SWOT analysis and implications for HRD professionals', *Human Resource Development International*, 10 (4), pp. 383–399.

 For further information, please visit the Online Resource Centre at
http://www.oxfordtextbooks.co.uk/orc/gallagher2e/

References and Bibliography

A

Adair, J. (1987) *How to manage your time*. Guildford, Surrey, UK: The Talbot Adair Press.

Akkerman, S., Petter, C. and de Laat, M. (2008) 'Organizing communities-of-practice: facilitating emergence', *Journal of Workplace Learning*, 20(6), pp. 383–399.

Amabile, T.M. (1995) 'KEYS: Assessing the climate for creativity', Instrument published for the Center for Creative Leadership, Greensboro, NC, *Journal of Management Studies*, 33, pp. 119-135.

— (1997) 'Motivating creativity in organizations: On doing what you love and loving what you do', *California Management Review*, 40(1), pp. 39–58.

Anderson, J.R. (1990) *Cognitive psychology and its applications*. New York: Freeman.

Anseau, J. (2007) *Rounding and significant figures—Commons Library standard note* [online]. Available at: http://www.parliament.uk/briefing-papers/SN04443 (accessed: 24 July 2012).

Argyle, M. (1993) *Bodily communication*. 2nd edn. London: Routledge.

— and Dean, J. (1965) 'Eye-contact, distance, and affiliation', *Sociometry*, 28, pp. 289–304.

Athayde, R. (2009) 'Measuring enterprise potential in young people', *Entrepreneurship: Theory & Practice*, 33(2), pp. 481–500.

B

Balchin, T. and Jackson, N. (2005) 'Developing students' creativity: Importance of creativity Styles' [online]. Available at: http://www.heacademy.ac.uk/resources/detail/id572_developing_students_creativity (accessed: 4 September 2009).

Bandura, A. (1997) *Self-efficacy: The exercise of control*. New York: W.H. Freeman and Company.

— and Schunk, D.H. (1981) 'Cultivating competence, self-efficacy and intrinsic interest through proximal self-motivation', *Journal of Personality and Social Psychology*, 41, pp. 586–598.

Barbour, J. (2012) 'No time: A physicist's view'. *The Times: Eureka*, 28, pp. 38–39.

Beaver, G. and Jennings, P. (2001) 'Human resource development in small firms: The role of managerial competence', *Entrepreneurship and Innovation*, June, pp. 93–101.

Beitler, M.A. and Mitlacher, L.W. (2007) 'Information sharing, self-directed learning and its implications for workplace learning: A comparison of business student attitudes in Germany and the USA', *Journal of Workplace Learning*, 19(8), pp. 526–536.

Bennett, R. (2002) 'Employers' demands for personal transferable skills in graduates: A content analysis of 1000 job advertisements and an associated empirical study', *Journal of Vocational Education and Training*, 54(4), pp. 457–475.

Belbin, M. (1981) *Management teams, why they succeed or fail*. London: Heinemann.

— (1996) *The coming shape of organization*. London: Butterworth Heinemann.

Berners-Lee, T. with Fischetti, M. (1999) *Weaving the web: The past, present and future of the world wide web by its inventor*. London: Orion Business Books.

The big read: Book of books: The nation's 100 favourite books (2003) BBC. London: Dorling Kindersley Ltd.

BIS: Department for Business Innovation and Skills (2012) *Foresight* [online]. BIS: http://www.bis.gov.uk/foresight (accessed: 19 March, 2012).

Bleakley, A. (2004) 'Your creativity or mine?: A typology of creativities in higher education and the value of a pluralistic approach', *Teaching in Higher Education*, 9(4), pp. 463–475.

Bloom, B. (1956) *Taxonomy of educational objections: Book 1: Cognitive domain*. New York: David McKay Company Inc.

Bolling, A.L. (1994) 'Using group journals to improve writing and comprehension', *Journal on Excellence in College Teaching*, 5(1), pp.: 47–55.

Bolton, P. (2009) *Guide to statistical tables* [online]. Available at: http://www.parliament.uk/briefing-papers/SN5073 (accessed: 24 July 2012).

— (2010a) *How to spot spin and inappropriate use of statistics—Commons Library standard note* [online]. Available at: http://www.parliament.uk/briefing-papers/SN04446 (accessed: 24 July 2012).

— (2010b) *How to understand and calculate percentages* [online]. Available at: http://www.parliament.uk/briefing-papers/SN04441 (accessed: 24 July 2012).

Book2Book (2012) *Press release: Miscellaneous announcements: Dolly Parton announces UK Imagination Library Selection Committee* [online]. Available at: http://www.booktrade.info/index.php/showcomments/65572 (accessed: 25 May 2012).

Boud, D., Keogh, K. and Walker, D. (eds) (1985) *Reflection: Turning experience into learning.* London: Kogan Page.

Boxall, P. (ed.) (2006) *1001 books you must read before you die.* London: Quintet Publishing Ltd.

Boyatzis, R.E., Stubbs, E.C. and Taylor, S.N. (2002) 'Learning cognitive and emotional intelligence competences through graduate management education', *Academy of Management Learning and Education*, 1(2), pp. 150–162.

Boyle, E. (2004) 'Press and publicity management: The Dyson case', *Corporate Communications*, 9(3), pp. 202–222.

Branthwaite, A. (2002) 'Investigating the power of imagery in marketing communication: Evidence-based techniques', *Qualitative Market Research: An International Journal*, 5(3), pp. 164–171.

Bridges, D. (1993) 'Transferable skills: A philosophical perspective', *Studies in Higher Education*, 18(1) pp. 43–52.

Brookfield, S.D., Kalliath, T. and Laiken, M. (2006) 'Exploring the connections between adult and management education', *Journal of Management Education*, 30(6), p. 831.

Brophy, D.R. (1998) 'Understanding, measuring and enhancing individual problem-solving efforts', *Creativity Research Journal*, 11, pp. 1230–1250.

Bryman, A. and Bell, E. (2007) *Business research methods.* 2nd edn. Oxford: Oxford University Press.

Buchanan, D. and Huczynski, A. (2004) *Organizational behaviour: An introductory text.* 5th edn. Harlow, Essex: Pearson Education Limited.

— — (2006) *Organizational behaviour: An introductory text.* 6th edn. London: Prentice Hall.

Buzan, T. (1989) *Use both sides of your brain.* 3rd edn. New York: Plenum.

— (1996) *The mind map book: How to use radiant thinking to maximize your brain's untapped potential.* New York: Plume.

Byron, K. (2008) 'Carrying too heavy a load? The communication and miscommunication of emotion by email', *Academy of Management Review*, 33(2), pp. 309–327.

C

Cannadine, D. (2007) *Winston Churchill: Blood, toil, tears and sweat. The great speeches:* London: Penguin.

Carter, H. (1922) 'Notes, diary and articles, referring to the Theban Royal Necropolis and the Tomb of Tutankhamen'. Oxford: Griffith Institute [online]. Available at: http://www.griffith.ox.ac.uk/gri/4sea1not.html (accessed: 12 May 2009).

CBI/NUS (2011) *Working towards your future: Making the most of your time in higher education.* CBL [online].

Available at: http://www.nus.org.uk/cy/news/news/your-guide-to-better-employability-skills/ (accessed: 28 August 2012).

Chartered Management Institute (2002) 'Graduate key skills and employability'. London: Chartered Management Institute [online]. Available at: http://managers.org.uk/research-analysis/research/current-research/graduate-key-skills-and-employability-2002 (accessed: 25 September 2012).

Chen, G., Donahue, L.M. and Klimoski, R.J. (2004) 'Training undergraduates to work in organizational teams', *Academy of Management Learning and Education*, 3(1), pp. 27–40.

Chermack, T.J. and Kasshanna, B.K. (2007) 'The use and misuse of SWOT analysis and implications for HRD professionals, *Human Resource Development International*, 10(4), December, pp. 383–399.

City of Sunderland College, Directorate of Learning Resources (2010) *Harvard referencing: Student style guide.* Sunderland: City of Sunderland College.

Clanchy, J. and Ballard, B. (1999) *How to write essays: A practical guide for students.* 3rd edn. Melbourne, Australia: Addison Wesley Longman.

Collins, A., Brown, J.S. and Newman, S.E. (1989) 'Cognitive apprenticeship: Teaching the crafts of reading, writing, and mathematics', in L.B. Resnick (ed.), *Knowing, learning, and instruction: Essays in honor of Robert Glaser.* Hillsdale, NJ: Lawrence Erlbaum Associates, pp. 453–494.

Compact Oxford English Dictionary for Students (2006) Oxford: Oxford University Press.

Cotton, J. (1995) *The theory of learning: An introduction.* London: Kogan Page.

Cowan, J. (2006) *On becoming an innovative university teacher: Reflection in action.* 2nd edn. Maidenhead, Berks: Society for Research into Higher Education and Open University Press.

Cracknell, R. (2007) *Measures of average and spread— Commons Library standard note* [online]. Available at: http://www.parliament.uk/briefing-papers/SN04444 (accessed: 24 July 2012).

Cropley, A.J. (2003) *Creativity in education and learning.* London: Kogan Page.

Crystal, D. (2006) *How language works.* London: Penguin Books.

Csikszentmihalyi, M. (1996) 'The new frontiers of happiness: The creative personality', *Psychology Today*, July/August, pp. 36–40.

Cunliffe, A. and Easterby-Smith, M. (2004) 'From reflection to practical reflexivity: Experiential learning as lived experience', in M. Reynolds and R. Vince (eds), *Organizing reflection.* Aldershot, UK: Ashgate, pp. 30–46.

D

Dacre Pool, L. and Sewell, P. (2007) 'The key to employability: Developing a practical model of graduate employability'. *Education and Training*, 49(4), pp. 277–289. Available at: http://www.uclan.ac.uk/information/uclan/employability/careeredge.php (accessed: 13 February 2012).

D'Andrea Tyson, L. (2005) 'On managers not MBAs', *Academy of Management Learning and Education*, 5(4), 2, pp. 235–236.

Daniels, T., Spiker, B.K. and Papa, M.J. (1997) *Perspectives on organizational communication*. 4th edn. Dubuque, IA: Brown & Benchmark.

De Bono, E. (1990) *Lateral thinking: Creativity step by step*. New York: Harper Collins.

Deakins, D. (1998) 'Learning and the entrepreneur', *International Journal of Entrepreneurial Behaviour & Research*, 4(2), Editorial.

Dearing, R. (1997) *The Dearing report*. London: The National Committee of Inquiry into Higher Education [online]. Available at: http://www.leeds.ac.uk/educol/ncihe/docsinde.htm (accessed: 23 November 2006).

DesmoinesRegister (2004) *Roweder, Otto* [online]. Available at: http://www.desmoinesregister.com/article/99999999/FAMOUSIOWANS/41217023/Rohwedder-Otto (accessed: 25 May 2012).

Dewey, L. (1909) 'How we think'. DC Heath and Co., p. 9. Reprinted in Fisher. A. (2001) *Critical thinking: An I introduction*. Cambridge: Cambridge University Press.

DfEE and QCA (1999) '*The National Curriculum: Handbook for primary teachers in England*', London: jointly published by DfEE and QCA, p. 22.

Dight, C. (2006) 'Seniority requires a new set of skills', 5 October. *The Times* [online]. Available at: http://www.timesonline.co.uk/article/0,8171-2387387.html (accessed: 22 November 2006).

Di Vesta F.J. and Gray, S.G. (1972) 'Listening and note taking', *Journal of Educational Psychology*, 63(1), pp. 8–14.

Dollywood.com (2012) *Imagination Library* [online]. Available at: http://www.dollywood.com/learn-about-dollywood/Imagination-Library.aspx (accessed: 25 May 2012).

Dreyfus, H. and Dreyfus, S. (1986) *Mind over machine: The power of intuition and experience in the age of the computer*. Oxford: Blackwell.

Drucker, P.F. (1985) *Innovation and entrepreneurship*. London: Heinemann.

E

Eldridge, K. and Cranston, H. (2009) 'Managing transnational education: Does national culture really matter?', *Journal of Higher Education Policy and Management*, 31(1), February, pp. 67–79.

F

Falzimi, M.W. (2008) 'The greatest thing since Otto Rohwedder', *Archival Ramblings*, 7 July [online]. Available at: http://www.njsmuseum.blogspot.com/2008/07/greatest-thing-since-otto-rohwedder.html (accessed: 27 May 2012).

Fiedler, F.E. (1967) *A theory of leadership effectiveness*. New York: McGraw-Hill.

Fisher, A. (2001) *Critical thinking: An introduction*. Cambridge: Cambridge University Press.

Fletcher, C. and Williams, R. (1985) *Performance appraisal and career development*. London and Brookfield: V.T. Hutchinson.

Freire, P. (1970) *Pedagogy of the oppressed*. Continuum Publishing Company. Reprint, London: Penguin Books. 1996.

Friedman, R.A. and Currall, S.C. (2003) 'Conflict escalation: Dispute exacerbating elements of email communication', *Human Relations*, 56(11), pp. 1325–1347.

G

Gallagher, K. and Watson, G. (2008) *Creating a research-based scenario in a group setting: Carbon footprint campaign*. University of Sunderland's Learning Enhancement Conference. 17 April.

Garavalia, L.S. and Gredler, M.E. (2002) 'An exploratory study of academic goal setting, achievement calibration and self-regulated learning', *Journal of Instructional Psychology*, 29(4), p. 221.

Gardner, H. (1993) *Frames of mind: The theory of multiple intelligence*. New York: Basic Books.

Garland, H. (1983) 'Influence of ability, assigned goals and normative information on personal goals and performance: A challenge to the goal attainability assumption', *Journal of Applied Psychology*, 68, pp. 20–30.

Gentry, W.A., Harris L.A., Baker, B.A. and Britain, Leslie J. (2008) 'Managerial skills: What has changed since the late 1980s?', *Leadership and Organization Development Journal*, 29(2), pp. 167–181.

Gilleard, C. (2006) 'Graduate careers: Bridging the gap between graduates and employers', 13 October. *Independent* [online]. Available at: http://education.independent.co.uk/magazines/article1869024.ece (accessed: 22 November 2006).

Gizowska, E. (2005) 'Greens we don't have to eat', 20 May. *The Times* [online]. Available at: http:www.timesonline.co.uk/tol/life_and_style/health/expert_advice524196.ece (accessed: 5 August 2008).

Gladwell, M. (2001) *The tipping point: How little things can make a big difference*. London: Abacus.

Glaser, E. (1941). 'An experiment in the development of critical thinking. Advanced School of Education at Teacher's College, Columbia University.' Reprinted in Fisher. A. (2001) *Critical thinking: An introduction*. Cambridge: Cambridge University Press.

Goleman, D. (1996) *Emotional intelligence: Why it can matter more than IQ*. London: Bloomsbury Publishing Plc.

—, Boyatzis, R. and McKee, A. (2002) *The new leaders: Transforming the art of leadership into the science of results*. (Reprint: London: Time Warner Books, 2005 edn). London: Little Brown.

Government Office for Science (2008) *Foresight mental capital and wellbeing project: Final project report* (executive summary). London: Government Office for Science.

The Great Idea Finder (2005) *Bread slicer* [online]. Available at: http://www.ideafinder.com/history/inventions/breadslicer.htm (accessed: 27 May 2012).

Greeno, J.G., Moore, J.L. and Smith, D.R. (1993) 'Transfer of situated learning', in D.K. Detterman and R.J. Sternberg (eds), *Transfer on trial: Intelligence, cognition and instruction*. Norwood, NJ: Ablex.

Guilford, J.P. (1950) 'Creativity', *American Psychologist*, 5, pp. 444–454.

H

Hames, T. (2007) 'Impress at interview', *The Times* (London edn), p. 35.

Hamilton, P.M. (2003) '"The Vital Connection": A rhetoric on equality', *Personnel Review*, 32(6), pp. 694–710.

Harpaz, I. (2002) 'Expressing a wish to continue or stop working as related to the meaning of work', *European Journal of Work and Organizational Psychology*, 11(2), pp. 177–198.

Hawkes, N. and Sierra, L. (2010) *Making sense of statistics* [online]. Available at: http://www.straightstatistics.org/resources/making-sense-statistics (accessed: 24 July 2012).

HEA (2012) *Pedagogy for employability*. York: The Higher Education Academy [online]. Available at: http://www.heacademy.ac.uk/news/detail/2012/pedagogy_for_employability (accessed: 28 August 2012).

HECSU and AGCAS (2011) *What do graduates do?* [online]. Higher Education Careers Services Unit: http://www.hecsu.ac.uk/reserach_reports_what_do_graduates_do_2011.htm (retrieved: 19 March, 2012).

Henderson, M. (2008) 'Do five simple things a day to stay sane, say scientists', 22 October, p. 5. *The Times*.

Herzberg, F. (1966) *Work and the nature of man*. New York: Staples Press.

Hilpern, K. (2006) 'Why firms are "dangerously disconnected" with graduates', 11 September. *Independent* [online]. Available at: http://education.independent.co.uk/magazines/article1478899.ece (accessed: 22 November 2006).

Hodkinson, P. (2005) 'Reconceptualising the relations between college-based and workplace learning', *Journal of Workplace Learning*, 17(8), pp. 521–532.

Hofstede, G. (1980) *Culture's consequences: International differences in work-related values*. Beverley Hills: Sage.

— (2001) *Culture's consequences: Company values, behaviors, institutions, and organizations across nations*. Beverly Hills, CA: Sage.

— and Bond, M. (1988) 'The Confucian connection: From cultural roots to economic growth', *Organizational Dynamics*, 16(4), pp. 4–21.

— and Hofstede, G.J. (2005) *Cultures and organizations: Software of the mind*. New York: McGraw Hill.

Honey, P. (2008) *Strengthen your strengths: A guide to enhancing your self-management skills*. Maidenhead, Berks: Peter Honey Publications.

— and Mumford, A. (2006) *The learning styles questionnaire: 80 item version*. Maidenhead, Berks: Peter Honey Publications Limited.

Hong, N. (2012) 'The energy factor in the Arctic dispute: A pathway to conflict or cooperation?', *Journal of World Energy Law & Business*, 5(1), pp. 13–26.

Hornby, N. (1992) *Fever Pitch*. London: Penguin Books.

I

Illeris, K. (2002) *The three dimensions of learning*. 2nd edn. Florida: Kreiger Publishing Company.

Institute of Directors (2007) '*Institute of Directors skills briefing—December 2007, Graduates' employability skills*' [online]. Available at: http://www.iod.com/intershoproot/eCS/Store/en/pdfs/policy_paper_graduates_employability_skills.pdf (accessed: 1 June 2009).

Intute website (no date) [online]. Available at: http://www.intute.ac.uk/about.html (accessed: 2 January 2009).

J

Jackson, N. (2004) 'Exploring the Concept of Metalearning'. York: LTSN Generic Centre [online]. Available at: http://www.heacademy.ac.uk/resources/detail/resource_database/id334_exploring_the_concept_of_metalearning (accessed: 4 October 2012).

Jumping for the jelly beans (1973) BBC Television. Produced by Peter Riding. Presented by Frederick Herzberg.

K

Kelly, A. (2001) 'The evolution of key skills: Towards a tawney paradigm', *Journal of Vocational Education and Training*, 53(1), p. 25.

Keynote (2002) *The Keynote Project*. Produced by Nottingham Trent University, the London Institute and the University of Leeds, funded under the Fund for the Development of Teaching and Learning by the Higher Education Funding Council for England and the Department for Employment and Learning [online]. Available at: http://www.leeds.ac.uk/textiles/keynote/pdfs/Keynote_PDP.pdf (accessed: 19 August 2008).

— (2009) *Drinks market 2009 report* [online]. Available at: http://www.keynote.co.uk/reports/s (accessed: 6 October 2012).

Knight, P. (2002) 'Notes on a creative curriculum', prepared for the Higher Education Academy's Imaginative Curriculum Project [online]. Available at: http://78.158.56.101/archive/palatine/resources/imagincurric/index.html (accessed: 4 October 2012).

Kolb, D.A. (1984) *Experiential learning*. London: Prentice Hall.

—, Rubin, I.M. and Osland, J. (1991) *Organizational behaviour: An experiential approach*. 5th edn. Englewood Cliffs, NJ: Prentice Hall, p. 59.

Koro-Ljungberg, M. (2001) 'Metaphors as a way to explore qualitative data', *Qualitative Studies in Education*, 14(3), 367–379.

L

Lakoff, G. and Johnson, M. (1980) *Metaphors we live by*. Chicago: Chicago University Press.

Le Maistre, C. and Pare, A. (2004) 'Learning in two communities: The challenge for universities and workplaces', *Journal of Workplace Learning*, 16 (1/2) pp. 44–52.

Lea, M.R. (1997) *Writing at university: A guide for students*. Buckingham: Open University Press.

Lipnack, J. and Stamps, J. (1997) *Virtual teams: Reaching across space, time and organizations with technology*. Canada: John Wiley & Sons.

Local Government Data Unit—Wales (2009) *A guide to presenting data* [online]. Available at: http://www.dataunitwales.gov.uk/presentingdata (accessed: 24 July 2012).

Locke, E.A., Zubritsky, E., Cousins, E. and Bobko, P. (1984) 'Effect of previously assigned goals on self-set goals and performance', *Journal of Applied Psychology*, 69, pp. 649–699.

Love, M. (2008) 'Frankly we'd rather go to Dollywood', 27 January. *Observer* [online]. Available at: http://www.guardian.co.uk/travel/2008/jan/27/usa.familyholidays?page=all (accessed: 27 July 2008).

M

McFadzean, E. (1999) 'Encouraging creative thinking', *Leadership and Organization Development Journal*, 20(7), pp. 374–383.

McGill, I. and Brockbank, A. (2004) *The handbook of action learning*. London: Routledge.

Machamer, P. (2009) 'Galileo Galilei', *The Stanford encyclopedia of philosophy* (Summer edn). Zalta, E. N. (ed.) (2009) [online]. Available at: http://plato.stanford.edu/archives/sum2009/entries/galileo (accessed: 4 August 2012).

Mahlios, M. and Maxson, M. (1998) 'Metaphors as structures for elementary and secondary preservice teachers' thinking', *International Journal of Educational Research*, 29, pp. 227–240.

Malatesha Joshi, R. (2005) 'Vocabulary: A critical component of comprehension', *Reading & Writing Quarterly*, 21, pp. 208–219.

Mallison, J. (2007) *Book Smart: Your essential reading list for becoming a literary genius in 365 days*. New York: McGraw-Hill.

Mento, A. J., Martinelli, P. and Jones, R.M. (1999) 'Mind mapping in executive education: Applications and outcomes', *Journal of Management Development*, 18(4), pp. 390–407.

Mingers, J. (2000) 'What is it to be critical?: Teaching a critical approach to management undergraduates', *Management Learning*, 31, pp. 219–237.

Mintzberg, H. (1973) *The nature of managerial work*. New York: Harper & Row.

Moon, J. (2006) *Learning journals: A handbook for reflective practice and professional development*. 2nd edn. London & New York: Routledge.

Morgan, G. (1986) *Images of organization*. London: Sage.

Morse, N.C. and Weiss, R.S. (1955) 'The function and meaning of work and job', *American Sociological Review*, 20, pp. 191–198.

Moss Kanter, R. (2005) *Confidence: How winning streaks and losing streaks begin and end*. London: Random House Books.

Mumford, A. (1997) *Management development: Strategies for action*. 3rd edn. London: Chartered Institute of Personnel and Development.

Murray, R. (2005) *Writing for academic journals*. Maidenhead, Berks: Open University Press.

N

NASA: Mars Climate Orbiter Mishap Investigation Board (1999) 'Phase 1 Report' [online]. Available at: ftp://ftp.hq.nasa.gov/pub/pao/reports/1999/MCO_report.pdf (accessed: 4 September 2009).

National Numeracy (2012) *What is numeracy?* [online]. Available at: http://www.nationalnumeracy.org.uk/what-is-numeracy/index.html (accessed: 23 July 2012).

nef (2011) *Five ways to wellbeing* [online]. Nef: Economics as if people and the planet mattered: http://www.neweconomics.org/publications/five-ways-to-wellbeing (accessed: 19 March 2012).

New Scientist (1999) 'Schoolkid blunder brought down mars probe', Issue 2207, 9 October [online]. Available at: http://www.newscientist.com/article/mg16422070.900-schoolkid-blunder-brought-down-mars-probe.html (accessed: 18 June 2009).

O

Oberg, J. (1999) 'Why the Mars probe went off course', *Spectrum Magazine*, December [online]. Available at: http://www.jamesoberg.com/mars/loss.html (accessed: 18 June 2009).

O'Connor, A. and Ramos, J.M. (2006) 'Empowering entrepreneurship through foresight and innovation: Developing a theoretical framework for empowerment in enterprise programs', *Journal of Developmental Psychology*, 11(3), pp. 207–231.

P

Padesky, C. and Greenberg, D. (1995) *Clinician's guide to mind over mood*. New York: Guilford Press.

Parry, V. (2008) '"Pollyanna" tips are based on hard evidence', 22 October, p. 5. *The Times*.

Pears, R. and Shields, G. (2008) *Cite them right*. Newcastle: Pear Tree Books.

— — (2010) *Cite them right: The essential referencing guide*. 8th edn. Basingstoke: Palgrave Macmillan.

Pease, A. and Pease, B. (2004) *The definitive book of body language: How to read others' attitudes by their gestures*. London: Orion Books Ltd.

Pedler, M., Burgoyne, J. and Boydell, T. (2007) *A manager's guide to self development*. 5th edn. Maidenhead, Berks: McGraw-Hill.

Perrin, J. (2006) *The villain: The life of Don Whillans*. London: Arrow Books Ltd.

Philpott, C. (2006) 'Transfer of learning between higher education institution and school-based components of PGCE courses of initial teacher education', *Journal of Vocational Education and Training*, 58(3), pp. 283–302.

Plain English Campaign (2008) [online]. Available at http://www.plainenglish,co.uk/guides.htm (accessed: 26 June 2008).

Plucker, J.A., Beghetto, R.A. and Dow, G.T. (2004) 'Why isn't creativity more important to educational psychologists? Potentials, pitfalls, and future directions in creativity research', *Educational Psychologist*, 39(2), pp. 83–96.

Prose, F. (2006) *Reading like a writer: A guide for people who love books and for those who want to write them*. New York: Harper Perennial.

R

Read, K. (2007) '"Corporate pathos": New approaches to quell hostile publics', *Journal of Communication Management*, 11(4), pp. 323–347.

Reay, D. (1994) *Understanding how people learn*. London: Kogan Page.

Reynolds, M. and Russ, V. (2004) 'Critical management education and action-based learning: Synergies and contradictions', *Academy of Management Learning*, 3(4), pp. 442–456.

Richardson, L. (1994) 'Writing: A method of inquiry', in N. Denzil and Y. Lincoln (eds), *Handbook of qualitative research*. London: Sage.

Richey, T. (1998) 'General morphological analysis: A general method for non-quantified modelling'. Adapted from the paper ' Fritz Zwicky, Morphologie and Policy Analysis', 16th EURO Conference on Operational Analysis, Brussels, 1988 [online]. Available at: http://www.swemorph.com/pdf/gma.pdf (accessed: 3 July 2009).

Robertson, M., Line, M., Jones, S. and Thomas, S. (2000) 'International students. Learning environments and perceptions: A case study using the Delphi technique. *Higher Education Research & Development*, 19(1), May, pp. 89–102.

Robinson, F. (1970) *Effective study*. 4th edn. New York: Harper & Row. (out of print)

Roe, N. (2003) 'Take the high road', 27 December. *The Times* [online]. Available at http://www.women.timesonline.co.uk/tol/life_and_style/women/body_and_soul/article837912.ece (accessed: 5 August 2008).

Roethlisberger, F.J. and Dixon, W.J. (1939) *Management and the worker*. Cambridge, MA: Harvard University Press.

Rogers, P.S., Campbell, N., Louhiala-Salminen, L., Rentz, K. and Suchan, J. (2007) 'The impact of perceptions of journal quality on business and management communication academics', *Journal of Business Communication*, 44(4) pp. 403–426.

Rotherham Metropolitan Borough Council (2011) *Rotherham's Imagination Library* [online]. Available at: http://www.rotherham.gov.uk/info/200071/parental_support/557/rotherhams-imagination-library (accessed: 25 May 2012).

Ruona, W.E.A., Leimbach, M., Holton, E F. and Bates, R. (2002) 'The relationship between learner utility reactions and predicted learning transfer among trainees', *International Journal of Training and Development*, 6(4), pp. 218–228.

Rupley, W.H. (2005) Introduction: 'Vocabulary knowledge: Its contribution to reading growth and development', *Reading & Writing Quarterly*, 21, pp. 203–207.

S

Sadler-Smith, E. (2006) *Learning and development for managers: Perspectives from research and practice.* Oxford: Blackwell.

Schein, E. (1984) 'Coming to a new awareness of organisational culture', *Sloan Management Review, Winter*: 25(2), pp. 3–16.

— (1985) *Organizational culture and leadership: A dynamic view.* San Francisco: Jossey-Bass.

Shannon, C. and Weaver, W. (1949) *The mathematical theory of communication.* Urbana: University of Illinois Press.

Shaw, M. (2005) 'Indicators of creativity in 18 QAA subject benchmark statements' [online]. Available at: http://www.heacademy.ac.uk (accessed: 25 September 2012).

Siemens, G. (2005) 'Connectivism: A learning theory for the digital age', *International Journal of Instructional Technology and Distance Learning*, 2(1), January [online]. Available at: http://www.itdl.org/Journal/Jan_05/article01.htm (accessed: 21 December 2008).

Simpson, J. (1998) *Touching the void.* London: Vintage.

Sperry, R.W. (1968) 'Hemispheric deconnection and unity in conscious awareness', *Scientific American*, 23, pp. 723–735.

Stein, J. (Jan 2007) 'The science of imagination', as given in '40 ways to improve your creativity'. *Independent*, January 2007.

Sternberg, R.J. and Lubart, T.I. (1999) 'The concept of creativity: Prospects and paradigms,' in R.J. Sternberg (ed.), *Handbook of creativity.* Cambridge: Cambridge University Press.

Stevens, M.J. and Campion, M.A. (1994) 'The knowledge, skill, and ability requirements for teamwork: Implications for human resource management', *Journal of Management*, 20(2), pp. 503–530.

—— (1999) 'Staffing work teams: Development and validation of a selection test for teamwork settings', *Journal of Management*, 25(2), 207–228.

Sun Tzu (trans. Thomas Cleary) (2005) *The art of war: Sun Tzu.* Boston an London: Shambhala.

T

Tariq, V. and Durrani, N. (2009) 'Every student counts: Promoting numeracy and enhancing employability',

MSOR Connections, 19(1), pp. 7–11 [online]. Available at: http://mathstore.gla.ac.uk/headocs/9107_tariq_v_and_durrani_n_studentcount.pdf. (accessed: 22 July 2009).

Taylor, F.W. (1911) *Principles of scientific management.* New York: Harper.

Timmons, J.A. (1989) *The entrepreneurial mind.* Andover, MA: Brick House Publishing.

Tingle, L. (2007) Dollywood. *BBC One Politics Show*, 30 November [online]. Available at: http://news.bbc.co.uk/1/hi/programmes/politics_show/711473.stm (accessed: 27 July 2008).

Torrington, D. and Hall, L. (1987) *Personnel management: A new approach.* New York: Prentice Hall.

Truss, L. (2003) *Eats, shoots, and leaves: The zero tolerance approach to punctuation.* London: Profile Books.

Trompenaars, F. and Hampden Turner, C. (1997) *Riding the waves of culture: Understanding cultural diversity in business.* London: Nicholas Brealey Publishing.

Tuckman, B. (1965) 'Developmental sequences in small groups', *Psychological Bulletin*, 63(6), pp. 384–399.

— and Jensen, M.A.C. (1977) 'Stages of small-group development revisited', *Group and Organization Studies* (pre-1986); December 1977, 2(4), pp. 419–427.

V

Vanderburg, R.M. (2006) 'Reviewing research on teaching writing based on Vygotsky's theories: What can we learn', *Reading & Writing Quarterly*, 22, pp. 375–393.

Verma, V.K. (1997) *Managing the project team: The human aspects of project management: Volume 3.* PA19073. London: Project Management Institute.

W

Webster, J. and Wong, W.K.P. (2008) 'Company traditional and virtual group forms: Identity, communication and trust in naturally occurring project teams', *The International Journal of Human Resource Management*, 19(1), pp. 41–62.

Wedgwood, M. (2008) 'Higher education for the workforce: Barriers and facilitators to employer engagement'. London: The Stationery Office (Department for Innovation, Universities & Skills). Available at: http://www.dcsf.gov.uk/research/data/uploadfiles/DIUS-RR-08-04.pdf (accessed: 4 September 2009).

Wenger, E. (2006) Communities of practice: a brief introduction [online]. Available at: http://www.ewenger.com/theory/communities_of_practice_intro.htm (accessed: 6 September 2009).

—, McDermott, R. and Snyder, W.H. (2002) *Cultivating communities of practice: A guide to managing knowledge.* Boston, MA: Harvard Business School Press.

Whigham, D. (2007) *Business data analysis using Excel.* Oxford: Oxford University Press.

Williams, C. (2003) *Overcoming anxiety: A five areas approach.* London: Hodder Arnold.

Wilson, F., Kickul, J. and Marlino, D. (2007) 'Gender, entrepreneurial self-efficacy, and entrepreneurial career intentions for entrepreneurship education', *Entrepreneurship: Theory & Practice,* 3(3), pp. 387–406.

Woolcock, N. (2012) 'Half of adults have math skills of a primary pupil', *The Times* (London edn), 2 March, p. 5.

Wunderer, R. (2001) 'Employees as "co-intrapreneurs"—a transformation concept', *Leadership and Organization Development Journal,* 22(5), pp. 193–211.

Y

Yorke, M. (2006) *Employability in higher education: What it is—what it is not.* Learning and Emplyability Series one. York: ESECT and HEA [online]. Available at: http://www.heacademy.ac.uk/resources/detail/subjects/adm/employability_resources_and_publications (accessed: 28 August 2012).

Young, R. (2007) *A basic outline of samples and sampling* [online]. Available at: http://www.parliament.uk/briefing-papers/SN04447 (accessed: 24 July 2012).

Young, T. (2005) *Technical writing A-Z: A commonsense guide to engineering reports and theses.* New York: ASME Press.

Z

Zalta, E.N. (ed.) (2009) [online]. Available at: http://plato.stanford.edu/archives/sum2009/entries/galileo (accessed: 4 August, 2012).

Index